E   ition

In an industry where staying employable means staying current, this book is an essential read and an efficient reference for web designers and developers. This book does not belong on your bookshelf. It belongs on your desk.

➤ **Matt Margolis**
  Manager, application development, Getty Images

The whole book feels like a well-stocked toolbox. It's accessible, well-presented, and packed with information. Brian is a confident expert and a masterful educator.

➤ **Tibor Simic**
  Developer, Inge-mark

I've been making websites for more than ten years, and I still learned a few tricks from reading this book. If you haven't yet taken advantage of the new features available in HTML5, now is the time. Brian's book will explain what you can and should use, and when.

➤ **Stephen Orr**
  Lead developer, Made Media

HTML5 and CSS3, Second Edition

Level Up with Today's Web Technologies

Brian P. Hogan

The Pragmatic Bookshelf

Dallas, Texas • Raleigh, North Carolina

Many of the designations used by manufacturers and sellers to distinguish their products are claimed as trademarks. Where those designations appear in this book, and The Pragmatic Programmers, LLC was aware of a trademark claim, the designations have been printed in initial capital letters or in all capitals. The Pragmatic Starter Kit, The Pragmatic Programmer, Pragmatic Programming, Pragmatic Bookshelf, PragProg and the linking g device are trademarks of The Pragmatic Programmers, LLC.

Every precaution was taken in the preparation of this book. However, the publisher assumes no responsibility for errors or omissions, or for damages that may result from the use of information (including program listings) contained herein.

Our Pragmatic courses, workshops, and other products can help you and your team create better software and have more fun. For more information, as well as the latest Pragmatic titles, please visit us at *http://pragprog.com.*

The team that produced this book includes:

Susannah Davidson Pfalzer (editor)
Potomac Indexing, LLC (indexer)
Candace Cunningham (copyeditor)
David J Kelly (typesetter)
Janet Furlow (producer)
Juliet Benda (rights)
Ellie Callahan (support)

Printed in the United States of America.
ISBN-13: 978-1-937785-59-8
Printed on acid-free paper.
Book version: P1.0—October 2013

Contents

Acknowledgments ix

Preface xi

1. An Overview of HTML5 and CSS3 1
   1.1   A Stronger Platform for Web Development   1
   1.2   The Road to the Future Is Bumpy   5

Part I — Improving User Interfaces

2. New Structural Tags and Attributes 13
   Tip 1.   Redefining a Blog Using Semantic Markup   15
   Tip 2.   Showing Progress toward a Goal with the \<meter\> Element   26
   Tip 3.   Creating Pop-Up Windows with Custom Data Attributes   30
   Tip 4.   Defining an FAQ with a Description List   34

3. Creating User-Friendly Web Forms 37
   Tip 5.   Describing Data with New Input Fields   39
   Tip 6.   Jumping to the First Field with Autofocus   49
   Tip 7.   Providing Hints with Placeholder Text   50
   Tip 8.   Validating User Input without JavaScript   54
   Tip 9.   In-Place Editing with contenteditable   59

4. Styling Content and Interfaces 67
   Tip 10.   Styling Tables with Pseudoclasses   69
   Tip 11.   Making Links Printable with :after and content   78
   Tip 12.   Building Mobile Interfaces with Media Queries   81
   Tip 13.   Creating Multicolumn Layouts   84

5. **Making Accessible Interfaces** **91**
    Tip 14.   Providing Navigation Hints with ARIA Roles   93
    Tip 15.   Creating an Accessible Updatable Region   98
    Tip 16.   Improving Table Accessibility   104

Part II — New Sights and Sounds

6. **Drawing in the Browser** **111**
    Tip 17.   Drawing a Logo on the Canvas   112
    Tip 18.   Graphing Statistics with RGraph   120
    Tip 19.   Creating Vector Graphics with SVG   126

7. **Embedding Audio and Video** **131**
    Tip 20.   Working with Audio   137
    Tip 21.   Embedding Video   141
    Tip 22.   Making Videos Accessible   146

8. **Eye Candy** **151**
    Tip 23.   Rounding Rough Edges   153
    Tip 24.   Working with Shadows, Gradients, and
                Transformations   157
    Tip 25.   Working with Fonts   164
    Tip 26.   Making Things Move with Transitions and
                Animations   169

Part III — Beyond Markup

9. **Saving Data on the Client** **183**
    Tip 27.   Saving Preferences with Web Storage   185
    Tip 28.   Storing Data in a Client-Side Database Using
                IndexedDB   190
    Tip 29.   Working Offline   203

10. **Creating Interactive Web Applications** **207**
    Tip 30.   Preserving History   209
    Tip 31.   Talking across Domains   213
    Tip 32.   Chatting with Web Sockets   219
    Tip 33.   Finding Yourself: Geolocation   227
    Tip 34.   Getting It All Sorted Out with Drag and Drop   231

11.	**Where to Go Next**	239
	11.1 Defining Layouts with the Flexible Box Model	240
	11.2 Cross-Origin Resource Sharing	242
	11.3 Web Workers	243
	11.4 Server-Sent Events	247
	11.5 Filter Effects	250
	11.6 WebGL	252
	11.7 Onward!	252
A1.	**Features Quick Reference**	253
	A1.1 New Elements	253
	A1.2 Attributes	254
	A1.3 Forms	254
	A1.4 Form-Field Attributes	255
	A1.5 Accessibility	255
	A1.6 Multimedia	256
	A1.7 CSS3	257
	A1.8 Client-Side Storage	259
	A1.9 Additional APIs	260
A2.	**jQuery Primer**	263
	A2.1 Loading jQuery	263
	A2.2 jQuery Basics	264
	A2.3 Methods to Modify Content	264
	A2.4 Creating and Removing Elements	267
	A2.5 Events	267
	A2.6 Document Ready	269
	A2.7 Use jQuery Wisely	270
A3.	**Encoding Audio and Video for the Web**	273
	A3.1 Encoding Audio	273
	A3.2 Encoding Video	274
A4.	**Resources**	275
	Bibliography	277
	Index	279

Acknowledgments

Second editions are supposed to be quick—just a chance to correct mistakes or make improvements and updates to the first edition. This, though, was almost like writing a new book, and there are so many people I need to thank who made my work much easier.

First, I want to thank you for reading this book. I hope it helps you tackle some cool and interesting projects of your own when you're done.

Next, the wonderful gang at The Pragmatic Bookshelf deserves not only my gratitude, but also a lot of the credit for this book. Susannah Pfalzer once again ensured that one of my books makes sense. She's an awesome development editor and I'm thankful for her time and attention to detail, especially on a book like this, where thousands of little details need attention. Dave Thomas and Andy Hunt had great feedback, and I'm grateful for their continued support. Thank you, all.

I was fortunate to have an absolutely amazing group of technical reviewers on this book. The comments and feedback were excellent, exhaustive, and full of great suggestions for improvement. Thank you to Cheyenne Clark, Joel Clermont, Jon Cooley, Chad Dumler-Montplaisir, Jeff Holland, Michael Hunter, Karoline Klever, Stephen Orr, Dan Reedy, Loren Sands-Ramshaw, Brian Schau, Matthew John Sias, Tibor Simic, Charley Stran, and Colin Yates, for all of your help. Not only were your reviews thorough, but they also offered great advice and insight, and impacted the final version of this book considerably.

Thanks to Jessica Janiuk for providing the screenshots for Android devices.

Thanks to my business associates Chris Warren, Chris Johnson, Mike Weber, Nick LaMuro, Austen Ott, Erich Tesky, Kevin Gisi, and Jon Kinney for their ongoing support.

Finally, my wife Carissa works really hard to make sure that I can work really hard. She's a silent partner in this and I'm eternally grateful for her love and support. Thank you, Carissa, for everything you do.

Preface

To a web developer, three months on the Web is like a year in real time. And that means it's been twelve web years since the last edition of this book.

We web developers are always hearing about something new. A few years ago HTML5 and CSS3 seemed so far off, but companies are using these technologies in their work today because browsers like Chrome, Safari, Firefox, Opera, and Internet Explorer are implementing pieces of the specifications.

HTML5 and CSS3 help lay the groundwork for solid, interactive web applications. They let us build sites that are simpler to develop, easier to maintain, and more user-friendly. HTML5 has elements for defining site structure and embedding content, which means we don't have to resort to extra attributes, markup, or plug-ins. CSS3 provides advanced selectors, graphical enhancements, and better font support that makes our sites more visually appealing without using font image-replacement techniques, complex Java-Script, or graphics tools. Better accessibility support will improve dynamic JavaScript client-side applications for people with disabilities, and offline support lets us start building working applications that don't need an Internet connection.

In this book, we'll get hands-on with HTML5 and CSS3 so you can see how to use them in your projects, even if your users don't have browsers that can support all of these features yet. Before we get started, let's take a second to talk about HTML5 and buzzwords.

HTML5: The Platform vs. The Specification

HTML5 is a specification that describes some new tags and markup, as well as some wonderful JavaScript application programming interfaces (APIs), but it's getting caught up in a whirlwind of hype and promises. Unfortunately, HTML5 *the standard* has evolved into HTML5 *the platform*, creating an awful lot of confusion among developers and customers. In some cases, pieces from the CSS3 specification, such as shadows, gradients, and transformations, are being called HTML. Browser-makers are trying to one-up each other with how much "HTML5" they support. People are starting to make strange requests like "Create the site in HTML5."

For the majority of the book, we'll focus on the HTML5 and CSS3 specifications themselves and how you can use the techniques they describe on all the common web browsers. In the last part of the book, we'll look into a suite of closely related specifications associated with HTML5 that are in use right now on multiple platforms, such as Geolocation and Web Sockets. Although these technologies aren't *technically* HTML5, they can help you build incredible things when combined with HTML5 and CSS3.

What's in This Book

Each chapter in this book focuses on a specific group of problems that we can solve with HTML5 and CSS3. Each chapter has an overview and a list summarizing the tags, features, or concepts covered in the chapter. The main content of each chapter is broken into *tips*, which introduce you to a specific concept and walk you through building a simple example using the concept. The chapters in this book are grouped topically. Rather than group things into an HTML5 part and a CSS3 part, it made more sense to group them based on the problems they solve. You'll find some chapters that specifically focus on CSS3, and you'll find CSS3 goodness sprinkled throughout other chapters.

Many tips contain a section called "Falling Back," which shows you methods for addressing users whose browsers don't directly support the feature we're implementing. We'll be using a variety of techniques to make these fallbacks work, from third-party libraries to our own JavaScript and jQuery solutions.

Each chapter wraps up with a section called "The Future," where we discuss how the concept can be applied as it becomes more widely adopted.

We'll start off with a brief overview of HTML5 and CSS3 and take a look at some of the new structural tags you can use to describe your page content. Then we'll work with forms, and you'll get a chance to use some form fields and features, such as autofocus and placeholders. From there, you'll get to play with CSS3's new selectors so you can learn how to apply styles to elements without adding extra markup to your content.

Then we'll explore HTML5's audio and video support, and you'll learn how to use the canvas to draw shapes. You'll also see how to use CSS3's shadows, gradients, and transformations, as well as how to work with fonts, transitions, and animations.

Next we'll use HTML5's client-side features, such as web storage, IndexedDB, and offline support to build client-side applications. We'll use web sockets to talk to a simple chat service, and discuss how HTML5 makes it possible to send messages and data across domains. You'll also get a chance to play with the Geolocation API and learn how to manipulate the browser's history.

This book focuses on what you can use today in modern browsers. Additional HTML5 and CSS3 features might not be ready for widespread use yet but are valuable nonetheless. You'll learn more about them in the final chapter, Chapter 11, *Where to Go Next*, on page 239.

In Appendix 1, *Features Quick Reference*, on page 253, you'll find a listing of all the features covered in this book, with a quick reference to the chapters that reference each feature. We'll be using a lot of jQuery in this book, so Appendix 2, *jQuery Primer*, on page 263, gives you a short primer. Appendix 3, *Encoding Audio and Video for the Web*, on page 273, is a small appendix explaining how to encode audio and video files for use with HTML5.

Browser Compatibility Lists

At the start of each chapter, you'll find a list of the HTML5 features we'll discuss. In these lists, browser support is shown in square brackets using a shorthand code and the minimum supported version number. The codes used are *C:* Chrome, *F:* Firefox, *S:* Safari, *IE:* Internet Explorer, *O:* Opera, *iOS:* iOS devices with Safari, and *A:* Android browser.

What's Not in This book

We won't talk about Internet Explorer versions before Internet Explorer 8. Microsoft has actively pushed people off of those old browsers.

We also won't cover every aspect of HTML5 and CSS3. Some things don't make sense to talk about because the implementations have changed or they're not practical yet. For example, the CSS grid layout is really exciting,[1] but it's not worth spending time on until browsers all get "on the same page." In this book I focus on showing how you can use HTML5 and CSS3 techniques right now to improve things for the widest possible audience.

Since this book doesn't have any basic HTML or CSS content, it's not a book for absolute beginners. It is aimed primarily at web developers who have a good understanding of HTML and CSS. If you're just getting started, go get a copy of *HTML and CSS: Design and Build Websites [Duc11]*, by Jon Duckett.

---

1. http://www.w3.org/TR/css3-grid-layout/

It covers the basics nicely. You should also look at *Designing with Web Standards [Zel09]*, by Jeffrey Zeldman.

I assume that you have a basic understanding of JavaScript and jQuery,[2] which we'll be using to implement many of our fallback solutions. Appendix 2, *jQuery Primer*, on page 263, is a brief introduction to jQuery that covers the basic methods we'll be using, but you should consider picking up the book *Pragmatic Guide to JavaScript [Por10]*, by Christophe Porteneuve, as a more in-depth reference for JavaScript. The last part of the book gets pretty JavaScript-heavy, but I'm confident you'll do just fine.

Changes in the Second Edition

The second edition of this book brings everything up-to-date and removes material that specifically targets Internet Explorer 7 and lower. You'll find more detail on HTML5 accessibility, more stable and proven fallback approaches, and nine new tips:

- Tip 2, *Showing Progress toward a Goal with the meter Element*, on page 26
- Tip 4, *Defining an FAQ with a Description List*, on page 34
- Tip 8, *Validating User Input without JavaScript*, on page 54
- Tip 19, *Creating Vector Graphics with SVG*, on page 126
- Tip 22, *Making Videos Accessible*, on page 146
- Tip 16, *Improving Table Accessibility*, on page 104
- Tip 26, *Making Things Move with Transitions and Animations*, on page 169
- Tip 28, *Storing Data in a Client-Side Database Using IndexedDB*, on page 190
- Tip 34, *Getting It All Sorted Out with Drag and Drop*, on page 231

Plus, you'll explore CSS's Flexible Box model, cross-origin resource sharing, web workers, server-sent events, and CSS filter effects in Chapter 11, *Where to Go Next*, on page 239.

In addition to the new content, the other tips have been updated with new fallback solutions as necessary, and you'll find a handy Node.js-based web server in this book's example-code download, which will make it easy for you to test all the projects across multiple browsers.

---

2.   http://www.jquery.com

How to Read This Book

Don't feel that you have to read this book from cover to cover. It's broken up into easily digestible tips that focus on one or two core concepts. In each chapter, you'll find several projects. If you download the example code from this book's website,[3] you'll find a template/ folder, which is a great place to start.

When you see code examples like this

```
html5_new_tags/index.html
<link rel="stylesheet" href="stylesheets/style.css">
```

the label above the code shows where you'll find the file in the example code. If you're reading this in electronic format, you can click that label to bring up the entire file so you can see the code in context. The label shows the location of the file in the example code; it may not always match the file you're working with.

Finally, follow along with the code in the book and don't be afraid to examine and tweak the finished examples. Let's get more specific about what you need to work with the examples in this book.

What You Need

You'll need Firefox 20 or later, Chrome 20 or higher, Opera 10.6, or Safari 6 to test the code in this book. You'll probably want all of these browsers to test everything we'll be building, since each browser does things a little differently. Having an Android or iOS device around is helpful, too, but it's not required.

Testing on Internet Explorer

You'll also need a way to test your sites with Internet Explorer 8 and later so you can ensure that the fallback solutions we create actually work. The easiest way to do this is to install Microsoft Windows on VirtualBox for testing.[4] Microsoft provides free virtual machines for testing web applications at Modern.IE, where you can download ready-to-go images for VirtualBox, Parallels, or VMware.[5] These machines work for thirty days and then need to be redownloaded.

Node.js and the Example Server

Testing some of the features in this book requires that you serve the HTML and CSS files from a web server, and testing others requires a more complex

---

3. http://pragprog.com/titles/bhh52e/
4. http://virtualbox.org
5. http://modern.ie

back end. In the downloadable example code for the book, you'll find a server you can use to make the examples easier to work with. To run this server you'll need to install Node.js by following the instructions on the Node.js website.[6] You'll want at least version 0.10.0 to avoid intermittent server crashes.

You'll also need npm, a command-line utility to install Node Packaged Modules, so you can install dependencies. This utility is included as part of a Node.js installation.

Once you've installed Node.js, visit the book's website and download the example code. Extract the archive, navigate to the location of the extracted files in the Terminal (or the Command Prompt if you're on Windows), and run this command, *without the $*, to download all of the dependencies:

```
$ npm install
```

Then type the following, again leaving off the $:

```
$ node server
```

to launch the server on port 8000. Load up *http://localhost:8000* in your browser and browse the demos. If you're testing on virtual machines, your machines should be able to connect using the actual IP address of the computer that's running the example server. Best of all, any files or folders you place in the same folder as the server file will get served, so you could follow along with this book by working out of the example-code folders.

A Note about JavaScript and jQuery Usage

In this book we'll use a lot of JavaScript. In the past, it's been common practice to load JavaScript files in the <head> section of the page and then use techniques like jQuery's document.ready() to wait until the Document Object Model (DOM) is ready for modification. However, it's recommended practice to load all scripts at the *bottom of the page*, as this can result in better performance. So that's what we'll do. All scripts, including jQuery, will go at the bottom of the page, except for a few cases where we must alter the DOM before any elements load.

In addition, we'll use jQuery where it makes sense. If we're simply looking for an element by its ID, we'll use document.getElementById(). But if we're doing event handling or more complex DOM manipulation that needs to work in Internet Explorer 8, we'll use jQuery.

---

6.   http://nodejs.org

To put it another way, we're going to "use the right tool for the job." It might lead to a little inconsistency at times, but that's the tradeoff when we start introducing fallback solutions to make old browsers fall in line. I'll be sure to explain why we're doing things as we go forward.

Online Resources

The book's website has links to an interactive discussion forum as well as errata for the book. The source code for all the examples in this book is linked on that page, as well.[7]

If you find a mistake, please create an entry on the Errata page so we can get it addressed. In the electronic version of this book, there are links in the footer of each page that you can use to easily submit errata.

Finally, be sure to visit this book's blog, Beyond HTML5 and CSS3.[8] I'll be posting related material, updates, and working examples from this book.

Ready to go? Great! Let's get started with HTML5 and CSS3.

---

7. http://www.pragprog.com/titles/bhh52e/
8. http://www.beyondhtml5andcss3.com/

CHAPTER 1

An Overview of HTML5 and CSS3

HTML5 and CSS3 are more than just two new standards proposed by the World Wide Web Consortium (W3C) and its working groups. They are the next iteration of technologies you use every day, and they're here to help you build better modern web applications. Before we dive deep into the details of HTML5 and CSS3, let's talk about some benefits of those standards, as well as some of the challenges we'll face.

1.1 A Stronger Platform for Web Development

A lot of the new features of HTML center on creating a better platform for web-based applications. From more descriptive tags and better cross-site and cross-window communication to animations and improved multimedia support, developers using HTML5 have a lot of new tools to build better user experiences.

Backward Compatibility

One of the best reasons for you to embrace HTML5 today is that it works in most existing browsers. Right now, even in Internet Explorer 6, you can start using HTML5 and slowly transition your markup. It'll even validate with the W3C's validation service (conditionally, of course, because the standards are still evolving).

If you've worked with HTML or XML, you've come across the doctype declaration before. It's used to tell validators and editors what tags and attributes you can use and how the document should be formed. Additionally, a lot of web browsers use it to determine how they will render the page. A valid doctype often causes browsers to render pages in "standards mode."

Following is the rather verbose *XHTML 1.0 Transitional* doctype used by many sites.

```
<!DOCTYPE html PUBLIC "-//W3C//DTD XHTML 1.0 Transitional//EN"
  "http://www.w3.org/TR/xhtml1/DTD/xhtml1-transitional.dtd">
```

Compared to this, the HTML5 doctype is ridiculously simple:

```
html5_why/index.html
<!DOCTYPE html>
```

Place that at the top of the document, and you're using HTML5. Of course, you can't use any of the new HTML5 elements that your target browsers don't yet support, but your document will validate as HTML5.

More-Descriptive Markup

Each version of HTML introduces some new markup, but never before have there been so many additions that directly relate to describing content. You'll learn about elements for defining headings, footers, navigation sections, sidebars, and articles in Chapter 2, *New Structural Tags and Attributes*, on page 13. You'll also learn about meters, progress bars, and how custom data attributes can help you mark up data.

Less Cruft

A lot of the elements in HTML5 have been streamlined and have more sensible defaults. You've already seen how much simpler the doctype is, but other things have gotten easier to type, as well. For example, for years we've been told we have to specify JavaScript <script> tags like this:

```
<script language="javascript" type="text/javascript">
```

But in HTML5, it's expected that you'll use JavaScript for all <script> tags, so you can safely leave those extra attributes off.

If we want to specify that our document contains UTF-8 characters, we only have to use a <meta> tag like

```
<meta charset="utf-8">
```

instead of the unwieldy and often copied-and-pasted

```
<meta http-equiv="Content-Type" content="text/html; charset=utf-8">
```

Improved User Interfaces

The user interface is such an important part of web applications, and we jump through hoops every day to make browsers do what we want. To style a table or round corners, we either use JavaScript libraries or add tons of additional markup so we can apply styles. HTML5 and CSS3 make that practice a thing of the past.

Joe asks:
But I Like My XHTML Self-Closing Tags. Can I Still Use Them?

You sure can! Look at Polyglot Markup.[a] Many developers fell in love with XHTML because of the stricter requirements on markup, compared to HTML. XHTML documents forced quoted attributes, made you self-close content tags, required that you use lowercase attribute names, and brought well-formed markup to the World Wide Web. Moving to HTML5 doesn't mean you have to change your ways. HTML5 documents will be valid if you use the HTML5-style syntax or the XHTML syntax. But before you dive in you need to understand the implications of using self-closing tags.

Most web servers serve HTML pages with the text/html MIME type because of Internet Explorer's inability to properly handle the application/xml+xhtml MIME type associated with XHTML pages. Because of this, browsers tend to strip off self-closing tags because they don't consider self-closing tags to be valid HTML. For example, if you had a self-closing script tag above a div, like this,

```
<script language="javascript" src="application.js" />
<h2>Help</h2>
```

the browser would remove the self-closing forward slash, and then the renderer would think that the h2 was *within* the script tag, *which never closes!* This is why you see script tags coded with an explicit closing tag, even though a self-closing tag is valid XHTML markup.

Be aware of possible issues like this if you do use self-closing tags in your HTML5 documents. Be sure to serve your files with the correct MIME type. You can learn more about these issues at http://www.webdevout.net/articles/beware-of-xhtml#myths.

---

a.   http://www.w3.org/TR/html-polyglot/

Better Forms

HTML5 promises better user-interface controls. For ages, we've been forced to use JavaScript and CSS to construct sliders, calendar date pickers, and color pickers. These are all defined as real elements in HTML5, just like drop-downs, checkboxes, and radio buttons. You'll learn how to use them in Chapter 3, *Creating User-Friendly Web Forms*, on page 37. Although this isn't quite ready for every browser, it's something you need to keep your eye on, especially if you develop web-based applications.

In addition to improved usability without reliance on JavaScript libraries, there's another benefit—improved accessibility. Screen readers and other browsers can implement these controls in specific ways so that they work easily for people with disabilities.

Improved Accessibility

Using the new HTML5 elements to clearly describe our content makes it easier for programs like screen readers to consume the content. A site's navigation, for example, is much easier to find if you can look for the <nav> tag instead of a specific <div> or unordered list. Footers, sidebars, and other content can be easily reordered or skipped altogether. Parsing pages in general becomes much less painful, which can lead to better experiences for people relying on assistive technologies. In addition, new attributes on elements can specify the roles of elements so that screen readers can work with them more easily. In Chapter 5, *Making Accessible Interfaces*, on page 91, you'll learn how to use those new attributes so that today's screen readers can use them.

Advanced Selectors

CSS3 has selectors that let you identify odd and even rows of tables, all selected checkboxes, or even the last paragraph in a group. You can accomplish more with less code and less markup. This also makes it much easier to style HTML you can't edit. In Chapter 4, *Styling Content and Interfaces*, on page 67, you'll see how to use these selectors effectively.

Visual Effects

Drop shadows on text and images help bring depth to a web page, and gradients can also add dimension. CSS3 lets you add shadows and gradients to elements without resorting to background images or extra markup. In addition, you can use transformations to round corners or skew and rotate elements. You'll see how all of those things work in Chapter 8, *Eye Candy*, on page 151.

Multimedia with Less Reliance on Plug-ins

You don't need Flash or Silverlight for video, audio, and vector graphics anymore. Although Flash-based video players are relatively simple to use, they don't work on Apple's mobile devices. That's a significant market, so you'll need to learn how to use non-Flash video alternatives. In Chapter 7, *Embedding Audio and Video*, on page 131, you'll see how to use HTML5 audio and video with effective fallbacks.

Better Applications

Developers have tried all kinds of things to make richer, more interactive applications on the Web, from ActiveX controls to Flash. HTML5 offers amazing features that, in some cases, completely eliminate the need for third-party technologies.

Cross-Document Messaging

Web browsers prevent us from using scripts on one domain to affect or interact with scripts on another domain. This restriction keeps end users safe from cross-site scripting, which has been used to do all sorts of nasty things to unsuspecting site visitors.

However, this prevents *all* scripts from working, even when we write them ourselves and know we can trust the content. HTML5 includes a workaround that is both safe and simple to implement. You'll see how to make this work in Tip 31, *Talking across Domains*, on page 213.

Web Sockets

HTML5 offers support for web sockets, which give you a persistent connection to a server. Instead of constantly polling a back end for progress updates, your web page can subscribe to a socket, and the back end can push notifications to your users. We'll play with that in Tip 32, *Chatting with Web Sockets*, on page 219.

Client-Side Storage

We tend to think of HTML5 as a web technology, but with the addition of the Web Storage and Web SQL Database application programming interfaces (APIs), we can build applications in the browser that can persist data entirely on the client's machine. You'll see how to use those APIs in Chapter 9, *Saving Data on the Client*, on page 183.

1.2 The Road to the Future Is Bumpy

A few roadblocks continue to impede the widespread adoption of HTML5 and CSS3.

Handling Old Versions of Internet Explorer

Internet Explorer still has a large user base, and versions prior to IE9 have very weak HTML5 and CSS3 support. Internet Explorer 10 improves this situation vastly, but it's not widely used yet and won't be made available to people using Windows Vista or earlier operating systems. That doesn't mean we can't use HTML5 and CSS3 in our sites anyway. We can make our sites work in Internet Explorer, but they don't have to work the same as the versions we develop for Chrome and Firefox. We'll just provide fallback solutions so we don't anger users and lose customers. You'll learn plenty of tactics throughout this book.

Accessibility

Our users must be able to interact with our websites, whether they are visually impaired, hearing impaired, on older browsers, on slow connections, or on mobile devices. HTML5 introduces some new elements, such as <audio>, <video>, and <canvas>. Audio and video have always had accessibility issues, but the <canvas> element presents new challenges. It lets us create images within the HTML document using JavaScript. This creates issues for the visually impaired but also causes problems for the 5 percent of web users who have disabled JavaScript.[1]

Cake and Frosting

I like cake. I like pie better, but cake is pretty good stuff. I prefer cake with frosting on it.

When you're developing web applications, you have to keep in mind that all the pretty user interfaces and fancy JavaScript stuff is the frosting on the cake. Your website can be really good without that stuff, and just like a cake, you need a foundation on which to put your frosting.

I've met some people who don't like frosting. They scrape it off the cake. I've also met people who use web applications without JavaScript for various reasons.

Bake these people a really awesome cake. Then add frosting for those who want it.

We need to be mindful of accessibility when we push ahead with new technologies, and provide suitable fallbacks for these HTML5 features, just like we would for people using Internet Explorer.

Deprecated Tags

HTML5 has introduced a lot of new elements, but the specification also deprecates quite a few common elements that you might find in your web pages.[2] You'll want to remove those moving forward.

First, several presentational elements are gone. If you find these in your code, get rid of them! Replace them with semantically correct elements and use CSS to make them look nice.

- basefont
- big
- center

---

1. http://visualrevenue.com/blog/2007/08/eu-and-us-javascript-disabled-index.html
2. http://www.w3.org/TR/html5-diff/

- font
- s
- strike
- tt
- u

Some of those tags are pretty obscure, but lots of pages maintained with visual editors such as Dreamweaver still contain occurrences of <font> and <center> tags.

In addition, support for frames has been removed. Frames have always been popular in enterprise web applications such as PeopleSoft, Microsoft Outlook Web Access, and even custom-built portals. Despite their widespread use, frames caused so many usability and accessibility issues that they just had to go. That means these elements are gone:

- frame
- frameset
- noframes

Look at ways to lay out your interfaces using CSS instead of frames. If you're using frames to ensure the same header, footer, and navigation appears on each page of your application, you should be able to accomplish the same thing with the tools provided by your web-development framework. For example, you could look into the position: fixed CSS property.

A few other elements are gone because there are better options available:

- acronym gets replaced by abbr.
- applet gets replaced by object.
- dir gets replaced by ul.

In addition, many attributes are no longer valid. These include presentational attributes such as the following:

- align
- link, vlink, alink, and text attributes on the body tag
- bgcolor
- height and width
- scrolling on the iframe element
- valign
- hspace and vspace
- cellpadding, cellspacing, and border on table

The profile attribute on the <head> tag is no longer supported either, and this is something you see in a lot of WordPress templates.

Finally, the longdesc attribute for <img> and <iframe> elements is gone, which is a bit of a disappointment to accessibility advocates, because longdesc was an accepted way of providing additional descriptive information to users of screen readers.

If you plan on using HTML5 with your existing sites, you'll want to look for these elements and remove them or replace them with more semantic ones. Be sure to validate your pages with the W3C Validator service;[3] this will help you locate deprecated tags and attributes.

Competing Corporate Interests

Internet Explorer is not the only browser slowing adoption of HTML5 and CSS3. Google, Apple, and the Mozilla Foundation have their own agendas, as well, and they're battling it out for supremacy. They're arguing over video and audio codec support, and they're including their opinions in their browser releases. For example, Safari will play MP3 audio with the <audio> tag, but ogg files won't work. Firefox, however, supports ogg files instead of mp3 files.

Eventually these differences will be resolved. In the meantime, we can make smart choices about what we support, either by limiting what we implement to the browsers our target audiences use or by implementing things multiple times, once for each browser, until the standards are finalized. It's not as painful as it sounds. You'll learn more about this in Chapter 7, *Embedding Audio and Video*, on page 131.

HTML5 and CSS3 Are Still Works in Progress

They're not final specifications, and that means anything in those specifications could change. Although Firefox, Chrome, and Safari have strong HTML5 support, if the specification changes, the browsers will change with it, and this could lead to some deprecated, broken websites. For example, over the last few years CSS3 box shadows have been removed from and readded to the specification, and the Web Sockets protocol has been modified, breaking client-server communications entirely.

If you follow the progress of HTML5 and CSS3 and stay up-to-date with what's happening, you'll be fine. The HTML5 specification is at http://www.w3.org/TR/html5/.

---

3.   http://validator.w3.org/

CSS3 is split across multiple modules, and you can follow its progress at http://www.w3.org/Style/CSS/current-work.

When you come across something that doesn't work in one of your target browsers, you just fill in the gaps as you go, using JavaScript and Flash as your putty. You'll build solid solutions that work for all your users, and as time goes on, you'll be able to remove the JavaScript and other fallback solutions without changing your implementations.

But before we think much about the future, let's start working with HTML5. A bunch of new structural tags are waiting to meet you in the next chapter.

Part I

Improving User Interfaces

In the first few chapters of this book, we'll talk about how we can use HTML5's and CSS3's features to improve the interfaces we present to our users. We'll see how we can create better forms, easily style tables, and improve the accessibility of our pages for assistive devices. We'll also see how we can use content generation to improve the usability of our print style sheets, and we'll explore in-place editing with the new contenteditable attribute.

CHAPTER 2

New Structural Tags and Attributes

I'd like to talk to you about a serious problem affecting many web developers today. *Divitis* is rampant—this chronic syndrome causes web developers to wrap elements with extra <div> tags with IDs such as banner, sidebar, article, and footer. It's also highly contagious. Developers pass Divitis among each other extremely quickly, and since <div>s are invisible to the naked eye, even mild cases of Divitis may go unnoticed for years.

Here's a common symptom of Divitis:

```
<div id="page">
  <div id="navbar_wrapper">
    <div id="navbar">
      <ul>
        <li><a href="/">Home</a></li>
        <li><a href="/products">Products</a></li>
        ...
      </ul>
    </div>
  </div>
</div>
```

Here we have an unordered list, which is already a block element, wrapped with two <div> tags that are also block elements. Remember, block elements fall on their own line, whereas inline elements do not force a line break, and so this <div> tag doesn't serve any purpose. The id attributes on these wrapper elements tell us what they do, but you can remove at least one of these wrappers to get the same result. Overuse of markup leads to bloat and pages that are difficult to style and maintain.

There is hope, though. The HTML5 specification provides a cure in the form of new semantic tags that describe their content. Because so many developers have made sidebars, headers, footers, and sections in their designs, the

HTML5 specification introduces new tags specifically designed to divide a page into logical regions.

In addition to these new structural tags, we'll talk about a few other tags, like <meter> and <progress>, and discuss how we can use the new custom-attributes feature in HTML5 so we can embed data into our elements instead of hijacking classes or existing attributes. In a nutshell, we're going to cover how to use the right tag for the right job. Together with HTML5, we can help wipe out Divitis in our lifetime.

In this chapter, we'll explore these new elements and features:

<header>
  Defines a header region of a page or section. *[C5, F3.6, S4, IE8, O10]*

<footer>
  Defines a footer region of a page or section. *[C5, F3.6, S4, IE8, O10]*

<nav>
  Defines a navigation region of a page or section. *[C5, F3.6, S4, IE8, O10]*

<section>
  Defines a logical region of a page or a grouping of content. *[C5, F3.6, S4, IE8, O10]*

<article>
  Defines an article or complete piece of content. *[C5, F3.6, S4, IE8, O10]*

<aside>
  Defines secondary or related content. *[C5, F3.6, S4, IE8, O10]*

Description lists
  Defines a list of names and associated values, like definitions and descriptions. *[All browsers]*

<meter>
  Describes a quantity within a range. *[C8, F16, S6, O11]*

<progress>
  Control that shows real-time progress toward a goal. *[C8, F6, S6, IE10, O11]*

Custom data attributes
  Allow the addition of custom attributes to any elements that use the data- pattern. *[All browsers support reading these via JavaScript's getAttribute() method.]*

Tip 1

Redefining a Blog Using Semantic Markup

Semantic markup is all about describing content. If you've been developing web pages for a few years, you've probably divided your pages into various regions such as header, footer, and sidebar so that you can more easily identify the regions of the page when applying style sheets and other formatting.

Semantic markup makes it easy for machines *and* people to understand the meaning and context of the content. The new HTML5 markup tags, such as <section>, <header>, and <nav>, help you do that, as well.

One place you're sure to find lots of content in need of structured markup is a blog. You're going to have headers, footers, multiple types of navigation (archives, blogrolls, and internal links), and, of course, articles or posts. Let's use HTML5 markup to mock up the front page of the blog for AwesomeCo, a company on the cutting edge of awesomeness.

When we're all done, we'll have something that looks like the following figure.

AwesomeCo Blog!

Latest Posts   Archives   Contributors   Contact Us

How Many Should We Put You Down For?

Posted by Brian on October 1st, 2013 at 2:39PM

The first big rule in sales is that if the person leaves empty-handed, they're likely not going to come back. That's why you have to be somewhat aggressive when you're working with a customer, but you have to make sure you don't overdo it and scare them away.

"Never give someone a chance to say no when selling your product."

One way you can keep a conversation going is to avoid asking questions that have yes or no answers. For example, if you're selling a service plan, don't ever ask "Are you interested in our 3 or 5 year service plan?" Instead, ask "Are you interested in the 3 year service plan or the 5 year plan, which is a better value?" At first glance, they appear to be asking the same thing, and while a customer can still opt out, it's harder for them to opt out of the second question because they have to say more than just "no."

25 Comments ...

Archives

- October 2013
- September 2013
- August 2013
- July 2013
- June 2013
- May 2013
- April 2013
- March 2013
- February 2013
- January 2013
- More

Copyright © 2013 AwesomeCo.

Home   About   Terms of Service   Privacy

Figure 1—The finished layout

To get an idea of what we're going to build, take a look at the following figure. We'll create a fairly typical blog structure, with a main header and horizontal navigation below the header. In the main section, each article has a header and a footer. An article may also have a pull quote, or an aside. There's a sidebar that contains additional navigation elements. Finally, the page has a footer for contact and copyright information. There's nothing new about this structure except that this time, instead of coding it up with lots of <div> tags, we're going to use specific tags to describe these regions.

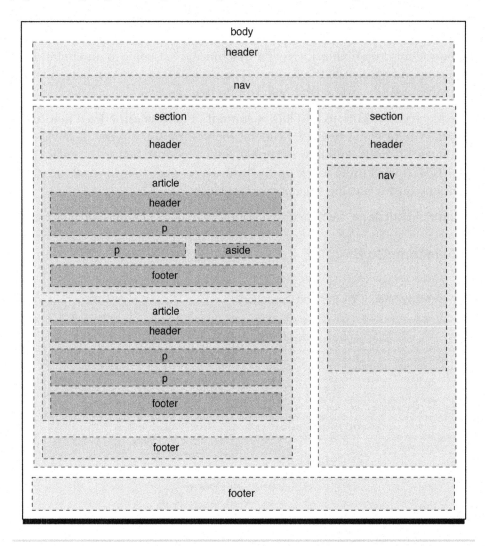

Figure 2—The blog structure using HTML5 semantic markup

It All Starts with the Right Doctype

We want to use HTML5's new elements, and that means we need to let browsers and validators know about the tags we'll be using. Create a new page called index.html, and place this basic HTML5 template into that file.

```
html5_new_tags/index.html
Line 1  <!DOCTYPE html>
     2  <html lang="en-US">
     3    <head>
     4      <meta charset="utf-8">
     5      <title>AwesomeCo Blog</title>
     6    </head>
     7
     8    <body>
     9    </body>
    10  </html>
```

Take a look at the doctype on line 1 of that example. This is all we need for an HTML5 doctype. If you're used to doing web pages, you're probably familiar with the long, hard-to-remember doctypes for XHTML, like this:

```
<!DOCTYPE html PUBLIC "-//W3C//DTD XHTML 1.0 Transitional//EN"
  "http://www.w3.org/TR/xhtml1/DTD/xhtml1-transitional.dtd">
```

Now take another look at the HTML5 doctype:

```
<!DOCTYPE html>
```

That's much simpler and much easier to remember.

The point of a doctype is twofold. First, it's to help validators determine what validation rules an HTML validator needs to use when validating the code. Second, a doctype forces Internet Explorer versions 6, 7, and 8 to go into "standards mode," which is vitally important if you're trying to build pages that work across all browsers. The HTML5 doctype satisfies both of these needs.

Notice the <meta> tag on line 4. This specifies the character encoding of our page. If we want to use Unicode characters, we need to include this at the top, above any lines that contain any text.

With our basic HTML5 template in place, let's start building out our blog.

Headers

Headers, not to be confused with headings such as <h1>, <h2>, and <h3>, may contain all sorts of content, from the company logo to the search box. Our blog header will contain only the blog's title for now.

```
html5_new_tags/index.html
Line 1 <header id="page_header">
    2   <h1>AwesomeCo Blog!</h1>
    3 </header>
```

You're not restricted to having just one header on a page. Each section or article can also have a header, so it can be helpful to use the ID attribute like I did on line 1 to uniquely identify your elements. A unique ID makes it easy to style elements with CSS or locate elements with JavaScript.

Footers

The <footer> tag defines footer information for a document or an adjacent section. You've seen footers before on websites. They usually contain information like the copyright date and who owns the site, although it's common for footers to contain complex navigation structures. The specification says we can have multiple footers in a document too, so that means we could use the footers within our blog articles.

For now, let's define a simple footer for our page. Since we can have more than one footer, we'll give this one an ID just like we did with the header. It'll help us uniquely identify this particular footer when we want to add styles to this element and its children.

```
html5_new_tags/index.html
<footer id="page_footer">
  <p>Copyright © 2013 AwesomeCo.</p>
</footer>
```

This footer simply contains a copyright date. However, like headers, footers on pages often contain other elements, including navigational elements.

Navigation

Navigation is vital to the success of a website. People simply aren't going to stick around if you make it too hard for them to find what they're looking for, so it makes sense for navigation to get its own HTML tag.

Let's add a navigation section to our document's header. We'll add links to the blog's home page, the archives, a page that lists the contributors to the blog, and a link to a contact page.

Your page can have multiple navigation elements. You often have navigation in the header and the footer, so now you can identify those explicitly. Our blog's footer needs links to the AwesomeCo home page, the company's "about us" page, and the company's terms of service and privacy policies. We'll add these as another unordered list within the page's <footer> element.

html5_new_tags/index.html

```
<footer id="page_footer">
  <p>Copyright © 2013 AwesomeCo.</p>
  <nav>
    <ul>
      <li><a href="#">Home</a></li>
      <li><a href="#">About</a></li>
      <li><a href="#">Terms of Service</a></li>
      <li><a href="#">Privacy</a></li>
    </ul>
  </nav>
</footer>
```

We'll use CSS to change how both of these navigation bars look, so don't worry about the appearance yet. The point of these new elements is to describe the content, not to describe how the content looks. That's what CSS is for. Let's keep working on the markup.

Sections and Articles

Sections are the logical regions of a page, and the <section> tag is here to replace the abused <div> tag when it comes to describing logical sections of a page.

html5_new_tags/index.html

```
<section id="posts">
</section>
```

Don't get carried away with sections, though. Use them to logically group your content! Here we've created a section that will hold all the blog posts. However, each post shouldn't be in its own section. We have a more appropriate tag for that.

Articles

The <article> tag is the perfect element to describe the actual content of a web page. With so many elements on a page, including headers, footers, navigational elements, advertisements, widgets, and social-media sharing buttons, it might be easy to forget that people come to a site because they're interested in the content you're providing. The <article> tag helps you describe that content.

So what's the difference between an <article> and a <section>? Think of a <section> as a logical part of a document with related content. Think of an <article> as actual content, such as a magazine article, blog post, or news item. Moreover, you should be able to syndicate the contents of an article; it should be able to stand on its own.

To put it another way, a <section> is like the sports section of a newspaper. The sports section has many articles, each one able to stand on its own. Each of those articles may again be divided into its own bunch of sections.

Some sections of a web page, like headers and footers, have proper tags. A section is a rather generic element you can use to logically group content.

Each of our articles will have a header, some content, and a footer. We define an entire article like this:

```
html5_new_tags/index.html
<article class="post">
  <header>
    <h2>How Many Should We Put You Down For?</h2>
    <p>Posted by Brian on
      <time datetime="2013-10-01T14:39">October 1st, 2013 at 2:39PM</time>
    </p>
  </header>
  <p>
    The first big rule in sales is that if the person leaves empty-handed,
    they're likely not going to come back. That's why you have to be
    somewhat aggressive when you're working with a customer, but you have
    to make sure you don't overdo it and scare them away.
  </p>
  <p>
    One way you can keep a conversation going is to avoid asking questions
    that have yes or no answers. For example, if you're selling a service
    plan, don't ever ask &ldquo;Are you interested in our 3 or 5 year
    service plan?&rdquo; Instead, ask &ldquo;Are you interested in the 3
    year service plan or the 5 year plan, which is a better value?&rdquo;
    At first glance, they appear to be asking the same thing, and while
    a customer can still opt out, it's harder for them to opt out of
    the second question because they have to say more than just
    &ldquo;no.&rdquo;
  </p>
  <footer>
    <p><a href="comments"><i>25 Comments</i></a> ...</p>
  </footer>
</article>
```

We can use <header> and <footer> elements inside of our articles, which makes it much easier to describe those specific sections. We can also divide our article into multiple sections using the <section> element.

Asides and Sidebars

Sometimes you have content that adds something extra to your main content, such as pull quotes, diagrams, additional thoughts, or related links. You can use the new <aside> tag to identify these elements.

```
html5_new_tags/index.html
<aside>
  <p>
    &ldquo;Never give someone a chance to say no when
    selling your product.&rdquo;
  </p>
</aside>
```

We'll place the callout quote in an <aside> element. We'll nest this <aside> within the article, keeping it close to its related content.

Our completed section, with the aside, looks like this:

```
html5_new_tags/index.html
<section id="posts">
  <article class="post">
    <header>
      <h2>How Many Should We Put You Down For?</h2>
      <p>Posted by Brian on
        <time datetime="2013-10-01T14:39">October 1st, 2013 at 2:39PM</time>
      </p>
    </header>
    <aside>
      <p>
        &ldquo;Never give someone a chance to say no when
        selling your product.&rdquo;
      </p>
    </aside>
    <p>
      The first big rule in sales is that if the person leaves empty-handed,
      they're likely not going to come back. That's why you have to be
      somewhat aggressive when you're working with a customer, but you have
      to make sure you don't overdo it and scare them away.
    </p>
    <p>
      One way you can keep a conversation going is to avoid asking questions
      that have yes or no answers. For example, if you're selling a service
      plan, don't ever ask &ldquo;Are you interested in our 3 or 5 year
      service plan?&rdquo; Instead, ask &ldquo;Are you interested in the 3
      year service plan or the 5 year plan, which is a better value?&rdquo;
      At first glance, they appear to be asking the same thing, and while
      a customer can still opt out, it's harder for them to opt out of
      the second question because they have to say more than just
      &ldquo;no.&rdquo;
    </p>
    <footer>
      <p><a href="comments"><i>25 Comments</i></a> ...</p>
    </footer>
  </article>
</section>
```

Now we just have to add the sidebar section.

Our blog has a sidebar on the right side that contains links to the archives for the blog. If you're thinking that we could use the aside tag to define the sidebar of our blog, think again. You *could* do it that way, but it goes against the spirit of the specification. The <aside> is designed to show content related to an article. It's a good place to show related links, a glossary, or a pull quote.

To mark up our sidebar that contains our archive list, we'll use another <section> tag and a <nav> tag.

```
html5_new_tags/index.html
<section id="sidebar">

  <nav>
    <h3>Archives</h3>

    <ul>
      <li><a href="2013/10">October 2013</a></li>
      <li><a href="2013/09">September 2013</a></li>
      <li><a href="2013/08">August 2013</a></li>
      <li><a href="2013/07">July 2013</a></li>
      <li><a href="2013/06">June 2013</a></li>
      <li><a href="2013/05">May 2013</a></li>
      <li><a href="2013/04">April 2013</a></li>
      <li><a href="2013/03">March 2013</a></li>
      <li><a href="2013/02">February 2013</a></li>
      <li><a href="2013/01">January 2013</a></li>
      <li><a href="all">More</a></li>
    </ul>

  </nav>

</section>
```

In our case, the links in our page's sidebar are a secondary navigation. Not every group of links needs to be wrapped with the <nav> element; we reserve that element specifically for navigation regions.

That's it for our blog's structure. Now let's turn our attention to the layout.

Styling the Blog

We apply styles to these new elements just like we'd style <div> elements. First we create a new stylesheet file called stylesheets/style.css and attach it to our HTML document by placing a stylesheet link in the header, like this:

```
html5_new_tags/index.html
<link rel="stylesheet" href="stylesheets/style.css">
```

`html5_new_tags/stylesheets/style.css`
```css
body{
  margin: 15px auto;
  font-family: Arial, "MS Trebuchet", sans-serif;
  width: 960px;
}

p{ margin: 0 0 20px 0;}

p, li{ line-height: 20px; }
```

Next we define the header's width.

`html5_new_tags/stylesheets/style.css`
```css
#page_header{ width: 100%; }
```

We style the main navigation links by transforming the bulleted lists into a horizontal navigation bar by floating all of the list items so they fall on the same line:

`html5_new_tags/stylesheets/style.css`
```css
#page_header > nav > ul, #page_footer > nav > ul{
  list-style: none;
  margin: 0;
  padding: 0;
}

#page_header > nav > ul > li, #page_footer nav > ul > li{
  margin: 0 20px 0 0;
  padding: 0;
  display: inline;
}
```

We add a little margin to the right side of each <li> so we get space between each menu entry. We're using the shorthand version of the margin rule, which reads top, right, bottom, left. Think of it like an analog clock; 12 is at the top, 3 is on the right, 6 is at the bottom, and 9 is on the left.

Next we style the main content to create a large content column and a smaller sidebar. The posts section needs to be floated left and given a width, and we need to float the callout inside the article. While we're doing that, let's bump up the font size for the callout.

`html5_new_tags/stylesheets/style.css`
```css
#posts{
  float: left;
  width: 74%;
}
```

```
#posts aside{
  float: right;
  font-size: 20px;
  line-height: 40px;
  margin-left: 5%;
  width: 35%;
}
```

Then we float the sidebar and define its width:

html5_new_tags/stylesheets/style.css
```
#sidebar{
  float: left;
  width: 25%;
}
```

Last, we need to clear the floats on the footer so that it sits at the bottom of the page. Remember that whenever we float something, the element gets removed from the normal document flow. Clearing an element tells the browser not to float that element.[1]

html5_new_tags/stylesheets/style.css
```
#page_footer{
  clear: both;
  display: block;
  text-align: center;
  width: 100%;
}
```

These are just basic styles. From here, I'm confident you can make this look much, much better.

Falling Back

Although this all works great in Internet Explorer 9, Firefox, Chrome, Opera, and Safari, the people in management aren't going to be too happy when they see the mess that Internet Explorer 8 makes out of our page. The content displays fine, but since Internet Explorer 8 doesn't understand these elements, it can't apply styles to them, and the whole page resembles something from the mid 1990s.

The only way to make Internet Explorer 8 and older style these elements is to use JavaScript to define the elements as part of the document. That turns out to be really easy. We add this code to the <head> section of the page so it executes before the browser renders any elements. We place it inside a *conditional comment*, a special type of comment that only Internet Explorer will read.

---

1. https://developer.mozilla.org/en-US/docs/Web/CSS/clear

```
html5_new_tags/index.html
<!--[if lte IE 8]>
<script>
  document.createElement("nav");
  document.createElement("header");
  document.createElement("footer");
  document.createElement("section");
  document.createElement("aside");
  document.createElement("article");
</script>
<![endif]-->
```

This particular comment targets any version of Internet Explorer older than version 9.0. If we reload our page, it looks correct now.

This approach creates a dependency on JavaScript, though, so you need to take that into consideration. The improved organization and readability of the document make it worth it, and since there are no accessibility concerns, because the contents still display and are read by a screen reader, you're only making the presentation seem grossly out-of-date to your users who have disabled JavaScript intentionally.

This approach is fine for adding support for a handful of elements or for understanding how you can add support. Remy Sharp's brilliant html5shiv takes this approach much further and might be more appropriate for incorporating fallback support if you're looking to support many more elements.[2]

---

2. http://code.google.com/p/html5shiv/

Tip 2

Showing Progress toward a Goal with the <meter> Element

AwesomeCo is holding a charity fundraiser in a few months and looking to get $5000 donated by the general public. Because AwesomeCo is such an awesome company, it's planning to kick in an additional $5000 if people pledge enough support to hit the original $5000 goal. AwesomeCo wants to display a progress meter on one of its pages. When we're done, we'll have something that looks like the following figure.

While we can certainly achieve that with some <div> tags styled with CSS, we can also use the new <meter> tag, which is designed specifically for this task.

The <meter> tag helps you semantically describe an actual meter. In order for your meter to be in harmony with the specification, you shouldn't use your meter for things with arbitrary minimum or maximum values, like height and weight. However, you *could* use <meter> for temperature if you treated it like a *thermometer*, where you would set low and high values.

In our case, we want to show how close we are to our goal of $5000. We have a minimum and a maximum value, so it's a perfect fit for us.

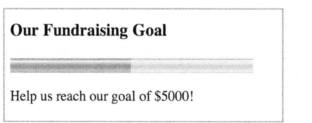

Figure 3—A meter to show progress toward our goal

Let's build a quick prototype by creating a new HTML5 document. We'll represent our meter with this code, hard-coding 2500.00 as our current value to demonstrate how it works right now.

```
html5_meter/index.html
<h3>Our Fundraising Goal</h3>
<meter title="USD" id="pledge_goal"
        value="2500.00" min="0" max="5000.00">
</meter>
<p>Help us reach our goal of $5000!</p>
```

We can control the width of the meter using CSS as follows. Create the file stylesheets/style.css and add this to it:

html5_meter/stylesheets/style.css

```
meter{
  width: 280px;
}
```

Don't forget to link to the CSS file in the <head> section of the HTML page:

html5_meter/index.html

```
<link rel="stylesheet" href="stylesheets/style.css">
```

When we look at this in the browser, we see a very nice meter. But meters aren't supported everywhere, so we need a good fallback solution.

Falling Back

Not every browser recognizes the <meter> tag. But we can easily solve that by constructing our own meter using jQuery and the information we embedded in the <meter> element. To do this we'll create a new file called javascripts/fallback.js that will hold our JavaScript solution. We need to load jQuery and this new file at the bottom of our page.

First, to detect if the browser supports the <meter> element, we create the meter element and check if the element has the max attribute defined. If it's undefined, we can assume that the browser doesn't understand enough of the <meter> to interpret our markup. We declare this as a function called noMeterSupport(), like this:

html5_meter/javascripts/fallback.js

```
var noMeterSupport = function(){
  return(document.createElement('meter').max === undefined);
}
```

Then we use jQuery to grab the values from the meter and construct a meter when there's no support for the <meter>.

Our meter is going to consist of an outer box that will represent the total length of the meter, which we'll call the fakeMeter; an inner box, which we'll call the fill; and a text label that shows the dollar amount. We'll also attach some styles to these elements. Once we have the new element in place, we replace the <meter> tag with our own.

html5_meter/javascripts/fallback.js

```
Line 1  if (noMeterSupport()) {
   -      var fakeMeter, fill, label, labelText, max, meter, value;
   -      meter = $("#pledge_goal");
   -      value = meter.attr("value");
```

```
5    max = meter.attr("max");
-    labelText = "$" + meter.val();

-    fakeMeter = $("<div></div>");
-    fakeMeter.addClass("meter");
10   label = $("<span>" + labelText + "</span>");
-    label.addClass("label");

-    fill = $("<div></div>");
-    fill.addClass("fill");
15   fill.css("width",(value / max * 100) + "%");
-    fill.append("<div style='clear:both;'><br></div>");
-    fakeMeter.append(fill);
-    fakeMeter.append(label);
-    meter.replaceWith(fakeMeter);
20 }
```

If this code is a little confusing, check out Appendix 2, *jQuery Primer*, on page 263, for a short overview of basic jQuery.

With the JavaScript in place, we can turn our attention to styling the meter.

html5_meter/stylesheets/style.css
```
.meter{
  border: 1px solid #000;
  display: block;
  position: relative;
  width: 280px;
}
```

We give it a border and a width, and we set its positioning to relative so we can then easily position the label inside of it. Then we define the inner fill with a gradient fill, like this:

html5_meter/stylesheets/style.css
```
.fill{
  background-color: #693;
  background-image: -webkit-gradient(
      linear,
      left bottom,
      left top,
      color-stop(0.37, rgb(14,242,30)),
      color-stop(0.69, rgb(41,255,57))
  );

  background-image: -moz-linear-gradient(
      center bottom,
      rgb(14,242,30) 37%,
      rgb(41,255,57) 69%
  );
}
```

That gradient syntax is a little complex and we'll talk about it in more detail in Chapter 8, *Eye Candy*, on page 151. Once we've styled the fill, we need to place the label for the dollar amount inside of the bar.

html5_meter/stylesheets/style.css
```css
.label{
  position: absolute;
  right: 0;
  top: 0;
  z-index: 1000;
}
```

We're absolutely positioning the label inside of the bar. It will sit on a layer above the fill. Our finished fallback meter looks like the following figure.

Our Fundraising Goal

$2500.00

Help us reach our goal of $5000!

Figure 4—Our fallback meter

Users without JavaScript enabled will still see the content we placed within the opening and closing meter element, which means we have to be mindful of what we place there.

Progress Bars

If you need to implement an upload progress bar in a web application, you should investigate the <progress> tag introduced in HTML5.

The <progress> tag is similar to <meter>, but it's designed to show active progress like you'd see if you were uploading a file (rather than a measurement that's not currently moving, like a snapshot of available storage on the server for a given user). The markup for a progress bar is very similar to the <meter> tag.

html5_meter/progress.html
```html
<progress id="progressbar" min="0" max="100" value="0"></progress>
```

Like <meter>, <progress> isn't supported by all browsers yet, To support it, you use JavaScript to grab the values in the meter and build your own visualization. Or you can use the HTML5-Progress polyfill by Lea Verou.[3]

---

3. http://lea.verou.me/polyfills/progress/

Tip 3

Creating Pop-Up Windows with Custom Data Attributes

If you've built any web applications that use JavaScript to grab information out of a document, you know that it can sometimes involve a bit of hackery and parsing to make things work. You'll end up inserting extra information into event handlers or abusing the rel or class attributes to inject behavior. Those days are now over thanks to the introduction of custom data attributes.

Custom data attributes all start with the prefix data- and are ignored by the validator for HTML5 documents. You can attach a custom data attribute to any element you'd like, whether it be metadata about a photograph, latitude and longitude coordinates, or, as you'll see in this tip, dimensions for a pop-up window. Best of all, you can use custom data attributes right now in nearly every web browser, since they can be easily grabbed with JavaScript.

Separating Behavior from Content, or Why onclick() Is Bad

Over the years, pop-up windows have gotten a bad reputation, and rightly so. They're often used to get you to look at an ad, to convince unsuspecting web surfers to install spyware or viruses, or, worse, to give away personal information that is then resold. It's no wonder most browsers have some type of pop-up blocker available.

Pop-ups aren't all bad, though. Web-application developers often rely on pop-up windows to display online help, additional options, or other important user-interface features. To make pop-ups less annoying, we need to implement them in an unobtrusive manner. When you look at AwesomeCo's human-resources page, you see several links that display policies in pop-up windows. Most of them look like this:

```
html5_popups_with_custom_data/original_example_1.html
<a href='#'
   onclick="window.open('help/holiday_pay.html',WinName,'width=300,height=300');">
   Holiday pay
</a>
```

This is a pretty common way to build links that spawn pop-ups. In fact, this is the way JavaScript newbies often learn to make pop-up windows. We should address a couple of problems with this approach before moving on, though.

Improve Accessibility

The very first problem you might notice is that the link's destination isn't set! If JavaScript is disabled, the link won't take the user to the page. That's a huge problem we need to address immediately. Don't *ever* omit the href attribute or give it a value like this under *any* circumstances. Give it the address of the resource that would normally pop up.

```
html5_popups_with_custom_data/original_example_2.html
<a href='help/holiday_pay.html'
  onclick="window.open(this.href,WinName,'width=300,height=300');">
  Holiday pay
</a>
```

The JavaScript code can then read the attached element's href attribute for the link's location.

The first step toward building accessible pages is to ensure that all the functionality works *without* JavaScript. Writing the interactive JavaScript on top of this foundation can be much easier.

Abolish the onclick()

Keep the behavior separate from the content, just like you keep the presentation information separate by using linked style sheets. Using onclick() is easy at first, but imagine a page with fifty links, and you'll see how the onclick() method gets out of hand. First, you're repeating that JavaScript over and over again.

And if you generate this code from some server-side code, you're making the resulting HTML much bigger than it needs to be.

Instead, we can give each of the anchors on the page a class that identifies it as a link.

```
html5_popups_with_custom_data/original_example_3.html
<a href="help/holiday_pay.html" class="popup">Holiday Pay</a>
```

To make handling events work smoothly across browsers, we'll use jQuery. At the bottom of the page, right above the closing <body> tag, bring in the jQuery library.

```
html5_popups_with_custom_data/original_example_3.html
<script
  src='http://ajax.googleapis.com/ajax/libs/jquery/1.9.1/jquery.min.js'>
</script>
```

Then right below that, add a new <script> tag that contains this code:

```
html5_popups_with_custom_data/original_example_3.html
$("a.popup").click(function(event){
  event.preventDefault();
  window.open(this.getAttribute('href'));
});
```

We use a jQuery selector to grab all elements with the class of popup, and then add an observer to each element's click event.

The function we pass to the click() method will be executed when someone clicks the link. The preventDefault method prevents the default click-event behavior. In this case, it prevents the browser from following the link and displaying a new page.

However, we've lost the information on how to size and position the window. We want a page designer who isn't very familiar with JavaScript to still be able to set the dimensions of a window on a per-link basis.

Custom Data Attributes to the Rescue!

Situations like this are common when building any JavaScript-enabled application. As we've seen, storing the window's desired height and width with the code is desirable, but the onclick() approach has lots of drawbacks. Instead we can embed these attributes on the element. All we have to do is construct the link like this:

```
html5_popups_with_custom_data/popup.html
<a href="help/holiday_pay.html"
   data-width="600"
   data-height="400"
   title="Holiday Pay"
   class="popup">Holiday pay</a>
```

Now we modify the click() event we wrote to grab the options from the link's custom data attributes and pass them to the window.open() method.

```
html5_popups_with_custom_data/popup.html
$("a.popup").click(function(event){
  event.preventDefault();
  var link = this;
  var href = link.getAttribute("href");
  var height = link.getAttribute("data-height");
  var width = link.getAttribute("data-width");

  window.open (href,"popup",
    "height=" + height +",width=" + width + "");
});
```

We use jQuery strictly to handle the click() event. The element we clicked on is represented by the keyword this within the click-handler function. Using getAttribute(), we retrieve the attributes we need from the elements to construct our pop-up window.

That's all there is to it! The link now opens in a new window.

Falling Back

These attributes work in older browsers right now as long as they support JavaScript. The custom data attributes won't trip up the browser, and your document will be valid. Since you're using the HTML5 doctype, the attributes that start with data- will all be ignored.

We can access custom data attributes another way, using dataset. This converts the custom data attributes into properties, which we access like this:

```
html5_popups_with_custom_data/popup_dataset.html
var height = link.dataset.height;
var width = link.dataset.width;
```

This is convenient, but you should be aware of a couple of issues. First and foremost, it doesn't work in Internet Explorer 10 or previous, so it's not a great fit for general-purpose solutions yet. Second, if you had a custom data attribute like data-mobile-image-size, we'd have to access it as dataset.mobileImageSize. The properties on dataset are converted to camel case.

A Word of Caution

In this example, we used custom data attributes to provide additional information to a client-side script. It's a clever approach to a specific problem and illustrates one way to use these attributes. It does tend to mix presentation information with markup, but it's a simple way to see how easy it is to use JavaScript to read values you embed in your page.

Defining an FAQ with a Description List

If there's one constant about content-driven sites, it's that there's a list of frequently asked questions (FAQs). The good sites fill their FAQs with questions people actually ask; the rest use the FAQ section to answer questions their main website copy should've already covered. Regardless of the FAQs' content, historically it's been challenging to come up with good markup when we implement them.

Web developers have used everything from ordered lists to <div> tags with classes and tons of styling, but those approaches aren't good semantic fits. We want to be able to link a question to an answer, and we can do this easily and semantically using the <dl> element.

In previous versions of HTML, the <dl> element was called a *definition list*, designed to associate a term to a definition. But in HTML5, <dl> is a *descriptive list*. Although the code is mostly the same, the specification change makes it more clear that we have flexibility in how we use this element.

This is great, because AwesomeCo needs an FAQ that explains what the company does. For this example, we'll make some things up and use dummy content.

The Structure

The structure for our FAQ will be pretty simple. We'll use the <dl> tag to define the FAQ itself, and we'll use the <dt> tag for each question. We'll place the answer to each question within the <dd> element.

```
html5_descriptionlist_faq/index.html
<article>
  <h1>AwesomeCo FAQ</h1>
  <dl>
    <dt>What is it that AwesomeCo actually does?</dt>
    <dd>
      <p>
        AwesomeCo creates innovative solutions for business that
        leverage growth and promote synergy, resulting in a better
        life for the global community.
      </p>
    </dd>
  </dl>
</article>
```

The default styling in most browsers works pretty well, as you can see in the following figure; each answer is indented underneath each question.

Figure 5—Our usnstyled FAQ

With this markup in place, we can apply styles without adding classes to the HTML elements. It's also easy for us to collapse the entries in the FAQ with JavaScript if we want to save real estate on smartphones.

Every browser supports the <dl> tag; the only thing that changed in HTML5 is how we're supposed to use it with content. There's no need for a fallback solution.

2.1 The Future

You can do some interesting things with these new tags and attributes. For example, we can easily identify and disable navigation and article footers using print style sheets:

```
nav, article>footer{display:none}
```

We can use scripting languages to quickly identify all of the articles on a page or on a site. But most important, we can mark up content with appropriate tags that describe it so we can write better style sheets and better JavaScript. Take a look at the specification, and you'll find a few more elements that browsers will eventually implement, including markup for dialog boxes (<dialog>), highlighted text (<mark>), and more.

Custom data attributes give developers the flexibility to embed all sorts of information in their markup. In fact, we'll use them again in Chapter 6, *Drawing in the Browser*, on page 111.

We can use them with JavaScript to determine whether a form tag should submit via Ajax, by simply locating any form tag with data-remote=true. We can also use them to display dates and times in a user's time zone while still caching the page. Simply put the date on the HTML page as UTC, and convert it to the user's local time on the client side. These attributes allow you to embed real, usable data in your pages, and you can expect to see more and more frameworks and libraries taking advantage of them. I'm sure you'll find lots of great uses for them in your own work.

And we can help wipe out Divitis once and for all!

CHAPTER 3

Creating User-Friendly Web Forms

If you've ever designed a complicated user interface, you know how limiting the basic HTML form controls are. You're stuck using text fields, select menus, radio buttons, checkboxes, and sometimes the even clunkier *multiple select* lists that you constantly have to explain to your users how to use. ("Hold down the Ctrl key and click the entries you want, unless you're on a Mac, in which case you use the Cmd key.")

So, you do what all good web developers do—you turn to jQuery UI,[1] or you roll your own controls and features using a combination of HTML, CSS, and JavaScript. But when you look at a form that has sliders, calendar controls, spinboxes, autocomplete fields, and visual editors, you quickly realize that you've created a nightmare for yourself. You'll have to make sure that the controls you include on your page don't conflict with any of the other controls you've included or any of the other JavaScript libraries on the page. You can spend hours implementing a calendar picker only to find out later that the color-picker control you used no longer works because that plug-in wasn't written carefully enough and isn't compatible with the latest version of jQuery your project is using.

If you're smiling, it's because you've been there. If you're fuming, I'm guessing it's for the same reason. There is hope, though. In this chapter, we're going to build some interfaces using new form-field types, and implement autofocusing and placeholder text. Then we'll look at how we can do some simple client-side validation. Finally, we'll discuss how to use the new contenteditable attribute to turn any HTML field into a user-input control.

Specifically, we'll cover the following features:

---

1.   http://jqueryui.com/

Email field [<input type="email">]
> Displays a form field for email addresses. *[O10.1, iOS, A3]*

URL field [<input type="url">]
> Displays a form field for URLs. *[O10.1, iOS5, A3]*

Range (slider) [<input type="range">]
> Displays a slider control. *[C5, S4, F23, IE10, O10.1]*

Number [<input type="number">]
> Displays a form field for numbers, often as a spinbox. *[C5, S5, O10.1, iOS5, A3]*

Color [<input type="color">]
> Displays a field for specifying colors. *[C5, O11]*

Date fields [<input type="date">]
> Displays a form field for dates. Supports date, month, or week. *[C5, S5, O10.1]*

Dates with times [<input type="datetime">]
> Displays a form field for dates with times. Supports datetime, datetime-local, or time. *[S5, O10.1]*

Search field [<input type="search">]]
> Displays a form field for search keywords. *[C5, S4, O10.1, iOS]*

Autofocus support [<input type="text" autofocus>]
> Support for placing the focus on a specific form element. *[C5, S4]*

Placeholder support [<input type="email" placeholder="me@example.com">]
> Support for displaying placeholder text inside of a form field. *[C5, F4, S4]*

Required fields [<input type="email" required>]
> Prevent submission of pages unless the fields are filled in. *[C23, F16, IE10, O12]*

Validation via regex [<input pattern="/^(\s|\d+)$/">]*
> Prevents submission of pages unless the field's contents match the pattern. *[C23, F16, IE10, O12]*

In-place editing support [<p contenteditable>lorem ipsum</p>]
> Support for in-place editing of content via the browser. *[C4, F3.5, S3.2, IE6, O10.1, iOS5, A3]*

Let's start by discussing some of the extremely useful form-field types.

Tip 5

Describing Data with New Input Fields

HTML5 introduces several new input types that you can use to better describe the type of data your users are entering. In addition to the standard text fields, radio buttons, and checkbox elements, you can use elements such as email fields, calendars, color pickers, spinboxes, and sliders. Browsers can use these new fields to display better controls to the user without the need for JavaScript. Mobile devices and virtual keyboards for tablets and touch screens can use the field types to display different keyboard layouts. For example, Safari on iOS displays alternate keyboard layouts when the user is entering data into the URL and email types, making special characters like @, ., :, and / easily accessible.

AwesomeCo is working on creating a new project-management web application to make it easier for developers and managers to keep up with the progress of the many projects they have going on. Each project has a name, a contact email address, and a staging URL so managers can preview the website as it's being built. There are also fields for the start date, priority, and estimated number of hours the project should take to complete. Finally, the development manager would like to give each project a color so he can quickly identify projects when he looks at reports.

Let's mock up a quick project preferences page using the new HTML5 fields. When we're done, our form will look something like this:

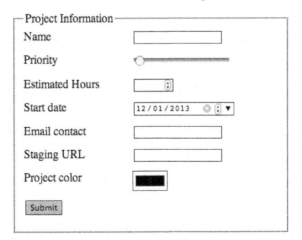

Describing the Form

Let's create a new HTML5 page with a basic HTML form that does a POST request, with the assumption that at some point there'll be a page that processes this form. Since there's nothing special about the project's name field, we'll use the trusty text type for this first input:

```
html5_forms/index.html
<form method="post" action="/projects/1">

  <fieldset id="personal_information">
    <legend>Project Information</legend>
    <ol>
      <li>
        <label for="name">Name</label>
        <input type="text" name="name" id="name">
      </li>
      <li>
        <input type="submit" value="Submit">
      </li>
    </ol>

  </fieldset>

</form>
```

We're marking up this form with labels wrapped in an ordered list. Labels are essential when creating accessible forms. The for attribute of the label references the id of its associated form element. This helps screen readers identify fields on a page. The ordered list provides a nice way of listing the fields without resorting to complex table or <div> structures. This also gives us a way to mark up the order in which we'd like people to fill out the fields. Once we build the entire form, we'll use some CSS rules to line things up.

Creating a Slider Using range

Sliders are common for letting users decrease or increase a numerical value and could be a great way to quickly allow managers to both visualize and modify the priority of the project. So let's implement a slider with the range type:

```
html5_forms/index.html
<label for="priority">Priority</label>
<input type="range" min="0" max="10"
       name="priority" value="0" id="priority">
```

We add this to the form within a new <li> element, just like the name field.

Chrome, Safari, and Opera each implement a slider widget, which looks like this:

Priority

Notice that we've also set the min and max range for the slider. That will constrain the value for the form field.

Handling Numbers with Spinboxes

We ask users to enter numbers a lot, and although typing numbers is fairly simple, spinboxes can simplify making minor adjustments. A spinbox is a control with arrows that increment or decrement the value in the box. Let's use the spinbox for the project's Estimated Hours field. In addition to the easier data entry it provides, using this field clearly describes the type of data the field holds.

html5_forms/index.html
```
<label for="estimated_hours">Estimated Hours</label>
<input type="number" name="estimated_hours"
       min="0" max="1000"
       id="estimated_hours">
```

Chrome, Safari, and Opera support the spinbox control, which looks like this:

Estimated Hours

The spinbox also lets people type in the value instead of using the arrows. And like with range sliders, we can set minimum and maximum values. However, those minimum and maximum ranges won't be applied to any value the user types into the field, so you'll need to restrict that with scripting or with HTML5's validation support, which we'll explore in Tip 8, *Validating User Input without JavaScript*, on page 54.

We can control the size of the increment step by giving a value to the step parameter. It defaults to 1 but can be any numerical value.

Dates

We need to record the start date of the project, and we want to make that as easy as possible. The date input type is a perfect fit here.

html5_forms/index.html
```
<label for="start_date">Start date</label>
<input type="date" name="start_date" id="start_date"
       value="2013-12-01">
```

It clearly describes the type of data the field will hold, but when implemented properly, the user will see a calendar widget, like the one Chrome displays:

Start date
Email contact
Staging URL
Project color
Submit

| December 2013 ▼ | | | | ◄ | ● | ► |
Sun	Mon	Tue	Wed	Thu	Fri	Sat
1	2	3	4	5	6	7
8	9	10	11	12	13	14
15	16	17	18	19	20	21
22	23	24	25	26	27	28
29	30	31	1	2	3	4

At the time of writing, Chrome and Opera are the only desktop browsers that currently support a full calendar picker, but some mobile browsers take advantage of this field to make it easy for users to select the month, date, and year. All other browsers simply render a text field.

Email

The email input type is designed to hold either a single email address or an email-address list, so it's the perfect candidate for our email field.

```
html5_forms/index.html
<label for="email">Email contact</label>
<input type="email" name="email" id="email">
```

Mobile devices get the most benefit from this type of form field, because the virtual keyboard layouts often change to make entering email addresses easier. Notice in the following that the @ symbol is prominent on both the iPhone and Android keyboards:

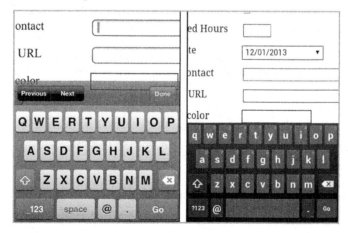

URL

Our form has a field for the project's staging URL. There's a field type designed to handle URLs, too. Adding the Staging URL field is as simple as adding this code:

```
html5_forms/index.html
<label for="url">Staging URL</label>
<input type="url" name="url" id="url">
```

Like the email field type, this field type is especially nice for your visitors on iOS or Android devices because these display a much different keyboard layout, with helper buttons for quickly entering web addresses, similar to the keyboard displayed when entering a URL into the mobile browser's address bar.

Color

Finally, we need to provide a way to enter a color code, and we'll use the color type for that.

```
html5_forms/index.html
<label for="project_color">Project color</label>
<input type="color" name="project_color" id="project_color">
```

At the time of writing, only some browsers display a color-picker control, but that shouldn't stop you from using this field. You're using proper markup to describe your content, and that's going to come in handy in the future, especially when you need to provide fallback support.

Styling the Form

We'll style the form with some basic CSS. Create a new file called stylesheets/style.css and link it in the <head> section of the form's page.

```
html5_forms/index.html
<link rel="stylesheet" href="stylesheets/style.css">
```

First we remove the numbering, margins, and padding from the list:

```
html5_forms/stylesheets/style.css
ol{
  list-style: none;
  margin: 0;
  padding :0;
}

ol li{
  clear: both;
  margin: 0 0 10px 0;
  padding: 0;
}
```

Then we align the labels and the input fields and add a little styling to the input fields.

```
html5_forms/stylesheets/style.css
label{
  float: left;
  width: 150px;
}

input{ border: 1px solid #333; }

input:focus{ background-color: #ffe; }
```

Using the :focus pseudoclass, we can apply styling to the field that currently has focus.

This gives us a presentable and semantic web form. We could go even farther and identify each of the field types using CSS.

Chrome and Opera support most of these new controls, but when you open the page in Firefox, Safari, or Internet Explorer, many of the fields will display as regular text fields.

Falling Back

Browsers that don't understand these new types simply fall back to the text type, so your forms will still be usable. At that point you can decide whether you want to use a widget or another library. For example, you can check if the browser supports the calendar control, and if it doesn't, you could add one using jQuery UI. Then as more browsers implement full-featured controls, you can remove your fixes. Let's go through the process by adding support for the color picker. The process will be basically the same for any other control for which we'd want to create a fallback.

Replacing the Color Picker

Thanks to CSS3's attribute selector, we can easily identify and replace the color picker using jQuery and the jQuery-simple-color plug-in.[2] We locate any <input> field with the type of color and apply the plug-in like this:

```
$('input[type=color]').simpleColor();
```

Since we used the new form types in our markup, we don't have to add an additional class name or other markup to identify the color pickers. CSS attribute selectors and HTML5 go together quite well.

---

2. http://recursive-design.com/projects/jquery-simple-color/

Typically, to use a plug-in like SimpleColor, we would download the plug-in, attach it to our page with a <script> tag, and then attach the plug-in to the element with a separate bit of JavaScript. But we want to use this color picker plug-in only if the browser doesn't support the control natively, so we'll use JavaScript to detect whether the browser supports input fields with a type of color. If it doesn't, then we'll load the plug-in dynamically.

First, since we're going to need jQuery, we'll load that by placing it right above the closing <body> tag:

html5_forms/index.html

```
<script
  src="http://ajax.googleapis.com/ajax/libs/jquery/1.9.1/jquery.min.js">
</script>
```

Then we create a new file called javascripts/fallbacks.js and link it to the bottom of the HTML page with a <script> tag, like this:

html5_forms/index.html

```
<script src="javascripts/fallbacks.js"></script>
```

Then, in javascripts/fallbacks.js we create a function to detect color support in the browser:

html5_forms/javascripts/fallbacks.js

```
Line 1  function hasColorSupport(){
    -     element = document.createElement("input");
    -     element.setAttribute("type", "color");
    -     var hasColorType = (element.type === "color");
    5     // handle partial implementation
    -     if(hasColorType){
    -       var testString = "foo";
    -       element.value = testString;
    -       hasColorType = (element.value != testString);
   10     }
    -     return(hasColorType);
    -   }
```

In this function we use JavaScript to create an element and set its type attribute to color. Then we retrieve the type attribute to see whether the browser allowed us to set the attribute. If it comes back with a value of color, then we have support for that type.

Things get interesting on line 6. Some browsers have partially implemented the color type. They support the field, but they don't actually display a color widget. We still end up with a text field on the page. So, in our detection method, we set the value for our input field and see whether the value sticks around. If it doesn't, we can assume that the browser has implemented a color picker because the input field isn't acting like a text box.

Finally, we call this detection function. To avoid loading the plug-in when we don't need it, we use JavaScript to inject a new <script> tag, which loads the plug-in and activates it when the script has loaded.

```
html5_forms/javascripts/fallbacks.js
var applyColorPicker = function(){
  $('input[type=color]').simpleColor();
};


if (!hasColorSupport()){
  var script = document.createElement('script');
  script.src = "javascripts/jquery.simple-color.js";

  if(script.readyState){    // IE support
    script.onreadystatechange = function () {
      if (this.readyState === 'loaded' || this.readyState === 'complete'){
        script.onreadystatechange = null;
        applyColorPicker();
      }
    };
  }else{
    // Other browsers
    script.onload = applyColorPicker;
  }

  document.getElementsByTagName("head")[0].appendChild(script);
}
```

Internet Explorer requires us to use onreadystatechange and detect the value of the readystate property. Other browsers simply let us attach a function name to the onload event. By including both we ensure our fallback works across the board.

Now things work fine in all browsers. We just need a little extra CSS to make the color picker line up with the other columns:

```
html5_forms/stylesheets/style.css
.simpleColorContainer, .simpleColorDisplay{
  float: left;
}
```

The process for creating fallbacks for other form fields is the same—we detect whether the browser supports the control natively, and, if it doesn't, we load the necessary library and apply the JavaScript version instead. Eventually you'll be able to phase out the JavaScript controls and rely completely on the controls in the browser. The solution we used works, but the detection technique we used is brittle. It targets a specific set of browsers and works only for the color control. Thankfully, there's a better solution.

Detecting Features with Modernizr

The Modernizr library can detect support for many HTML5 and CSS3 features.[3] It doesn't add the missing functionality, but it does provide several mechanisms similar to the solution we implemented for detecting things that are more bulletproof than solutions we might roll ourselves.

We load Modernizr in the <head> of our document after our CSS references. Modernizr makes a Modernizr object available to us, which we can use to detect features and load fallbacks. For example, here's how we do our color-picker fallback with Modernizr:

```
if(Modernizr.inputtypes.color){
  // we have color support
}else{
  // we don't have color support.
}
```

However, we need to load additional libraries when we don't have support. We can use Modernizr's load() method to detect a feature and load other scripts, then execute our own code when the code loads. Here's how we do it:

```
html5_forms/modernizr/javascripts/fallbacks.js
var applyColorPicker = function(){
  $('input[type=color]').simpleColor();
};

Modernizr.load(
  {
    test: Modernizr.inputtypes.color,
    nope: "javascripts/jquery.simple-color.js",
    callback: function(url, result){
      if (!result){
        applyColorPicker();
      }
    }
  }
);
```

The load() method can take a JavaScript object that defines a specific feature test and what should happen when the feature exists or is missing. We use yep to load scripts when the feature is supported, and nope to load scripts when the feature is missing. We can also define a callback function that runs

---

3.   http://www.modernizr.com/

once the external file was loaded. In our case we check for support for the color control, and if it's unavailable, we load the jQuery plug-in. Then, in the callback, we use the result variable, which will be true if our browser supports the color plug-in, and false if it doesn't. In other words, the result is the result of the test that we ran. We technically don't have to evaluate the result variable here, because callback only gets fired when a script is loaded. In our case, we're loading scripts only when we have no support. However, we could use the yep option, which would let us load additional scripts if the browser supported the color field. Those scripts would also invoke the callback, and then we'd be able to tell what happened in the callback by looking at result.

The load() function is built on top of the yepnope.js library, and so to learn how it works, look at the yepnope.js documentation.[4]

In order to use the load() method we have to build a custom version of Modernizr using an online tool.[5] This builder includes the Yepnope library. In the example-code download, I've included a complete version of Modernizr, but that's not a good fit for production because you should include only the components of Modernizr you need for your specific project.

Before you start throwing Modernizr in your projects, be sure you take some time to understand how it works by exploring its source code. Whether you wrote the code yourself or not, if you use it in your project, you're responsible for it. For example, Modernizr wasn't ready to handle Safari's partial support of the color field right away, so people had to quickly jump in and fix their sites while they waited for Modernizr to update. When the next version of Chrome or Firefox comes out, you may have to hack together a solution to support any changes. Who knows—maybe you'll be able to contribute that solution back to Modernizr!

Because of the complexity involved with detecting features across browsers, we'll use Modernizer throughout this book wherever it makes sense to do so.

Aside from new form-field types, HTML5 introduces a few other attributes for form fields that can help improve usability. Let's take a look at autofocus next.

---

4. http://yepnopejs.com/
5. http://modernizr.com/download/

Tip 6

Jumping to the First Field with Autofocus

You can really speed up data entry if you place the user's cursor in the first field on the form when the page loads. Many search engines do this using JavaScript, and now HTML5 provides this capability as part of the language.

All you have to do is add the autofocus attribute to any form field:

```
html5_forms/autofocus/index.html
<label for="name">Name</label>
<input type="text" name="name" autofocus id="name">
```

You don't need to say autofocus="true" or autofocus="autofocus". If the autofocus attribute is present, the browser will apply the feature.

You can have only one autofocus attribute on a page for it to work reliably. If you have more than one, the browser will focus the user's cursor onto the last autofocused form field.

Falling Back

We can detect the presence of the autofocus attribute and then set focus on the element with a little bit of JavaScript when the user's browser doesn't have autofocus support. This is probably the easiest fallback solution you'll come across. Add this to javascripts/fallbacks.js:

```
html5_forms/autofocus/javascripts/fallbacks.js
if (!Modernizr.autofocus){
  $('input[autofocus]').focus();
}
```

This uses jQuery to focus the field. We could do this with plain JavaScript, but we've already loaded jQuery, and we can use attribute selectors to grab the field with autofocus instead of adding a specific class or ID to the field.

Autofocus makes it easier for users to start working with your forms when they load, but you may want to give them a little more detail about the type of information you'd like them to provide. Let's take a look at the placeholder attribute next.

Providing Hints with Placeholder Text

Placeholder text provides users with instructions on how they should fill in the fields. It's not meant to be a replacement for the <label> tag; it's meant to give users an example.

AwesomeCo's support site requires users to sign up for an account, and one of the biggest problems with the sign-ups is that users keep trying to use insecure passwords. Let's use placeholder text (see the following figure) to give users a little guidance on our password requirements. For consistency's sake, we'll add placeholder text to the other fields too.

```
┌─Create New Account──────────────────┐
│ First Name                          │
│ ┌─────────────────────────────┐     │
│ │John'                        │     │
│ └─────────────────────────────┘     │
│ Last Name                           │
│ ┌─────────────────────────────┐     │
│ │'Smith'                      │     │
│ └─────────────────────────────┘     │
│ Email                               │
│ ┌─────────────────────────────┐     │
│ │user@example.com             │     │
│ └─────────────────────────────┘     │
│ Password                            │
│ ┌─────────────────────────────┐     │
│ │8–10 characters              │     │
│ └─────────────────────────────┘     │
│ Password Confirmation               │
│ ┌─────────────────────────────┐     │
│ │Type your password a         │     │
│ └─────────────────────────────┘     │
│ ┌──────────┐                        │
│ │ Sign Up  │                        │
│ └──────────┘                        │
└─────────────────────────────────────┘
```

Figure 6—Placeholders can help users understand what you're asking them to do.

To include placeholder text, we add the placeholder attribute to each input field, like this:

```
html5_placeholder/index.html
<input id="email" type="email"
       name="email" placeholder="user@example.com">
```

Once we add placeholder text to each field, the entire form's markup looks like this:

```
html5_placeholder/index.html
<form id="create_account" action="/signup" method="post">
  <fieldset id="signup">
    <legend>Create New Account</legend>
    <ol>
      <li>
        <label for="first_name">First Name</label>
        <input id="first_name" type="text"
               autofocus
               name="first_name" placeholder="'John'">
      </li>
      <li>
        <label for="last_name">Last Name</label>
        <input id="last_name" type="text"
               name="last_name" placeholder="'Smith'">
      </li>
      <li>
        <label for="email">Email</label>
        <input id="email" type="email"
               name="email" placeholder="user@example.com">
      </li>
      <li>
        <label for="password">Password</label>
        <input id="password" type="password" name="password" value=""
               autocomplete="off" placeholder="8-10 characters" />
      </li>
      <li>
        <label for="password_confirmation">Password Confirmation</label>
        <input id="password_confirmation" type="password"
               name="password_confirmation" value=""
               autocomplete="off" placeholder="Type your password again" />
      </li>
      <li><input type="submit" value="Sign Up"></li>
    </ol>
  </fieldset>
</form>
```

You may have noticed we've added the autocomplete attribute to the password fields on this form. HTML5 introduces an autocomplete attribute that tells web browsers they should not attempt to automatically fill in data for the field. Some browsers remember data that users have previously typed in, and in some cases, we want to tell the browsers that we'd rather not let users do that.

Since we're once again using the ordered-list element to hold our form fields, we'll add some basic CSS to make the form look nicer.

```
html5_placeholder/stylesheets/style.css
fieldset{
  width: 216px;
}

fieldset ol{
  list-style: none;
  padding:0;
  margin:2px;
}

fieldset ol li{
  margin:0 0 9px 0;
  padding:0;
}

/* Make inputs go to their own line */
fieldset input{
  display:block;
}
```

Now users of Safari, Opera, and Chrome will have helpful text inside the form fields. Let's make Firefox and Internet Explorer play along.

Falling Back

There are lots of proposed solutions for making placeholders work in old browsers, but one of the simplest solutions is the jQuery Placeholder plug-in.[6] We'll use this plug-in the same way we added fallback support for color pickers—by detecting support for placeholders and loading and activating the plug-in only when there's no support.

Let's add support to our form by creating a new file called javascripts/fallbacks.js, which will hold our detection and fallback code. Then we link that file to the HTML page with a <script> tag at the bottom of the page:

```
html5_placeholder/index.html
<script
  src='http://ajax.googleapis.com/ajax/libs/jquery/1.9.1/jquery.min.js'>
</script>
<script src='javascripts/fallbacks.js'></script>
```

We'll use Modernizr just like we did in *Detecting Features with Modernizr*, on page 47, which means we need to include the Modernizr library in the <head> section of our page so it applies things properly:

---

6. https://github.com/mathiasbynens/jquery-placeholder

html5_placeholder/index.html

```
<script src='javascripts/modernizr.js'></script>
```

In javascripts/fallbacks.js we declare a function that invokes the jQuery Placeholder plug-in:

html5_placeholder/javascripts/fallbacks.js

```
var applyPlaceholders = function(){
  $("input").placeholder();
}
```

Then we use Modernizr to detect placeholder support, load the plug-in, and invoke the fallback:

html5_placeholder/javascripts/fallbacks.js

```
Modernizr.load(
  {
    test: Modernizr.placeholder,
    nope: "javascripts/jquery.placeholder.js",
    callback: function(url, result){
      if (!result){
        applyPlaceholders();
      }
    }
  }
);
```

Now we have a pretty decent solution that makes placeholder text a viable option for your web apps, no matter what browser you use.

Placeholders are a great way to give users hints about the way we'd like them to enter data. But we may want to give a little more guidance than that, by making sure the users fill in fields the correct way.

Tip 8

Validating User Input without JavaScript

When we build web forms, we're trying to get data from our users and store it or process it and turn it into useful information. Some of the data we ask for might be required, and other bits might be optional. Sometimes that data needs to be in a certain format, and we want to validate the data before we store it so we can give the user a chance to make corrections. Traditionally, developers validate user input in server-side code, because client-side validation techniques with JavaScript can be easily disabled. Server-side validation results in a clumsy, slow user experience because users have to fill in the fields, submit the form, and wait for the whole page to refresh to see what they did wrong. To give quick feedback to users, developers end up writing client-side validation with JavaScript anyway, effectively writing validation twice. This has its own set of problems.

HTML5 introduces a couple of attributes for form elements that we can use to validate user input on the client side, so we can catch simple input errors before the user sends the requests to the server *without writing JavaScript*.

The AwesomeCo support site's signup page is a great place for us to test out these new attributes. Users need to provide their first name, last name, and email address. They also need to enter a password. Let's start by ensuring the first name, last name, and email fields are filled in.

We require that a user fills in a form field by adding the required attribute to the element just like we do with the <autofocus> attribute. So, we can add the required attribute to the First Name, Last Name, and Email fields on the original signup form.

```
html5_validation/index.html
<li>
  <label for="first_name">First Name</label>

  <input id="first_name" type="text"
    autofocus="true"
    required
    name="first_name" placeholder="'John'">
</li>
<li>
  <label for="last_name">Last Name</label>
```

```
  <input id="last_name" type="text"
    required
    name="last_name" placeholder="'Smith'">
</li>
<li>
  <label for="email">Email</label>

  <input id="email" type="email"
    required
    name="email" placeholder="user@example.com">
</li>
```

Browsers that support this attribute then prevent the form from submitting if the fields are not filled in. We get a nice error message, and we don't have to write a single line of JavaScript validation. Here's how Chrome handles this:

We've also designated the Email field as a required field, and by doing that we get an additional benefit; users need to enter something that looks like an email address.

This is another great reason to use form fields that describe our data.

That takes care of the first three required fields, but we want to ensure the Password field meets the eight-character-minimum requirement.

Validation with Regular Expressions

The pattern attribute lets us specify a regular expression against which we can validate the user data. The browser already knows how to validate email addresses and URLs, but we have specific rules for the Password field So, we add the pattern attribute to the Password field, using a regular-expression rule that enforces our password requirements of eight or more characters with at least one number, an uppercase letter, and one special character.

```
html5_validation/index.html
<li>
  <label for="password">Password</label>
  <input id="password" type="password" name="password" value=""
    autocomplete="off" placeholder="8-10 characters"
    pattern="^(?=.{8,})(?=.*[a-z])(?=.*[A-Z])(?=.*[\d])(?=.*[\W]).*$"
    title="Password must be 8 or more characters with at
          least one number, an uppercase letter, and one special character"
  />
</li>
```

Notice that we use the title attribute here to give a descriptive message as to what the user should enter.

And now when we try to enter something that doesn't match we get an error message. The title attribute's contents get added to the error message.

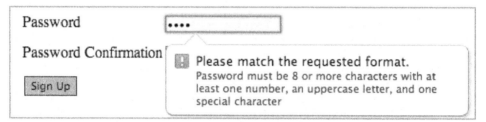

We'll want to make the Password Confirmation field use the same pattern.

```
html5_validation/index.html
<li>
  <label for="password_confirmation">Password Confirmation</label>
  <input id="password_confirmation" type="password"
    name="password_confirmation" value=""
    autocomplete="off" placeholder="Type your password again"
    pattern="^(?=.{8,})(?=.*[a-z])(?=.*[A-Z])(?=.*[\d])(?=.*[\W]).*$"
    title="Password confirmation must be 8 or more characters with at
          least one number, an uppercase letter, and one special character"
  />
</li>
```

One thing we can't do with these validation attributes is ensure that the password and its confirmation are the same. That's something we would need to handle with JavaScript.

Styling the Fields

Our form already has basic styles, but we now have some additional information on the fields that we can use to make it more apparent when the user has encountered errors. Some browsers, like Firefox, highlight the invalid fields when they lose focus. Other browsers don't provide any feedback until the form is submitted. Using just a little CSS, we can provide instant feedback to users.

We simply use the pseudoclasses :valid and :invalid in some style declarations:

html5_validation/stylesheets/style.css
```
input[required]:invalid, input[pattern]:invalid{
  border-color: #A5340B;
}


input[required]:valid, input[pattern]:valid{
  border-color: #0B9900;
}
```

Now when our users change the contents of the fields, they'll get some visual feedback.

Falling Back

The simplest fallback solution is to do absolutely nothing. Browsers will ignore the required and pattern attributes, so you can let your server-side validation catch any errors. But if you want to do better than that, you can use the values of the required and pattern attributes to build your own validation. Or you can use a library like H5F, which is incredibly robust and which you can drop onto your page and activate.[7] And unlike with other libraries, there's no need to do browser detection, because it automatically detects and leverages any existing browser support.

To use this library, we need to include it and activate it. We'll use Modernizr again to detect the feature and load the library. Even though H5F does its own detection, we still want to minimize loading external scripts, and we're already using Modernizr for the placeholder fallbacks. We can modify our existing load() function like this:

html5_validation/javascripts/fallbacks.js
```
➤ Modernizr.load([
    {
      test: Modernizr.placeholder,
      nope: "javascripts/jquery.placeholder.js",
      callback: function(url, result){
        if (!result){
          applyPlaceholders();
        }
      }
    }
➤   ,
```

---

7. https://github.com/ryanseddon/H5F

```
➤    {
➤      test: Modernizr.pattern && Modernizr.required,
➤      nope: "javascripts/h5f.min.js",
➤      callback: function(url, result){
➤        if (!result) {
➤          configureHSF();
➤        }
➤      }
➤    }
➤  ]);
```

Then, to activate H5F we write this code:

```
html5_validation/javascripts/fallbacks.js
var configureHSF = function(){
  H5F.setup(document.getElementById("create_account"));
};
```

The load() function takes a string, an object, or an array of objects. We're passing two objects to Modernizr.load() now instead of one. To do that, we have to place both objects in an array. That's why the objects are wrapped in square brackets.

We use document.getElementById() here because H5F needs a regular Document Object Model element. If we used jQuery to fetch the element, we'd get a jQuery object instead of the Element object and H5F wouldn't know what to do.

Client-side validation lets users see that they made mistakes, without waiting for a server response or a page refresh. But remember that this feature could be disabled or unavailable or simply incorrectly implemented, so you still need to make sure you have a server-side strategy for validating data.

Form fields aren't the only way to let users type data into a web page. Let's look at how we can let users enter text into regular HTML elements.

Tip 9

In-Place Editing with contenteditable

We're always looking for ways to make it easier for people to interact with our applications. For example, sometimes we want our site's users to edit information about themselves without having to navigate to a different form. We traditionally implement in-place editing by watching text regions for clicks and replacing those regions with text fields. These fields send the changed text back to the server via Ajax. HTML5's contenteditable attribute takes care of the data-entry part automatically. We'll still have to write some JavaScript to send the data back to the server so we can save it, but we no longer have to create and toggle hidden forms.

One of AwesomeCo's current projects lets users review their account profiles. It displays their name, city, state, postal code, and email address. Let's add some in-place editing to this profile page so that we end up with an interface like in the figure here.

User information

Edit Your Profile

Name	Hugh Mann
City	Anytown
State	OH
Postal Code	92110
Email	boss@awesomecompany.com

Figure 7—In-place editing made easy

Before we get started, I want you to know that implementing a feature that relies on JavaScript without first implementing a server-side solution goes against everything I believe in when it comes to building accessible web applications. We're doing it this way here because I want to focus on the features of the contenteditable attribute, *and this is not production code.* Always, and I mean *always*, build the solution that does not require JavaScript first, *then* build the version that relies on scripting, and finally be sure to write automated tests for both paths so that you're more likely to catch bugs if you change one version and not the other. Whenever possible, build your Java-Script solution on top of the non-JavaScript solution. You'll end up with better markup, better code, and better accessibility in the long run.

The Profile Form

HTML5 introduces the contenteditable attribute that is available on almost every element. Simply adding this attribute to an element turns the element into an editable field. So, let's construct the profile form. Create a new HTML page called show.html with a standard HTML template:

```
html5_content_editable/show.html
<!DOCTYPE html>
<html lang="en-US">
  <head>
    <meta charset="utf-8">
    <title>Show User</title>
    <link rel="stylesheet" href="stylesheets/style.css">
  </head>
  <body id="forms">
  </body>
</html>
```

Inside the <body> tag, we add the editable fields.

```
html5_content_editable/show.html
<h1>User information</h1>
<div id="status"></div>
<ul data-url="/users/1">
  <li>
    <b>Name</b>
    <span id="name" contenteditable>Hugh Mann</span>
  </li>
  <li>
    <b>City</b>
    <span id="city" contenteditable>Anytown</span>
  </li>
  <li>
    <b>State</b>
    <span id="state" contenteditable>OH</span>
  </li>
  <li>
    <b>Postal Code</b>
    <span id="postal_code" contenteditable>92110</span>
    </li>
  <li>
    <b>Email</b>
    <span id="email" contenteditable>boss@awesomecompany.com</span>
  </li>
</ul>
```

We'll make this look a little nicer with some CSS, too. In addition to some basic styling to line up the fields, we'll identify the editable fields so they change color when our users hover over or select them. Create a new file called stylesheets/style.css with this code:

html5_content_editable/stylesheets/style.css

```
Line 1  ul{list-style:none;}

        li > b, li > span{
           display: block;
        5    float: left;
             width: 100px;
        }

        li > span{
        10    width:500px;
              margin-left: 20px;
        }

        li > span[contenteditable]:hover{
        15    background-color: #ffc;
        }

        li > span[contenteditable]:focus{
              background-color: #ffa;
        20    border: 1px shaded #000;
        }

        li{clear:left;}
```

On line 3 we make the label and the <span> line up. Then we add the hover and focus effects on lines 14 and 18 by using CSS attribute selectors.

That's it for the front end. Users can modify the data on the page easily. Now we have to save it.

Persisting the Data

Although users can change the data, their changes will be lost if they refresh the page or navigate away. We need an approach to submitting those changes to our back end, and we can do that easily with jQuery. If you've ever done any Ajax before, this won't be anything new to you.

First we'll create a new file called javascripts/edit.js, and then we'll link that file and the jQuery library to the bottom of our HTML page, right above the closing <body> tag:

html5_content_editable/show.html

```
<script
    src="http://ajax.googleapis.com/ajax/libs/jquery/1.9.1/jquery.min.js">
</script>
<script src="javascripts/edit.js"></script>
```

Then we can write the code to save our data when it changes:

html5_content_editable/javascripts/edit.js

```
$("#edit_profile_link").hide();
var status = $("#status");
$("span[contenteditable]").blur(function(){
  var field = $(this).attr("id");
  var value = $(this).text();

  var resourceURL = $(this).closest("ul").attr("data-url");

  $.ajax({
    url: resourceURL,
    dataType: "json",
    method: "PUT",
    data: field + "=" + value,
    success: function(data){
      status.html("The record was saved.");
    },
    error: function(data){
      status.html("The record failed to save.");
    }
  });
});
}
```

We add an event listener to every span on the page that has the contenteditable
attribute. So, when the user tabs away from a field, all we have to do is submit
the data to our server-side script using jQuery's ajax() method. When we coded
up the web page we added the server-side URL to the data-url attribute of the
<ul> tag, so we grab that URL and construct our request to the server. This
is just an example—we don't have a back end to save this, and writing one
is beyond the scope of this book. However, you'll learn about a few ways you
can save user data on client machines in Chapter 9, *Saving Data on the Client*,
on page 183.

Falling Back

We've done a bunch of things that won't work for some of our audience. First,
we've created a dependency on JavaScript to save the edited results back to
the server, which is a bad thing. Rather than worrying much about situations
that might prevent a user from using our technique, let's just give users the

option to go to a separate page with its own form. Sure, it's more coding, but think about the possible scenarios:

- A user doesn't have a browser that supports contenteditable.

- A user is using a modern browser but still disabled JavaScript simply because he doesn't like JavaScript (it happens more often than you'd think).

- A user is behind firewall software that filters out JavaScript. Believe it or not, such firewalls exist and they make life miserable for both users and developers.

When it comes down to it, making a form that does a POST request to the same action that handled the Ajax update makes the most sense. How you do this is up to you, but many frameworks let you detect the type of request by looking at the accept headers to determine whether the request came from a regular POST request or an XMLHttpRequest. That way, you keep the server-side code DRY.[8] We'll hide the link to this form if the browser supports contenteditable and JavaScript.

So, we create a new page called edit.html, and code up a standard edit form that posts to the same update action that our Ajax version uses.

```
html5_content_editable/edit.html
<!DOCTYPE html>
<html lang="en-US">
  <head>
    <meta charset="utf-8">
    <title>Editing Profile</title>
    <link rel="stylesheet" href="stylesheets/style.css">
  </head>
  <body>
    <form action="/users/1" method="post" accept-charset="utf-8">
      <fieldset id="your_information">
        <legend>Your Information</legend>
        <ol>
         <li>
           <label for="name">Your Name</label>
           <input type="text" name="name" value="" id="name">
         </li>
         <li>
           <label for="city">City</label>
           <input type="text" name="city" value="" id="city">
         </li>
```

---

8. DRY stands for "Don't Repeat Yourself" and is a term coined by Dave Thomas and Andy Hunt in *The Pragmatic Programmer* [HT00].

```
        <li>
          <label for="state">State</label>
          <input type="text" name="state" value="" id="state">
        </li>
        <li>
          <label for="postal_code">Postal Code</label>
          <input type="text" name="postal_code" value="" id="postal_code">
        </li>
        <li>
          <label for="email">Email</label>
          <input type="email" name="email" value="" id="email">
        </li>
      </ol>

    </fieldset>
    <p><input type="submit" value="Save"></p>
  </form>

  </body>
</html>
```

We'll add some styles to stylesheets/style.css to make this form look good, using similar styles to the ones we've used for our other forms:

html5_content_editable/stylesheets/style.css
```
ol{
  padding :0;
  margin: 0;
  list-style: none;
}

ol > li{
  padding: 0;
  clear: both;
  margin: 0 0 10px 0;
}

label{
  width: 150px;
  float: left;
}
/* EN:edit_styles */
```

Then we'll add a link to edit.html on show.html.

html5_content_editable/show.html
```
<h1>User information</h1>
<section id="edit_profile_link">
  <p><a href="edit.html">Edit Your Profile</a></p>
</section>
<div id="status"></div>
```

With the link added, we need to modify our script. We want to hide the link to the edit page and enable the Ajax support only if we have support for editable content. The detection is relatively simple and doesn't need Modernizr at all. We just need to see if there's a contenteditable attribute on an element.

```
html5_content_editable/javascripts/edit.js
➤ var hasContentEditableSupport = function(){
➤   return(document.getElementById("edit_profile_link").contentEditable != null)
➤ };
➤
➤ if(hasContentEditableSupport()){
➤   $("#edit_profile_link").hide();
    var status = $("#status");
    $("span[contenteditable]").blur(function(){
      var field = $(this).attr("id");
      var value = $(this).text();

      var resourceURL = $(this).closest("ul").attr("data-url");

      $.ajax({
        url: resourceURL,
        dataType: "json",
        method: "PUT",
        data: field + "=" + value,
        success: function(data){
          status.html("The record was saved.");
        },
        error: function(data){
          status.html("The record failed to save.");
        }
      });
    });
➤ }
```

With that in place, our users have the ability to employ a standard interface or a quicker "in-place" mode. Just remember to implement the fallback interface. Browsers that don't understand contenteditable will ignore it (as they will many other HTML5 features), leaving your users unable to work with your site.

3.1 The Future

Right now, if you add a JavaScript-based date picker to your site, your users have to learn how it works. If you've ever shopped online for plane tickets and made hotel reservations, you're already familiar with the different ways people implement custom form controls on sites. It's akin to using an ATM—the interface is often different enough to slow you down.

Imagine, though, if each website used the HTML5 date field, and the browser had to create the interface. Each site a user visited would display the exact same date picker. Screen-reading software could even implement a standard mechanism to allow the blind to enter dates easily. We covered quite a few new form fields in this chapter, but we didn't cover all of them. We can use the search type for search boxes, the tel type for telephone numbers, and the time and datetime types for times and dates with times, respectively. All of these field types can present specific user interfaces to our visitors, and they describe the content much better than plain-old text types.

Now think about how useful placeholder text and autofocus can be for users once it's everywhere. Placeholder text can help screen readers explain to users how form fields should work, and autofocus could help people navigate more easily without a mouse, which is handy for the blind, but also for users with motor impairments who may not use the mouse.

Once more browsers support the built-in validation features, users will have the same experience across pages; error messages will be consistent, and users won't be looking around to figure out where they made mistakes.

The ability for developers to turn any element into an editable region makes it easy to do in-place editing, but it could change how we build interfaces for content-management systems.

The modern Web is all about interactivity, and forms are an essential part of that interactivity. HTML5's enhancements give us a whole new set of tools we can employ to help our users.

CHAPTER 4

Styling Content and Interfaces

For far too long, we developers have hacked around CSS to get the effects we need in our code. We've used JavaScript or server-side code to stripe table rows or put focus and blur effects on our forms. We've had to litter our tags with additional class attributes just so we could identify which of our fifty form inputs we want to style.

But no more! CSS3 has amazing selectors that make some of this work trivial. A selector is a pattern that you use to help you find elements in the HTML document so you can apply styles to those elements. We'll use these new selectors to style a table. Then we'll take a look at how we can use some other CSS3 features to improve our site's print style sheets, and we'll split content into multiple columns.

We'll look at these CSS features in this chapter:

:nth-of-type [p:nth-of-type(2n+1){color: red;}]
> Finds all n elements of a certain type. *[C2, F3.5, S3, IE9, O9.5, iOS3, A2]*

:first-child [p:first-child{color:blue;}]
> Finds the first child element. *[C2, F3.5, S3, IE9, O9.5, iOS3, A2]*

:nth-child [p:nth-child(2n+1){color: red;}]
> Finds a specific child element counting forward. *[C2, F3.5, S3, IE9, O9.5, iOS3, A2]*

:last-child [p:last-child{color:blue;}]
> Finds the last child element. *[C2, F3.5, S3, IE9, O9.5, iOS3, A2]*

:nth-last-child [p:nth-last-child(2){color: red;}]
> Finds a specific child element counting backward. *[C2, F3.5, S3, IE9, O9.5, iOS3, A2]*

:first-of-type [p:first-of-type{color:blue;}]
> Finds the first element of the given type. *[C2, F3.5, S3, IE9, O9.5, iOS3, A2]*

:last-of-type [p:last-of-type{color:blue;}]
> Finds the last element of the given type. *[C2, F3.5, S3, IE9, O9.5, iOS3, A2]*

Column support [#content{ column-count: 2; column-gap: 20px; column-rule: 1px solid #ddccb5; }] Divides a content area into multiple columns. *[C2, F3.5, S3, O11.1, iOS3, A2]*

:after [span.weight:after { content: "lbs"; color: #bbb; }]
> Used with content to insert content after the specified element. *[C2, F3.5, S3, IE8, O9.5, iOS3, A2]*

Media queries [media="only all and (max-width: 480)"]
> Apply styles based on device settings. *[C3, F3.5, S4, IE9, O10.1, iOS3, A2]*

Tip 10

Styling Tables with Pseudoclasses

A *pseudoclass* in CSS is a way to select elements based on information that lies outside the document or information that can't be expressed using normal selectors. You've probably used pseudoclasses like :hover before to change the color of a link when the user hovers over it with the mouse pointer. CSS3 has several new pseudoclasses that make locating elements much easier.

AwesomeCo uses a third-party billing and invoicing system for products it ships. You see, one of AwesomeCo's biggest markets is conference swag, such as pens, cups, shirts, and anything else you can slap your logo on. You've been asked to make the invoice more readable. Right now, the developers are producing a standard HTML table that looks like the one in the figure here.

Item	Price	Quantity	Total
Coffee mug	$10.00	5	$50.00
Polo shirt	$20.00	5	$100.00
Red stapler	$9.00	4	$36.00
Subtotal			$186.00
Shipping			$12.00
Total Due			$198.00

Figure 8—The current invoice uses an unstyled HTML table.

It's a pretty standard invoice with prices, quantities, row totals, a subtotal, a shipping total, and a grand total for the order. It would be easier to read if every other row were colored differently. It would also be helpful if the grand total were a different color so that it stands out more.

The code for the table looks like this. Copy it into your own file so you can work with it.

css3_advanced_selectors/index.html
```
<table >
  <tr>
    <th>Item</th>
    <th>Price</th>
```

```
      <th>Quantity</th>
      <th>Total</th>
    </tr>
    <tr>
      <td>Coffee mug</td>
      <td>$10.00</td>
      <td>5</td>
      <td>$50.00</td>
    </tr>
    <tr>
      <td>Polo shirt</td>
      <td>$20.00</td>
      <td>5</td>
      <td>$100.00</td>
    </tr>
    <tr>
      <td>Red stapler</td>
      <td>$9.00</td>
      <td>4</td>
      <td>$36.00</td>
    </tr>
    <tr>
      <td colspan="3">Subtotal</td>
      <td>$186.00</td>
    </tr>
    <tr>
      <td colspan="3">Shipping</td>
      <td>$12.00</td>
    </tr>
    <tr>
      <td colspan="3">Total Due</td>
      <td>$198.00</td>
    </tr>
  </table>
```

First, let's get rid of the hideous default table border. Create a new file called stylesheets/style.css and link it up:

css3_advanced_selectors/index.html
```
<link rel="stylesheet" href="stylesheets/style.css">
```

css3_advanced_selectors/stylesheets/style.css
```
table{
  border-collapse: collapse;
  width: 600px;
}

th, td{ border: none; }
```

Also, style the header by giving it a black background with white text.

css3_advanced_selectors/stylesheets/style.css
```
th{
  background-color: #000;
  color: #fff;
}
```

Apply that style, and the table looks like this:

Item	Price	Quantity	Total
Coffee mug	$10.00	5	$50.00
Polo shirt	$20.00	5	$100.00
Red stapler	$9.00	4	$36.00
Subtotal			$186.00
Shipping			$12.00
Total Due			$198.00

With the table's borders and spacing cleaned up, we can start using the pseudo-classes to style individual rows and columns. We'll start by striping the table.

Striping Rows with :nth-of-type

We've all seen "zebra striping" in tables. It's useful because it gives users horizontal lines to follow. This kind of styling is best done in CSS, the presentation layer. That has traditionally meant introducing additional class names to our table rows, like "odd" and "even." We don't want to pollute our table's markup like that, because the HTML5 specification encourages us to avoid using class names that define presentation. Using some new selectors, we can get what we want without changing our markup at all, truly separating presentation from content.

The nth-of-type selector finds every nth element of a specific type using either a formula or keywords. We'll get into the formula in more detail soon, but first let's focus on the keywords, because they're easier to grasp immediately.

We want to stripe every other row of the table with a different color, and the easiest way to do that is to find every even row of the table and give it a background color. We then do the same thing with the odd rows. CSS3 has even and odd keywords that support this exact situation.

css3_advanced_selectors/stylesheets/style.css
```
tr:nth-of-type(even){
  background-color: #F3F3F3;
}
tr:nth-of-type(odd) {
  background-color:#ddd;
}
```

So, this selector says, "Find me every even table row and color it. Then find every odd row and color that, too." That takes care of our zebra striping without resorting to any scripting or extra class names on rows.

With the styles applied, our table looks like this:

Item	Price	Quantity	Total
Coffee mug	$10.00	5	$50.00
Polo shirt	$20.00	5	$100.00
Red stapler	$9.00	4	$36.00
Subtotal			$186.00
Shipping			$12.00
Total Due			$198.00

Now let's work on aligning the columns in the table.

Aligning Column Text with :nth-child

By default, all of the columns in our invoice table are left-aligned. Let's right-align every column except for the first column. This way, our price and quantity columns will be right-aligned and easier to read. To do the right-alignment, we can use nth-child, but first we have to learn how it works.

The nth-child selector looks for child elements of an element and, like nth-of-type, can use keywords or a formula.

The formula is an+b, where a is a multiple, n is a counter starting at 0, and b is the offset. That description is not particularly helpful without some context, so let's look at it in the context of our table.

If we wanted to select all of the table rows, we could use this selector:

```
table tr:nth-child(n)
```

We're not using any multiple, nor are we using an offset.

However, if we wanted to select all rows of the table except for the first row, which is the row containing the column headings, we would use this selector that uses an offset:

```
table tr:nth-child(n+2)
```

The counter is 0, but the offset is 2, which means we don't start at the beginning of the table; we start at the second row.

If we wanted to select every other row of our table, we'd use a multiple, or 2n.

```
table tr:nth-child(2n)
```

If you wanted every third row, you'd use 3n.

You can also use the offset so that you can start further down the table. This selector would find every other row, starting with the fourth row:

```
table tr:nth-child(2n+4)
```

So, we can align every column *except* the first one with this rule:

```
css3_advanced_selectors/stylesheets/style.css
td:nth-child(n+2), th:nth-child(n+2){
  text-align: right;
}
```

We use two selectors separated by a comma so we can apply this style to the <th> tags as well as the <td> tags.

At this point, our table is really shaping up:

Item	Price	Quantity	Total
Coffee mug	$10.00	5	$50.00
Polo shirt	$20.00	5	$100.00
Red stapler	$9.00	4	$36.00
Subtotal			$186.00
Shipping			$12.00
Total Due			$198.00

Now let's style the last row of the table.

Bolding the Last Row with :last-child

The invoice is looking pretty good right now, but one of the managers would like the bottom row of the table to be bolder than the other rows so it stands out more. We can use last-child for that too, which grabs the last child in a group.

Applying a bottom margin to paragraphs so that they are evenly spaced on a page is a common practice among web developers. This can sometimes lead to an extra bottom margin at the end of a group, and that might be undesirable. For example, if the paragraphs are sitting inside of a sidebar or callout box, we may want to remove the bottom margin from the last paragraph so that there's not wasted space between the bottom of the last paragraph and the box's border. The last-child selector is the perfect tool for this. We can use it to remove the margin from the last paragraph.

```
p{ margin-bottom: 20px }
#sidebar p:last-child{ margin-bottom: 0; }
```

Let's use this same technique to bold the contents of the last row.

css3_advanced_selectors/stylesheets/style.css
```
tr:last-child{
  font-weight: bolder;
}
```

Let's do the same thing with the last column of the table. This will help the line totals stand out, too.

css3_advanced_selectors/stylesheets/style.css
```
td:last-child{
  font-weight: bolder;
}
```

Finally, we'll make the total's font size bigger by using last-child with descendant selectors. We'll find the last column of the last row and style it with this:

css3_advanced_selectors/stylesheets/style.css
```
tr:last-child td:last-child{
  font-size:24px;
}
```

Item	Price	Quantity	Total
Coffee mug	$10.00	5	$50.00
Polo shirt	$20.00	5	$100.00
Red stapler	$9.00	4	$36.00
Subtotal			$186.00
Shipping			$12.00
Total Due			**$198.00**

We're almost done, but there are a few things left to do with the last three rows of the table.

Counting Backward with :nth-last-child

We'd like to highlight the shipping row of the table when there's a discounted shipping rate. We'll use nth-last-child to quickly locate that row. You saw how you can use nth-child and the formula an+b to select specific child elements in *Aligning Column Text with :nth-child*, on page 72. The nth-last-child selector works exactly the same way, except that it counts backward through the children, starting at the last child first. This makes it easy to grab the second-to-last element in a group. It turns out we need to do just that with our invoice table.

So, to find our shipping row, we'd use this code:

css3_advanced_selectors/stylesheets/style.css
```
tr:nth-last-child(2){
  color: green;
}
```

Here we're specifying a specific child, the second to the last.

There's one more thing we should do with this table, though. Earlier we right-aligned all the columns except for the first column, and although that looks fine for the rows of the table with the item descriptions and prices, it makes the last three rows of the table look a little funny. Let's right-align the bottom three rows as well. We can do that by using nth-last-child with a negative value for n and a positive value for a in our formula, like this:

css3_advanced_selectors/stylesheets/style.css
```
tr:nth-last-child(-n+3) td{
  text-align: right;
}
```

You can think of this as a range selector; it's using the offset of 3, and since we're using nth-last-child, it's grabbing every element before the offset. If you were using nth-child, this formula would grab every row up to the offset.

Our newly styled table (see the next figure) looks much better now, and we didn't have to change the underlying markup one bit.

Item	Price	Quantity	Total
Coffee mug	$10.00	5	$50.00
Polo shirt	$20.00	5	$100.00
Red stapler	$9.00	4	$36.00
		Subtotal	$186.00
		Shipping	$12.00
		Total Due	$198.00

Figure 9—Our styled table, with striping and alignment done entirely with CSS3

Many of the selectors we used to accomplish this are not yet available to people using Internet Explorer, so we need a workaround for them.

Falling Back

Current versions of Internet Explorer, Opera, Firefox, Safari, and Chrome all understand these selectors, but Internet Explorer 8 and earlier will ignore these entirely. You'll need a good fallback solution, and you have a choice to make.

Do Nothing

The easiest solution is to do nothing. Since the content would be completely readable without the additional styling we're providing, we could just leave out Internet Explorer 8 users. Of course, there's another technique if doing nothing isn't the right approach for you.

Change the HTML Code

The most obvious solution that works everywhere is to modify the underlying code. You could attach classes to all the cells in the table and apply basic CSS to each class. This is the worst choice, because it mixes presentation and content and is exactly the kind of thing we're using CSS3 to avoid. Someday we wouldn't need all that extra markup, and it would be painful to remove it.

Use Selectivizr

The jQuery library already understands most of the CSS3 selectors we used, so we could quickly write a method to style the table that way, but there's an easier way.

Keith Clark wrote a great library called Selectivizr that adds support for CSS3 selectors to Internet Explorer.[1] All we need to do is add it to our page.

The Selectivizr library can use jQuery, Prototype, or several other libraries under the hood, but jQuery supports all the pseudoclasses we've used here.

To use it, we download Selectivizr and then link it in the <head> section of the HTML document. Since this is for Internet Explorer only, we can place the link in a conditional comment so it'll be downloaded only by your IE users.

css3_advanced_selectors/index.html
```
<script
  src='http://ajax.googleapis.com/ajax/libs/jquery/1.9.1/jquery.min.js'>
</script>
<!--[if (gte IE 5.5)&(lte IE 8)]>
  <script src="javascripts/selectivizr-min.js"></script>
<![endif]-->
```

Note that we're loading jQuery here too, and in this particular case we have to load jQuery in the <head> of the document. We could place the jQuery call in the conditional comment, but chances are good we'll need jQuery for other things anyway.

With this fallback in place, things look great in Internet Explorer, as the following figure shows.

---

1.   http://selectivizr.com/

Item	Price	Quantity	Total
Coffee mug	$10.00	5	$50.00
Polo shirt	$20.00	5	$100.00
Red stapler	$9.00	4	$36.00
		Subtotal	$186.00
		Shipping	$12.00
		Total Due	$198.00

Figure 10—Our table looks great in Internet Explorer.

Although this will require the user to have JavaScript turned on, the table styling is there mainly to make the content easier to see. As we already discussed, lack of styling doesn't prevent anyone from reading the invoice.

Styling elements is a whole lot easier with these advanced selectors, especially if you're not allowed to modify the HTML you're targeting due to a framework, packaged product, or office politics. When you're styling interfaces, use the semantic hierarchy and these new selectors before you introduce additional markup. You will find your code much easier to maintain.

We can also use CSS to add content to a web page. Let's see how.

Tip 11

Making Links Printable with :after and content

CSS can style existing elements, but it can also inject content into a document using the :before and :after pseudoelements and the content property. There are a few cases where content generation with CSS makes sense, and the most obvious one is when appending the URL of a hyperlink next to the link's text when a user prints the page. When you're looking at a document on the screen, you can just hover over a link and see where it goes by looking at the status bar. However, when you look at a printout of a page, you have absolutely no idea where those links go.

AwesomeCo is working up a new page for its forms and policies, and one of the members of the redesign committee insists on printing out a copy of the site each time the committee meets. He wants to know exactly where all of the links go on the page so that he can determine whether they need to be moved. With just a little bit of CSS, we can add that functionality, and it will work in Internet Explorer 8, Firefox, Safari, and Chrome.

The page itself has nothing more than a list of links on it right now. Eventually it'll get put into a template.

```
css3_print_links/index.html
    <ul>
      <li>
        <a href="travel/index.html">Travel Authorization Form</a>
      </li>
      <li>
        <a href="travel/expenses.html">Travel Reimbursement Form</a>
      </li>
      <li>
        <a href="travel/guidelines.html">Travel Guidelines</a>
      </li>
    </ul>

</body>
```

If you were to look at that page on a printout, you'd see the text of the links, and they'd be underlined, but you'd have no way to know what pages those links go to. Let's fix that.

Creating a Printer-Only Style Sheet

When we add a style sheet to a page, we can specify the media type that the styles apply to. Most of the time, we use the screen type. However, we can use the print type to define a style sheet that loads only when the page is printed (or when someone uses the Print Preview function).

css3_print_links/index.html

```
<link rel="stylesheet" href="print.css" type="text/css" media="print">
```

We then create a print.css style sheet file with this simple rule:

css3_print_links/stylesheets/print.css

```
a:after {
  content: " (" attr(href) ") ";
}
```

For every link on the page, this adds the value of the href inside parentheses after the link's text. When you print it from a modern browser, it looks like this:

Forms and Policies

- Travel Authorization Form (travel/index.html)
- Travel Reimbursement Form (travel/expenses.html)
- Travel Guidelines (travel/guidelines.html)

If you want to see it in action without using up paper, you can use your browser's Print Preview feature, which also triggers this style sheet.

Best of all, Internet Explorer 8 and up support creating content this way, so there's no need for a fallback.

The double-colon syntax

The :before and :after pseudoelements were introduced in the CSS2.1 specification.[2] In early drafts, they appear with two colons, like this:

```
a::after{
  content: " (" attr(href) ") ";
}
```

---

2. http://www.w3.org/TR/CSS21/generate.html#before-after-content

This syntax isn't supported in many browsers, so the specification calls on browser vendors to support both the single- and double-colon syntax.

You can use content in other ways, too. For example, you might use it to add visual labels to text. One common use for this is to employ content to put the words "external link" next to URLs that link out to other sites. You have to be careful not to cross the line from design to content. The CSS content property should be used for design-related things only, not for injecting actual page content.

We've covered how to make a web page look different when it's sent to a printer, but now let's see how to change the page content's appearance based on the screen size.

Tip 12

Building Mobile Interfaces with Media Queries

We've been able to define media-specific style sheets for quite a while, but we've been limited to the type of output, as you saw in Tip 11, *Making Links Printable with :after and content*, on page 78, when we defined our print style sheet. CSS3's media queries let us change a page's presentation based on the screen size our visitors use.[3] Web developers have used JavaScript for years to obtain information about the user's screen size. But we can start to do that with style sheets alone. We can use media queries to determine the following:

- Resolution
- Orientation (portrait or landscape mode)
- Device width and height
- Width and height of the browser window

Because of this, media queries make it very easy for us to create alternative style sheets for users of various screen sizes, and media queries are a key ingredient of responsive web design, the popular practice of building one site that changes its appearance and flow based on the user's screen resolution. Popular frameworks like Bootstrap rely on media queries heavily.[4]

Joe asks:
What About the Handheld Media Type?

The Handheld media type was designed to let us target mobile devices like we target printers, but most mobile devices want to show you the "real Internet," so they ignore that media type, serving the style sheet associated with the screen media type instead.

It turns out that the AwesomeCo executive staff has finally gotten tired of hearing complaints from customers and employees about how web pages look like garbage on smartphones. The marketing director would love to see a mobile-ready version of the blog template we built in Tip 1, *Redefining a Blog Using Semantic Markup*, on page 15. We can do a prototype of that quickly.

---

3. http://www.w3.org/TR/css3-mediaqueries/
4. http://twitter.github.com/bootstrap/

Our current blog is a two-column layout, with a main content region and a sidebar. The easiest way to make this more readable on a mobile browser is to remove the floating elements so that the sidebar falls beneath the main content. That way, the reader won't have to scroll sideways on the device. This is a dead-simple responsive design solution.

To make this work, we'll add this code to the bottom of the blog's style sheet:

```
css3_mediaquery/stylesheets/style.css
@media only screen and (max-device-width: 480px) {
  body{ width:480px; }
  nav, section, header, footer{ margin: 0 10px 0 10px; }

  #sidebar, #posts{
    float: none;
    width: 100%;
  }
}
```

You can think of the code we put within the media-query braces as its own style sheet, invoked when the conditions of the query are met. In this case, we resize the body of the page and turn our two-column layout into a single-column layout.

We could also use media queries when we link the style sheet, so we can keep our mobile style sheet in a separate file, like this:

```
<link rel="stylesheet" type="text/css"
  href="stylesheets/mobile.css" media="only screen and (max-device-width: 480px)">
```

With that, our blog immediately becomes more readable on tiny screens, although the viewport is still zoomed way out. We can fix that by adding this tag right below the web page's <title> tag:

```
css3_mediaquery/index.html
<meta name="viewport"
      content="width=device-width, initial-scale=1, maximum-scale=1">
```

Figure 11, *Our blog page on the iPhone*, on page 83 shows how our page looks now. It's far from perfect, but it's a great start.

You can use this approach to build style sheets for other displays, as well, such as kiosks and tablets, so that your content is more easily readable on those platforms. However, taking a page of content designed for a large screen and trying to shrink it will result in lots of problems for you. A *mobile-first* approach, where you design for the small screen first and then add more content for larger screens, is best. This method forces you to think long and hard about both your content and your audience.

Figure 11—Our blog page on the iPhone

Falling Back

Media queries are supported in Firefox, Chrome, Safari, Opera, and Internet Explorer 9 and up. You'll have to rely on JavaScript fallback solutions to load additional style sheets based on the user's device. Our example targets iPhones, so we don't need a fallback solution—our content is readable without the media query.

The excellent Respond.js library provides support for min- and max-width media queries,[5] and is a great fallback for Internet Explorer 8, but it's probably not necessary in most cases since those types of media queries are meant for smaller screens, and devices *not* running Internet Explorer 8. That said, you could still use media queries to handle presentation on various screen sizes, from small monitors to sizable wall displays.

Media queries give us the power to control how the page displays on various screen sizes. But sometimes on larger screens content areas can be really wide. Let's look at how we can divide those content areas into multiple columns.

---

5.   https://github.com/scottjehl/Respond

Tip 13

Creating Multicolumn Layouts

The print industry has had columns for years, and web designers have looked at those publications with envy. Narrow columns make it easier for readers to read your content, and with displays getting wider, developers are looking for ways to preserve comfortable column widths. After all, nobody wants to follow multiple lines of text across the monitor any more than they want a line of text to flow across the whole page of a newspaper. There have been some pretty clever solutions in the past ten years, but none of those solutions are as simple and easy as the method the CSS3 specification provides.

Splitting Columns

Each month, AwesomeCo publishes a newsletter for its employees. The company uses a popular web-based email system. Email-based newsletters don't quite look good and are hard to maintain. They've decided to put the newsletter on the intranet site and are planning to send emails to employees, with a link to pull up the newsletter in their browsers. For a mocked-up version of this newsletter, see the following figure.

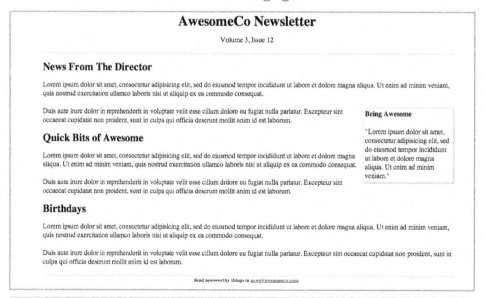

Figure 12—Our single-column newsletter is hard to read because it's very wide.

The new director of communications, who has a background in print publications, has decided that she would like the newsletter to look more like an actual newsletter, with two columns instead of one.

If you've ever tried to split some text into multiple columns using divs and floats, you know how hard that can be. The first big hurdle is deciding where to split the text. In publishing software such as InDesign, you can link text boxes together so that when one fills up with text, the text flows smoothly into the linked text area. We don't have anything quite like that on the Web yet, but we have something that works really well and is quite easy to use. We can split an element's contents into multiple columns, each with the same width.

We'll start with the markup for the newsletter. It's fairly basic HTML. Since its content will change once it's written, we'll use placeholder text for the content:

```
css3_columns/condensed_newsletter.html
<body>
  <div id="container">
    <header id="header">
      <h1>AwesomeCo Newsletter</h1>
      <p>Volume 3, Issue 12</p>
    </header>
    <section id="newsletter">
      <article id="director_news">
        <header>
          <h2>News From The Director</h2>
        </header>
        <div>
          <p>
            Lorem ipsum dolor sit amet...
          </p>
          <aside class="callout">
            <h4>Being Awesome</h4>
            <p>
              &quot;Lorem ipsum dolor sit amet, ....&quot;
            </p>
          </aside>
          <p>
            Duis aute irure dolor in ...
          </p>
        </div>
      </article>
      <article id="awesome_bits">
        <header>
          <h2>Quick Bits of Awesome</h2>
        </header>
```

```
      <div>
        <p>
          Lorem ipsum dolor sit amet...
        </p>
      </div>
    </article>
    <article id="birthdays">
      <header>
        <h2>Birthdays</h2>
      </header>
      <div>
        <p>
          Lorem ipsum dolor sit amet...
        </p>
      </div>
    </article>
  </section>
  <footer id="footer">
    <h6>
      Send newsworthy things to
      <a href="mailto:news@aweseomco.com">news@awesomeco.com</a>.
    </h6>
  </footer>
</div>
</body>
```

To split this into a two-column layout, we need to add a few new properties to our style sheet:

- column-count lets us specify how many columns we want to divide our content into.
- column-gap defines how much space should be placed in between the columns.
- column-rule gives us a border between the columns.

Let's add this to our style sheet to split the content into two columns with a little gutter between them:

css3_columns/stylesheets/style.css
```
#newsletter{
  -webkit-column-count: 2;
  -webkit-column-gap: 20px;
  -webkit-column-rule: 1px solid #ddccb5;
    -moz-column-count: 2;
    -moz-column-gap: 20px;
    -moz-column-rule: 1px solid #ddccb5;
        column-count: 2;
        column-gap: 20px;
        column-rule: 1px solid #ddccb5;
}
```

The next figure shows that now we have something much more readable.

AwesomeCo Newsletter

Volume 3, Issue 12

News From The Director

Lorem ipsum dolor sit amet, consectetur adipisicing elit, sed do eiusmod tempor incididunt ut labore et dolore magna aliqua. Ut enim ad minim veniam, quis nostrud exercitation ullamco laboris nisi ut aliquip ex ea commodo consequat.

Duis aute irure dolor in reprehenderit in voluptate velit esse cillum dolore eu fugiat nulla pariatur. Excepteur sint occaecat cupidatat non proident, sunt in culpa qui officia deserunt mollit anim id est laborum.

Quick Bits of Awesome

Lorem ipsum dolor sit amet, consectetur adipisicing elit, sed do eiusmod tempor incididunt ut labore et dolore magna aliqua. Ut enim ad minim

Being Awesome

"Lorem ipsum dolor sit amet, consectetur adipisicing elit, sed do eiusmod tempor incididunt ut labore et dolore magna aliqua. Ut enim ad minim veniam."

veniam, quis nostrud exercitation ullamco laboris nisi ut aliquip ex ea commodo consequat.

Duis aute irure dolor in reprehenderit in voluptate velit esse cillum dolore eu fugiat nulla pariatur. Excepteur sint occaecat cupidatat non proident, sunt in culpa qui officia deserunt mollit anim id est laborum.

Birthdays

Lorem ipsum dolor sit amet, consectetur adipisicing elit, sed do eiusmod tempor incididunt ut labore et dolore magna aliqua. Ut enim ad minim veniam, quis nostrud exercitation ullamco laboris nisi ut aliquip ex ea commodo consequat.

Duis aute irure dolor in reprehenderit in voluptate velit esse cillum dolore eu fugiat nulla pariatur. Excepteur sint occaecat cupidatat non proident, sunt in culpa qui officia deserunt mollit anim id est laborum.

Send newsworthy things to news@awesomeco.com.

Figure 13—Our new two-column newsletter

We can add more content, and the browser will automatically determine how to split the content evenly. Also, notice that the floated elements float to the columns that contain them.

To make these columns work across multiple browsers, we've had to define the properties multiple times, prefixing each rule for a specific type of browser.

Vendor-Specific Prefixes

While the World Wide Web Consortium was busy figuring out what features needed to go into the CSS specification, browser-makers added new features themselves and decided to prefix their own implementations. Some of those implementations ended up becoming the standards, solidifying prefixing as a viable practice that continues today. These prefixes let browser-makers introduce features early before they become part of a final specification, and since these features may not follow the specification, the browser-makers can implement the actual specification while keeping their own implementation as well. Most of the time, the vendor-prefixed version matches the CSS specification, but occasionally you'll encounter differences. Unfortunately for you, that means you'll need to declare some properties more than once for each type of browser. Here are the most common vendor prefixes:

- Firefox uses the -moz- prefix.

- Chrome and Safari, as well as many mobile browsers and recent versions of Opera, use the -webkit- prefix.

- Older versions of Opera use the -o- prefix.

Don't blindly use these prefixes, though. As browsers implement more of the standards, these prefixes are less necessary and create dead weight in your CSS. Keep an eye on the browsers your visitors use, and prune these selectors out of your style sheets if you don't need them anymore. You can employ Can I Use... to determine if you need prefixes.[6]

> **Joe asks:**
> # Can I Specify Different Widths for Each Column?
>
> Nope. Your columns must each be the same size. I was a little surprised, too, at first, so I double-checked the specification, and at the time of writing there is no provision for specifying multiple column widths.
>
> However, when you think about how columns are traditionally used, it makes sense. Columns are not intended to be a hack to easily make a sidebar for your website any more than tables are. Columns are meant to make reading long sections of text easier, and equal-width columns are perfect for that.

Falling Back

CSS3 columns don't work in Internet Explorer 9 and older, and it's probably fine to not have a fallback solution since the content is still readable. But if you've got your heart set on consistency across browsers, you can use CSS3MultiColumn, which adds support for basic multicolumn features.[7]

Simply load it *after* your style sheets, and it does the rest of the work for you. Since it only has to target Internet Explorer 9 and below, we can get away with wrapping it in a conditional comment, along with the JavaScript to make Internet Explorer 8 recognize our HTML5 elements:

css3_columns/newsletter.html
```
<!--[if lte IE 9]>
<script>
  // support for styling HTML5 elements
  document.createElement("section");
```

---

6.   http://caniuse.com/
7.   https://github.com/BetleyWhitehorne/CSS3MultiColumn

```
    document.createElement("header");
    document.createElement("footer");
    document.createElement("article");
    document.createElement("aside");
</script>

<script src="javascripts/css3-multi-column.min.js"></script>
<![endif]-->
```

Refresh the page in Internet Explorer, and you'll see your two-column newsletter, as in the following figure.

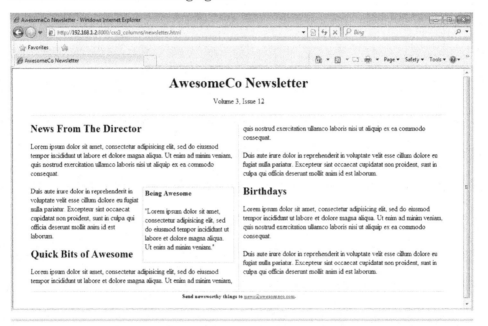

Figure 14—Our Internet Explorer version works, but needs some minor adjustments.

Visitors without JavaScript will still be able to read the content as before, so everybody wins.

Separating your content into multiple columns can make your content easier to read. However, if your page is long, your users might find it annoying to have to scroll back to the top to read the next column. Use this with care.

4.1 The Future

The things we talked about in this chapter improve the user interface; people can still work with our products if their browsers don't support these new features, but the table won't styled with stripes, the newsletter won't be laid out in multiple columns, and people will have to pinch and zoom on their smartphones to easily read the content. It's good to know that we can use the presentation layer to aid readability instead of having to resort to Java-Script hacks, or, worse, lots of additional markup.

Almost all browsers support these selectors now, with the exception of Internet Explorer 8 and below. When the specifications become final, the vendor-specific prefixes like -moz- and -webkit- will go away. Once that happens, you'll be able to remove your fallback code.

CHAPTER 5

Making Accessible Interfaces

Many of the new elements in HTML5 help us more accurately describe our content. This becomes more important when other programs start interpreting our code. For most of us, the program that reads the web page is our graphical web browser, but we can't forget about people who have to interact with our content and applications through other means. We need to make our web content accessible to as many people as possible.

Some people use software called *screen readers* to translate the graphical contents of the screen to audio that's read aloud. Screen readers work with the operating system or the web browser to identify content, links, images, and other elements on the screen. Whereas sighted users can easily scan the page for content, people using screen readers have the text read to them in a linear, top-down fashion.

Screen readers have made amazing advances, but they are always lagging behind the current trends. Live regions on pages, where polling or Ajax requests alter content on the page, are difficult to detect. More complex pages can be difficult to navigate because of the screen reader needing to read a lot of the content aloud. And because the elements on the page are read in a linear fashion, items like headers, navigation areas, and all of those widgets at the top of pages are reread on each page refresh.

Web Accessibility Initiative—Accessible Rich Internet Applications (WAI-ARIA) is a specification that provides ways to improve the accessibility of websites, especially web applications, and reduce the pain points users of assistive technology often encounter.[1] It is especially useful if you're developing applications with JavaScript controls and Ajax. Some parts of the WAI-ARIA

---

1. http://www.w3.org/WAI/intro/aria.php

specification have been rolled into HTML5,[2] while others remain separate and can complement the HTML5 specification. Many screen readers are already using features of the WAI-ARIA specification, including JAWS, Window-Eyes, and even Apple's built-in VoiceOver feature. WAI-ARIA also introduces additional markup that assistive technology can use as hints for discovering regions that are updatable.

In this chapter, we'll see how HTML5 and WAI-ARIA can improve the experience of our visitors who use these assistive devices. Most importantly, the techniques in this chapter require no fallback support, because many screen readers are already able to take advantage of these techniques.

We'll cover the following techniques:

The role attribute [<div role="document">]
> Identifies responsibility of an element to screen readers. *[C3, F3.6, S4, IE8, O9.6]*

aria-live [<div aria-live="polite">]
> Identifies a region that updates automatically, possibly by Ajax. *[F3.6 (Windows), S4, IE8]*

aria-hidden [<div aria-hidden="true">]
> Identifies a region that a screen reader should ignore. *[F3.6 (Windows), S4, IE8]*

aria-atomic [<div aria-live="polite" aria-atomic="true">]
> Identifies whether the entire contents of a live region should be read, or just the elements that changed should be read. *[F3.6 (Windows), S4, IE8]*

<scope> [<th scope="col">Time</th>]
> Associates a table header with columns or rows of the table. *[All browsers]*

<caption> [<caption>This is a caption</caption>]
> Creates a caption for a table. *[All browsers]*

aria-describedby [<table aria-describedby="summary">]
> Associates a description with an element. *[F3.6 (Windows), S4, IE8]*

---

2.   http://www.w3.org/TR/html5/dom.html#wai-aria

Tip 14

Providing Navigation Hints with ARIA Roles

Most websites share a common structure: there's a header, a navigation section, some main content, and a footer. Most of these sites are coded just like that, in a linear fashion. Unfortunately, this means screen readers may have to read the site to their users in that order. Since most sites repeat the same header and navigation on each page, users will have to hear these elements each time they visit another page.

The recommended fix is to provide a hidden "skip navigation" link that screen readers will read aloud, which simply links to an anchor somewhere near the main content. However, that's not built in, and it's not something that everyone knows (or remembers) how to do.

HTML5's role attribute lets us assign a "responsibility" to each element on your page. A screen reader can then easily parse the page and categorize all of those responsibilities, creating a simple index for the page. For example, it can find all the navigation roles on the page and present them to a user so she can quickly navigate around the application.

These roles come from the WAI-ARIA specification and have been incorporated into the HTML5 specification.[3] There are two classifications of roles that you can put to use right now: landmark roles and document-structure roles.

Landmark Roles

Landmark roles identify "points of interest" on a site, such as the banner, search area, or navigation, that screen readers can quickly identify.

Role	Use
application	Identifies a region of a page that contains a web application as opposed to a web document
banner	Identifies the banner area of your page
complementary	Identifies page content that complements the main content but is meaningful on its own

---

3.   http://www.w3.org/TR/wai-aria/roles

Role	Use
contentinfo	Identifies where information about the content, such as copyright information and publication date, exists
form	Identifies the section of a page that contains a form, using both native HTML form elements as well as hyperlinks and scripted controls
main	Identifies where your page's main content begins
navigation	Identifies navigational elements on your page
search	Identifies the search area of your page

Let's apply a few of these roles to the AwesomeCo blog template we worked on in Tip 1, *Redefining a Blog Using Semantic Markup*, on page 15.

For the overall header, we apply the banner role like this:

html5_aria/blog/index.html
```
<header id="page_header" role="banner">
  <h1>AwesomeCo Blog!</h1>
</header>
```

All that's needed is the addition of role="banner" to the existing <header> tag.

We can identify our navigation the same way:

html5_aria/blog/index.html
```
<nav role="navigation">
  <ul>
    <li><a href="#">Latest Posts</a></li>
    <li><a href="#">Archives</a></li>
    <li><a href="#">Contributors</a></li>
    <li><a href="#">Contact Us</a></li>
  </ul>
</nav>
```

The HTML5 specification says that some elements have default roles and can't be overridden. The nav element must have the role of navigation, and this role technically doesn't need to be specified. Screen readers aren't quite ready to accept that default yet, but many of them do understand these ARIA roles. So, to be safe, we'll be very specific.

Our main content and sidebar regions can be identified as follows:

html5_aria/blog/index.html
```
<section id="posts" role="main">
</section>
```

html5_aria/blog/index.html

```
<section id="sidebar" role="complementary">

  <nav>
    <h3>Archives</h3>
    <ul>
      <li><a href="2013/10">October 2013</a></li>
      <li><a href="2013/09">September 2013</a></li>
      <li><a href="2013/08">August 2013</a></li>
      <li><a href="2013/07">July 2013</a></li>
      <li><a href="2013/06">June 2013</a></li>
      <li><a href="2013/05">May 2013</a></li>
      <li><a href="2013/04">April 2013</a></li>
      <li><a href="2013/03">March 2013</a></li>
      <li><a href="2013/02">February 2013</a></li>
      <li><a href="2013/01">January 2013</a></li>
      <li><a href="all">More</a></li>
    </ul>
  </nav>
</section> <!-- sidebar -->
```

We identify the publication and copyright info in our footer using the contentinfo role, like this:

html5_aria/blog/index.html

```
<footer id="page_footer" role="contentinfo">
  <p>Copyright © 2013 AwesomeCo.</p>
</footer> <!-- footer -->
```

If we had a search for our blog, we could identify that region as well. Now that we've identified the landmarks, let's take this a step further and help identify some of the document elements.

Joe asks:
Do We Need These Landmark Roles If We Have Elements Such As nav and header?

The landmark roles may seem redundant, but they provide you with the flexibility you need for situations where you can't use the new elements.

Using the search role, you can direct your users to the region of the page that not only contains the search field, but also links to a site map, a drop-down list of "quick links," or other elements that will help your users find information quickly as opposed to directing them to the search field.

There are a lot more roles introduced by the specification than there are new elements and form controls.

Document-Structure Roles

Document-structure roles help screen readers identify parts of static content easily, which can help better organize content for navigation.

Role	Use
article	Identifies a composition that forms an independent part of a document.
definition	Identifies a definition of a term or subject.
directory	Identifies a list of references to a group, like a table of contents. Used for static content.
document	Identifies the region as content, as opposed to a web application.
group	Identifies a collection of user-interface objects that assistive technology should not include in a page summary.
heading	Identifies a heading for a section of a page.
img	Identifies a section that contains elements of an image. This may be image elements as well as captions and descriptive text.
list	Identifies a group of non-interactive list items.
listitem	Identifies a single member of a group of non-interactive list items.
math	Identifies a mathematical expression.
note	Identifies content that is parenthetical or ancillary to the main content of the resource.
presentation	Identifies content that is for presentation and can be ignored by assistive technology.
row	Identifies a row of cells in a grid.
rowheader	Identifies a cell containing header information for a row in a grid.
toolbar	Identifies a toolbar in a web application.

Many of the roles are implicitly defined by HTML tags, such as articles and headings. However, the document role isn't, and it's an extremely helpful role, especially in applications with a mix of dynamic and static content. For example, a web-based email client may have the document role attached to the element that contains the body of the email message. This is useful because screen readers often have different methods for navigating using the keyboard. When the screen reader's focus is on an application element, it may need to allow key presses through to the web application. However, when the focus is on static content, it could allow the screen reader's key bindings to work differently.

We can apply the document role to our blog by adding it to the <body> tag:

```
html5_aria/blog/index.html
<body role="document">
```

This can help ensure that a screen reader will treat this page as static content.

Falling Back

These roles are already usable on the latest browsers with the latest screen readers, so you can start working with them now. Browsers that don't support them are just going to ignore them, so you need to test these with screen-reading software on various browsers. You can't just assume that by placing these roles on the page, you're ensuring they'll work in every situation.

To try things out, you'll want to test with JAWS, which is the most widely used screen reader. Though JAWS is not free, you can get a time-limited demo.[4] You'll want to test JAWS with both Internet Explorer and Firefox, as things behave differently in each browser.

A free, open source alternative called NVDA is becoming quite popular, and you should consider testing with it, as well.[5]

Roles help screen readers identify important regions or elements on a page. They can also give the screen readers hints about the current state of an element. But modern applications have dynamic content, and we can let screen readers know that a page has updated. Let's explore how that works.

---

4. http://www.freedomscientific.com/downloads/jaws/jaws-downloads.asp
5. http://www.nvda-project.org/

Tip 15

Creating an Accessible Updatable Region

We use JavaScript heavily in our web applications these days. Popular frameworks like Backbone and Ember let us build powerful single-page applications, making more-responsive user interfaces that don't cause the page to refresh.[6,7] On these types of pages, the standard practice is to fire off some sort of visual effect to give the user a clue that something has changed on the page. However, a person using a screen reader isn't going to be able to see any visual cues. In the past, these people would often disable JavaScript in their browsers and would then interact with a fallback solution provided by a developer, but a 2012 survey by WebAIM shows that many users of screen-reading software do not disable JavaScript anymore. That means they'll use the same interface as everyone else, so we need to be able to let these people know when things on the interface have changed.[8]

The WAI-ARIA specification provides a nice solution called *live regions* that currently works in Internet Explorer, Firefox, and Safari with various popular screen readers.

The AwesomeCo executive director of communications wants a new home page. It should have links to a Services section, a Contact section, and an About section. He insists that the home page shouldn't scroll because "people hate scrolling." He would like you to implement a prototype for the page with a horizontal menu that changes the page's main content when clicked. That's easy enough to implement, and with the aria-live attribute, we can do something we haven't been able to do well before—implement this type of interface in a way that's friendly to screen readers.

Let's build a simple interface like the one in the following figure. We'll put all the content on the home page, and if JavaScript is available to us, we'll hide all but the first entry. We'll make the navigation links point to each section using page anchors, and we'll use jQuery to change those anchor links into events that swap out the main content. People with JavaScript will see what our director wants, and people without will still be able to see all the content on the page. Best of all, screen readers will know things changed.

---

6.   http://backbonejs.org/
7.   http://emberjs.com/
8.   http://webaim.org/projects/screenreadersurvey4/

AwesomeCo

Welcome   Services   Contact   About

Contact

The contact section

Copyright © 2013 AwesomeCo.

Home   About   Terms of Service   Privacy

Figure 15—A mock-up of the home page using jQuery to change the main content

Creating the Page

We'll start by creating a basic HTML5 page and we'll add our Welcome section, which will be the default section displayed to users when they visit the page. Here's the code for the page with the navigation bar and the jump links:

```
html5_aria/homepage/index.html
<!DOCTYPE html>
<html lang="en-US">
  <head>
    <meta charset="utf-8">
    <title>AwesomeCo</title>
    <link rel="stylesheet" href="stylesheets/style.css">
  </head>
  <body>
    <header id="header" role="banner">
      <h1>AwesomeCo </h1>
      <nav>
        <ul>
          <li><a href="#welcome">Welcome</a></li>
          <li><a href="#services">Services</a></li>
          <li><a href="#contact">Contact</a></li>
          <li><a href="#about">About</a></li>
        </ul>
      </nav>
    </header>
    <section id="content"
             role="document" aria-live="assertive" aria-atomic="true">

      <section id="welcome">
        <header>
          <h2>Welcome</h2>
        </header>
        <p>The welcome section</p>
      </section>
    </section>
```

```
<footer id="footer" role="contentinfo">
  <p>Copyright © 2013 AwesomeCo.</p>
  <nav>
    <ul>
       <li><a href="#">Home</a></li>
       <li><a href="#">About</a></li>
       <li><a href="#">Terms of Service</a></li>
       <li><a href="#">Privacy</a></li>
    </ul>
  </nav>
</footer>

  </body>
</html>
```

The Welcome section has an ID of welcome, which matches the anchor in the navigation bar. We declare our additional page sections in the same fashion.

html5_aria/homepage/index.html

```
<section id="services">
  <header>
    <h2>Services</h2>
  </header>
  <p>The services section</p>
</section>

<section id="contact">
  <header>
    <h2>Contact</h2>
  </header>
  <p>The contact section</p>
</section>

<section id="about">
  <header>
    <h2>About</h2>
  </header>
  <p>The about section</p>
</section>
```

This markup wraps our four content regions:

html5_aria/homepage/index.html

```
<section id="content"
         role="document" aria-live="assertive" aria-atomic="true">
```

The attributes on this line tell screen readers that this region of the page has content that may update.

Now let's add some CSS to the page to create the layout we need. It'll be similar to the CSS for the blog. In stylesheets/style.css, add the basic styling to the body:

```
html5_aria/homepage/stylesheets/style.css
body{
  width: 960px;
  margin: 15px auto;
}

p{
  margin: 0 0 20px 0;
}

p, li{
  line-height: 20px;
  font-family: Arial, "MS Trebuchet", sans-serif;
}
```

Then add the styles to create the horizontal navigation in the header:

```
html5_aria/homepage/stylesheets/style.css
#header{
  width: 100%;
}

#header > nav > ul, #footer > nav > ul{
  list-style: none;
  margin: 0;
  padding: 0;
}
#header > nav > ul > li, #footer > nav > ul > li{
  padding:0;
  margin: 0 20px 0 0;
  display:inline;
}
```

And finally, style the footer so it sits at the bottom and so its text is centered.

```
html5_aria/homepage/stylesheets/style.css
footer#footer{
  clear: both;
  width: 100%;
  display: block;
  text-align: center;
}
```

Now let's see what we can do about making the inner content change when we click one of our links.

Polite and Assertive Updating

There are two types of methods for alerting the user to changes on the page when using aria-live. The polite method is designed to not interrupt the user's workflow. For example, if the user's screen reader is reading a sentence and another region of the page updates and the mode is set to polite, then the screen reader will finish reading the current sentence. However, if the mode is set to assertive, then the updated region is considered high priority, and the screen reader will stop and begin reading the new content. It's really important that you use the appropriate type of interruption when you're developing your site. Overuse of assertive can disorient and confuse your users. Use assertive only if you absolutely must. In our case, it's the right choice because we'll be hiding the other content regions.

Atomic Updating

A second parameter, aria-atomic=true, instructs the screen reader to read the entire contents of the changed region. If we set it to false, it would tell the screen reader to read only nodes that changed. We're replacing the entire contents, so telling the screen reader to read it all makes sense in this case. If we were replacing a single list item or appending to a table with Ajax, we would want to use false instead.

Hiding Regions

To hide the regions, we need to write a little bit of JavaScript and attach it to our page. We'll create a file called application.js, and then include this file as well as the jQuery library on our page.

html5_aria/homepage/index.html
```
<script
    src="http://ajax.googleapis.com/ajax/libs/jquery/1.9.1/jquery.min.js">
</script>

<script src="javascripts/application.js"></script>
```

Our application.js file contains this simple script:

html5_aria/homepage/javascripts/application.js
```
Line 1  var configureTabSelection = function(){
    -     $("#services, #about, #contact").hide().attr("aria-hidden", true);
    -     $("#welcome").attr("aria-hidden",false);
    -
    5     $("nav ul").click(function(event){
    -       var target = $(event.target);
    -       if(target.is("a")){
    -         event.preventDefault();
    -         if ( $(target.attr("href")).attr("aria-hidden") ){
```

```
10          activateTab(target.attr("href"));
          };
        };
      });
    };

    var activateTab = function(selector){
      $("[aria-hidden=false]").hide().attr("aria-hidden", true);
      $(selector).show().attr("aria-hidden", false);
    };
20
    configureTabSelection();
```

On line 2, we hide the Services, About, and Contact sections. We also apply the aria-hidden attribute and give it the value of true for each of the sections. On the next line we apply the same attribute to the default Welcome section, but with a value of false. Adding these attributes helps assistive technology discover which elements are hidden, and it makes it really easy for us to identify which sections need to be turned off and on when we do the toggle.

We capture any clicks of the navigation bar on line 5, and then on 7 we determine which element was clicked. If the user clicked a link, we check to see whether the corresponding section is hidden. The href attribute of the clicked link can help us locate the corresponding section using jQuery selectors, which you can see on line 9.

If it's hidden, we call the activateTab() method, which takes a CSS selector. This method hides everything else and then shows the selected section by using jQuery's show() and hide() methods. It also swaps the value for the aria-hidden attributes.

That's all there is to it. The screen readers should detect the region changes.

Falling Back

Like roles, this solution can be used right now by the latest versions of screen readers. By following good practices such as unobtrusive JavaScript, we have a simple implementation that can work for a reasonably wide audience. When you're doing any modification of the user interface with JavaScript, you should apply ARIA roles to your elements to keep screen readers up-to-date with the element's state.

We often display data in tabular format, so let's explore how we can ensure that data is accessible.

Tip 16

Improving Table Accessibility

For years, HTML tables have been a great source of pain when it comes to accessibility. It's easy for sighted people to glance at a table and get the context. It can be much more difficult for people using screen readers to understand the big picture. To make matters worse, before CSS let us lay out our content, developers used tables to define the various regions of the page. This created huge problems for screen-reading software because it had to navigate around the tables and figure out how to read them. Unfortunately, even today, some websites rely on tables for layouts, prompting the HTML5 specification to create a special ARIA role for a layout table:

```
<table role="presentation">
  ...
</table>
```

Even though controlling a page's layout with tables is a horrible practice because it mixes presentation and content, the truth of the matter is that because people have used tables for layout so much, screen-reading software has gotten pretty good about navigating around them. This presentation role helps things out.

Despite the fact that this new role exists, tables aren't for layout. They're designed to let us mark up tabular data, and depending on the complexity of the table, we may need to help the screen readers give the site's visitor some more context. We'll do that by making associations between headers and their associated rows and columns more clear, and we'll add a caption and a description to the table.

AwesomeCo is holding its annual conference, AwesomeConf, in late December, and one of the pages on the site displays the conference schedule for the event, using an HTML table. We've been asked to ensure that this table is readable by screen readers, because in the past some attendees complained on the end-of-conference survey that the site had accessibility issues. The following figure shows the current conference schedule, displayed as an HTML table.

Conference Schedule

Time	Room 100	Room 101	Room 152	Room 153
8:00 AM	Opening Remarks and Keynote - Ballroom			
9:00 AM	Creating Better Marketing Videos	Embracing Social Media	Pop Culture And You	Visualizing Success
10:00 AM	Build a Solid Fundraising Campaign	Print Is Dead	Mobile First? Not So Fast!	Proving What Works
11:00 AM	Making Connections	Marketing Panel	Clear Content	Improving Experiences
12:00	Lunch			

Use this grid to find the session you want to attend. Note that the keynote and lunch are in the ballroom.

Figure 16—AwesomeConf schedule page

Here's a snippet of the code from the current page.

html5_accessible_tables/original_index.html

```html
<h1>Conference Schedule</h1>

<table>
  <tr>
    <th>Time</th>
    <th>Room 100</th>
    <th>Room 101</th>
    <th>Room 152</th>
    <th>Room 153</th>
  </tr>
  <tr>
    <th>8:00 AM</th>
    <td colspan="4">Opening Remarks and Keynote  - Ballroom</td>
  </tr>
  <tr>
    <th>9:00 AM</th>
    <td>Creating Better Marketing Videos</td>
    <td>Embracing Social Media</td>
    <td>Pop Culture And You</td>
    <td>Visualizing Success</td>
  </tr>
</table>
<section>
  <p>
    Use this grid to find the session you want
    to attend.  Note that the keynote and lunch
    are in the ballroom.
  </p>
</section>
```

It's a pretty standard table, but it has headings on both the x- and y-axes. This can present a problem for some screen reader–and-browser combinations. Let's make the heading associations more clear, both in our code and to screen readers.

Associating Headings with Columns

For simple tables, the <th> tag is enough to denote a header. The browsers and screen readers use a somewhat complex algorithm to locate the associated row or column. In more complex tables, we can use the scope attribute to explicitly state that a heading is for a column or a row. Here's how:

```
html5_accessible_tables/accessible_index.html
<tr>
➤   <th scope="col">Time</th>
➤   <th scope="col">Room 100</th>
➤   <th scope="col">Room 101</th>
➤   <th scope="col">Room 152</th>
➤   <th scope="col">Room 153</th>
  </tr>

  <tr>
➤   <th scope="row">8:00 AM</th>
    <td colspan="4">Opening Remarks and Keynote   - Ballroom</td>
  </tr>

  <tr>
➤   <th scope="row">9:00 AM</th>
    <td>Creating Better Marketing Videos</td>
    <td>Embracing Social Media</td>
    <td>Pop Culture And You</td>
    <td>Visualizing Success</td>
  </tr>
```

For all of the column headings, we specify scope="col". For the row headings, we use scope="row". This makes it easier for screen readers to associate columns, but we can also improve the overall accessibility of the table by describing more clearly what it does.

Explaining Tables with Captions and Descriptions

If we're presenting a table of information, it's a good idea to use some kind of heading or title above or below the table to explain what it does. By putting the title of the table inside a <caption> tag, we allow screen readers to use this to announce the table more clearly. We place the <caption> tag right below the opening <table> tag, like this:

> **Joe asks:**
> ## What About the id and <headers> Attributes?
>
> For many years, it was considered a best practice to associate table headers to columns by assigning a unique id to each header, and then referencing that id in each table cell using the <headers> attribute, like this:
>
> ```
> <table>
>   <tr>
>     <th id="name">Name</th>
>     <th id="email"></th>
>   </tr>
>   <tr>
>     <td headers="name">Ted</td>
>     <td headers="email">ted@puzzlesthebar.com</td>
>   </tr>
>   <tr>
>     <td headers="name">Barney</td>
>     <td headers="email">barney@puzzlesthebar.com</td>
>   </tr>
> </table>
> ```
>
> For simple tables with lots of rows of data, this approach vastly increases the markup on the page without adding any benefits over using scope. This should be reserved for incredibly complex tables, such as those with nested headers. And if you have tables that are that complex, you should see if you can restructure the information in a more understandable manner.

html5_accessible_tables/accessible_index.html

```
➤ <caption>
➤   <h1>Conference Schedule</h1>
➤ </caption>
  <tr>
```

Sometimes a caption isn't enough to explain what's going on with the table. We can use the aria-describedby role to link a table to a section of descriptive content on the page. Our table has a nice descriptive block of text already set aside in a <section> tag. Let's add an id attribute to that section:

```
➤ <section id="schedule_instructions">
    <p>
      Use this grid to find the session you want
      to attend.  Note that the keynote and lunch
      are in the ballroom.
    </p>
  </section>
```

With that id in place we can alter the <table> tag to reference that descriptive section:

```
<table aria-describedby="schedule_instructions">
```

Including captions and additional descriptions with tables helps people who use screen readers understand the context of the tables more clearly and improves usability for sighted users, as well. The <caption> element has been available in browsers for years, and browsers that don't understand the aria-describedby attribute will just ignore it, so there's no reason not to use these techniques with data tables right now.

5.1 The Future

HTML5 and the WAI-ARIA specification have paved the way for a much more accessible Web. With the ability to identify changing regions on the page, developers can create richer JavaScript applications without worrying so much about accessibility issues. Thanks to the ease of use, these roles are being included in popular JavaScript frameworks like Ember, jQuery Mobile, and many more, meaning that developers using those frameworks will be automatically building more-accessible applications.

Part II

New Sights and Sounds

In the second part of this book, we'll shift from talking about structure and interfaces to looking at how we can use HTML5 and CSS3 to draw, work with multimedia files, and create our own interface elements. We'll start off by spending some time making graphics using HTML5's new <canvas> tag, and then we'll work with the <audio> and <video> tags. We'll finish up by using CSS3 to do shadows, gradients, transformations, and animations.

Drawing in the Browser

If we wanted an image in a web application, we'd traditionally open our graphics software of choice, create an image, and embed it on our page with an <img> tag. If we wanted animations, we'd use Flash. HTML5's <canvas> element lets us create images, or even animations, in the browser programmatically using JavaScript. We can use the canvas to create simple or complex shapes or even create graphs and charts without resorting to server-side libraries, Flash, or other plug-ins. Coincidentally, we'll do both of these things in this chapter.

First, to get familiar with how we use JavaScript and the <canvas> tag, we'll draw some simple shapes as we construct a version of the AwesomeCo logo. Then we'll use a graphing library that's specifically designed to work with the canvas to create a bar graph of browser statistics. We'll also discuss some of the special fallback challenges that we'll face because the canvas is more of a programming interface than an element. Then we'll look at how to create the same logo using Scalable Vector Graphics (SVG), an alternative approach to drawing in the browser. We'll look at the following features:

<canvas> [<canvas><p>Alternative content</p></canvas>]
> Supports creation of raster-based graphics via JavaScript. *[C4, F3, S3.2, IE9, O10.1, iOS3.2, A2]*

<svg> [<svg><!-- XML content --></svg>]
> Supports creation of vector-based graphics via XML. *[C4, F3, S3.2, IE9, O10.1, iOS3.2, A2]*

Tip 17

Drawing a Logo on the Canvas

Let's begin our exploration of the HTML5 canvas by learning how to draw simple shapes and lines. Before we can draw anything, we have to add the <canvas> tag to our page. The <canvas> tag doesn't do anything by itself. Adding one to our page gives us a blank slate we can draw on using JavaScript code. We define a canvas with a width and height like this:

```
html5_canvas/canvas_simple_drawing.html
<canvas id="my_canvas" width="150" height="150">
  Fallback content here
</canvas>
```

Unfortunately, you can't use CSS to control or alter the width and height of a <canvas> element without distorting the contents, so you need to decide on your canvas dimensions when you declare it, or you need to adjust everything programatically.

We use JavaScript to put shapes on the canvas. Even if we provided fallback content to browsers that don't support the <canvas> tag, we still need to prevent the JavaScript code from trying to manipulate it. The best way to do that is to run our JavaScript only when the browser supports <canvas>. Here's how:

```
html5_canvas/canvas_simple_drawing.html
var canvas = document.getElementById('my_canvas');
if (canvas.getContext){
  var context = canvas.getContext('2d');

}else{
  // do something to show the canvas's hidden contents
  // or let the browser display the text within the <canvas> element.
}
```

We locate the <canvas> element by its id and then we call the getContext() method. If we get a response from the getContext() method, we grab the 2D context for the canvas so we can add objects. If we don't have a context, we don't want to run any code. We're building a framework to handle fallbacks from the beginning, because unlike in other situations, our users will see JavaScript errors if we try to access the context on browsers that don't support it.

Once we have the canvas's context, we add elements to that context, which causes them to be rendered to the screen. For example, to add a red box, we write code like this:

html5_canvas/canvas_simple_drawing.html
```
context.fillStyle = "rgb(200,0,0)";
context.fillRect (10, 10, 100, 100);
```

We first set a fill color, which is the color of our box. Then we create the box itself. The canvas's 2D context is a grid, with the top-left corner as the default origin. When we create a shape like a box, we specify the starting x- and y-coordinates and the width and height.

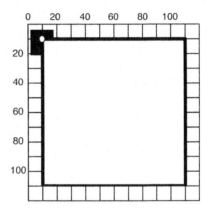

Each shape is added onto its own layer, so you could create three boxes with a 10-pixel offset, like this:

html5_canvas/canvas_simple_drawing.html
```
context.fillStyle = "rgb(200,0,0)";
context.fillRect (10, 10, 100, 100);
context.fillStyle = "rgb(0,200,0)";
context.fillRect (20, 20, 100, 100);

context.fillStyle = "rgb(0,0,200)";
context.fillRect (30, 30, 100, 100);
```

and they'll stack on top of each other, like this:

We can create complex images on the canvas by combining simple shapes, lines, arcs, and text. Let's do a more complex example by re-creating the AwesomeCo logo using the canvas. The logo is pretty simple, as the following figure shows.

Figure 17—The AwesomeCo logo

The logo consists of a string of text, an angled path, a square, and a triangle. Let's start by creating a new HTML5 document for this logo. We'll do everything in the same file for simplicity. We'll add a <script> block right above the closing <body> tag, which will hold our code for creating the logo.

html5_canvas/logo.html
```
<!DOCTYPE html>
<html lang="en">
  <head>
    <meta charset="utf-8">
    <title>AwesomeCo Logo Test</title>
  </head>
  <body>
      <script>
      </script>
  </body>
</html>
```

We'll start our JavaScript by creating a JavaScript function for drawing the logo, which detects whether we can use the 2D canvas.

html5_canvas/logo.html
```
 var drawLogo = function(){
   var canvas = document.getElementById("logo");
   var context = canvas.getContext("2d");
};
```

We invoke this method after first checking for the existence of the <canvas> element, like this:

html5_canvas/logo.html
```
var canvas = document.getElementById("logo");

if (canvas.getContext){
  drawLogo();
}
```

We're looking for an element on the page with the ID of logo, so we'd better make sure we add our canvas element to the document so it can be found and our detection will work.

html5_canvas/logo.html
```
<canvas id="logo" width="900" height="80">
  <h1>AwesomeCo</h1>
</canvas>
```

Let's start drawing our logo.

Drawing Lines

We draw lines on the canvas by playing a game of "connect the dots." We specify a starting point on the canvas grid and then specify additional points on the grid to move to. As we move around the canvas, the dots get connected, like this:

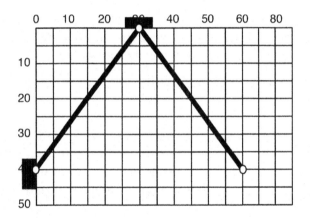

We use the beginPath() method to start drawing a line, and then we create our path:

html5_canvas/logo.html
```
context.fillStyle = "#FF0000";
context.strokeStyle = "#FF0000";

context.lineWidth = 2;
context.beginPath();
context.moveTo(0, 40);
context.lineTo(30, 0);
context.lineTo(60, 40 );
context.lineTo(285, 40 );

context.fill();
context.closePath();
```

Before we start drawing anything, we set the stroke and fill colors for the canvas. The stroke is the color of any lines we create. The fill color is the color that shapes, like rectangles or triangles, get filled in with. Think of the stroke as the color of a shape's perimeter, and the fill color as the shape's area.

When we're done defining the points of our path, we call the stroke() method to draw the line that connects the points. We then call the closePath() method to complete the path we've drawn. Our completed line looks like this:

Next let's add the "AwesomeCo" text to the canvas.

Adding Text

Before we can add text to the canvas, we have to choose a font and a font size. Then we have to place the text at the appropriate coordinates on the grid. We add the text "AwesomeCo" to our canvas like this:

```
html5_canvas/logo.html
context.font = "italic 40px 'Arial'";
context.fillText("AwesomeCo", 60, 36);
```

We define the text type, size, and font before we apply it to the canvas. We use the fillText() method so we get text that's filled in with the fill color we set earlier, and we place the text 60 pixels across and 36 pixels down so it sits right on the path we just drew, to the right of the large triangle but just above the line, like this:

Now let's draw the box-and-triangle combination that sits within the big triangle.

Moving the Origin

Instead of creating a complex shape by drawing a path, we'll make this box and triangle by creating a small square and placing a white triangle on top of the square. When we draw shapes and paths, we can specify the x- and y-coordinates from the origin at the top-left corner of the canvas, but we can also just move the origin to a new location. This makes it easy for us to draw these new shapes right where we want to without having to transpose the coordinates for every point on the shape.

Let's draw the smaller inner square by moving the origin.

html5_canvas/logo.html
```
context.save();
context.translate(20,20);
context.fillRect(0,0,20,20);
```

The square is placed inside of the larger triangle, like this:

Notice that before we move the origin, we call the save() method. This saves the previous state of the canvas so we can revert easily. It's like a restore point, and you can think of it as a stack. Every time you call save(), you get a new entry. When we're all done, we'll call restore(), which will restore the top save point on the stack.

Now let's use a path to draw the inner triangle, but instead of using a stroke, we'll use a fill to create the illusion that the triangle is cutting into the square.

html5_canvas/logo.html
```
context.fillStyle   = "#FFFFFF";
context.strokeStyle = "#FFFFFF";

context.lineWidth = 2;
context.beginPath();
context.moveTo(0, 20);
context.lineTo(10, 0);
context.lineTo(20, 20 );
context.lineTo(0, 20 );

context.fill();
context.closePath();
context.restore();
```

Here we set the stroke and fill to white (#fff) before we begin drawing. This overrides the previous color values we set. Then we draw our lines, and since we moved the origin previously, we're relative to the top-left corner of the square we just drew.

AwesomeCo

We've got our completed logo, but we can make it stand out more.

Adding Gradients to Objects

We set the stroke and fill color for the drawing tools when we started, like this:

```
html5_canvas/logo.html
context.fillStyle = "#FF0000";
context.strokeStyle = "#FF0000";
```

But that's a little boring. Let's create gradients and assign those to strokes and fills:

```
html5_canvas/logo_gradient.html
var gradient = context.createLinearGradient(0, 0, 0, 40);
gradient.addColorStop(0,    "#AA0000"); // darker red
gradient.addColorStop(1,    "#FF0000"); // red
context.fillStyle = gradient;
context.strokeStyle = gradient;
```

We create a gradient object and set the gradient's color stops. In this example, we're just going between two shades of red, but we could do a rainbow if we wanted. (Please do *not* do a rainbow.)

Note that we have to set the color of things before we draw them.

At this point, our logo is complete, and we have a better understanding of how to draw simple shapes on the canvas. However, versions of Internet Explorer prior to 9 don't have any support for the <canvas> tag. Let's fix that.

Falling Back

Google released a library called ExplorerCanvas that makes most of the Canvas application programming interface available to Internet Explorer users.[1] At the time of writing, the most stable release, version 3.0, doesn't support adding text at all, and hasn't been updated since 2009. So we'll use the version from the Subversion repository, which works much better but still has some limitations (which you can read about in the library's source code).[2] To make it work, we include this library in the <head> section of the page:

```
html5_canvas/logo_gradient.html
<!--[if lte IE 8]>
<script src="javascripts/excanvas.js"></script>
<![endif]-->
```

and then we add these lines right above where we detect the canvas:

---

1. http://code.google.com/p/explorercanvas/
2. http://explorercanvas.googlecode.com/svn/trunk/excanvas.js

```
html5_canvas/logo_gradient.html
var canvas = document.getElementById("logo");
```

```
➤ var G_vmlCanvasManager; // so non-IE browsers won't error
➤ if (G_vmlCanvasManager != undefined) { // IE 8
➤   G_vmlCanvasManager.initElement(canvas);
➤ }
  if (canvas.getContext){
    drawLogo();
  }
```

These lines force the ExplorerCanvas library to attach its behavior to the canvas element we defined. Sometimes ExplorerCanvas doesn't quite finish up its Document Object Model (DOM) manipulation tricks before we're ready to use it. If we were using jQuery and had placed the drawLogo() function inside of jQuery's document.ready() handler, we wouldn't need these lines.

With these changes, things work just fine in Internet Explorer 8.

For something this simple, we could just place a PNG version of the logo inside the <canvas> tag for the fallback content. Browsers that don't support <canvas> would just display the image.

Now that you see how easy it is to create simple shapes on the canvas, let's look at another use.

Graphing Statistics with RGraph

The canvas is great for drawing images, but the fact that we build objects on the canvas using JavaScript means we can use this for data visualization as well. Let's use the canvas to create a simple graph.

There are lots of ways to draw graphs on a web page. In the past, developers used Flash for graphs all the time, but that has the limitation of not working on some mobile devices, like the iPad and iPhone. Some server-side solutions work well, but those might be too processor-intensive if you're working with real-time data. A standards-based client-side solution like the canvas is a great option as long as we're careful to ensure it works in older browsers. You've already seen how to draw squares, but drawing something complex requires a lot more JavaScript. We need a graphing library to help. The RGraph library makes it ridiculously simple to draw graphs using the HTML5 canvas.[3] It's a pure JavaScript solution, though, so it won't work for user agents that don't have JavaScript available; but then again, neither will the canvas. Here's the code for a simple bar graph:

```
html5_canvas/rgraph_bar_example.html
<canvas width="500" height="250" id="test">[no canvas support]</canvas>

<script src="javascripts/RGraph.common.js" ></script>
<script src="javascripts/RGraph.bar.js" ></script>

<script type="text/javascript" charset="utf-8">
  var bar = new RGraph.Bar('test', [50,25,15,10]);
  bar.Set('chart.gutter', 50);
  bar.Set('chart.colors', ['red']);
  bar.Set('chart.title', "A bar graph of my favorite pies");
  bar.Set('chart.labels', ["Banana Creme", "Pumpkin", "Apple", "Cherry"]);
  bar.Draw();
</script>
```

All we have to do is create a couple of JavaScript arrays to hold the data, and RGraph draws the graph on the canvas for us. Using this data, we get a graph like in the following figure.

---

3.   http://www.rgraph.net/

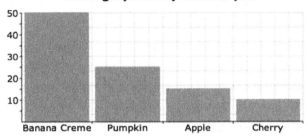

Figure 18—A client-side bar graph using the canvas

AwesomeCo is updating the company website, and senior management would like to see a graph of the most popular web browsers as determined by the traffic the site gets. The back-end programmers will be able to get the data in real time, but first they'd like to see whether we can come up with a way to display the graph in the browser, so they've provided us with some test data. Our goal is to transform that test data into a useful graph.

Describing Data with HTML

We could hard-code the values for the browser statistics in the JavaScript code, but then only users with JavaScript would be able to see the values. Instead, let's put the data right on the page as text. We can read the data with JavaScript and feed it to the graphing library later.

```
html5_canvas/canvas_graph.html
<div id="graph_data">
  <h1>Browser share for this site</h1>
  <ul>
    <li>
      <p data-name="Safari" data-percent="10">
        Safari - 10%
      </p>
    </li>
    <li>
      <p data-name="Internet Explorer" data-percent="30">
        Internet Explorer - 30%
      </p>
    </li>
    <li>
      <p data-name="Firefox" data-percent="15">
        Firefox - 15%
      </p>
    </li>
    <li>
```

```
      <p data-name="Google Chrome" data-percent="45">
        Google Chrome - 45%
      </p>
    </li>
  </ul>
</div>
```

We're using the HTML5 data attributes to store the browser names and the percentages. Although we have that information in the text, it's much easier to work with programmatically since we won't have to parse strings.

The following figure shows that the graph data is nicely displayed and readable even without the graph. This will be your fallback content for mobile devices and other users where either the <canvas> tag or JavaScript is not available.

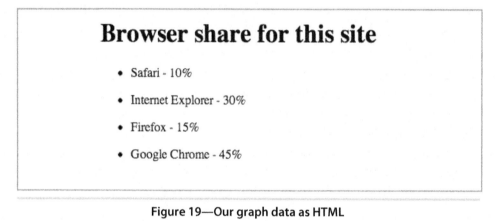

Browser share for this site

- Safari - 10%
- Internet Explorer - 30%
- Firefox - 15%
- Google Chrome - 45%

Figure 19—Our graph data as HTML

Now let's use this marked-up data to build a graph.

Turning Our HTML into a Bar Graph

We're going to use a bar graph, so we'll require the RGraph bar-graph library as well as the main RGraph library. We'll also use jQuery to grab the data out of the document. Finally, we'll put the code that builds our graph in a file called javascripts/graph.js.

We load the libraries we need right above the closing <body> tag:

html5_canvas/canvas_graph.html

```
<script
  src="http://ajax.googleapis.com/ajax/libs/jquery/1.9.1/jquery.min.js">
</script>
<script src="javascripts/RGraph.common.js" ></script>
<script src="javascripts/RGraph.bar.js" ></script>
<script src="javascripts/graph.js" ></script>
```

To build the graph, we need to grab the graph's title, the labels, and the data from the HTML document and pass it to the RGraph library. RGraph takes in arrays for both the labels and the data. We can use jQuery to quickly build those arrays. Add this code to javascripts/graph.js:

```
html5_canvas/javascripts/graph.js
Line 1  var canvasGraph = function(){
   -      var title = $('#graph_data h1').text();
   -      var labels = $("#graph_data>ul>li>p[data-name]").map(function(){
   -         return this.getAttribute("data-name");
   5      });
   -      var percents = $("#graph_data>ul>li>p[data-percent]").map(function(){
   -         return parseInt(this.getAttribute("data-percent"));
   -      });
   -      var bar = new RGraph.Bar('browsers', percents);
   10     bar.Set('chart.gutter', 50);
   -      bar.Set('chart.colors', ['red']);
   -      bar.Set('chart.title', title);
   -      bar.Set('chart.labels', labels);
   -      bar.Draw();
   15     $('#graph_data').hide();
   -  }
```

First, on line 2, we grab the text for the header. Then, on line 3, we select all the elements that have the data-name attribute. We use jQuery's map function to turn the values from those elements into an array.

We use that same logic on line 6 to grab an array of the percentages.

On line 7, we're forcing the value from the data attribute to be an integer. We could also use jQuery's data() method, which can read HTML5's data attributes and automatically convert the value to the appropriate data type.

With the data collected, RGraph has no trouble drawing our graph (see Figure 20, *Our graph rendered on the canvas*, on page 124).

Displaying Alternative Content

In *Describing Data with HTML*, on page 121, we could have placed the graph between the starting and ending <canvas> tags. This would hide these elements on browsers that support the canvas element while displaying them to browsers that don't. However, the content would still be hidden if the user's browser supports the canvas element but the user has disabled JavaScript.

Let's leave the data outside the canvas element and then hide it with jQuery once we've checked that the browser supports the canvas. We'll use standard JavaScript instead of Modernizr to detect canvas support, since it's really easy.

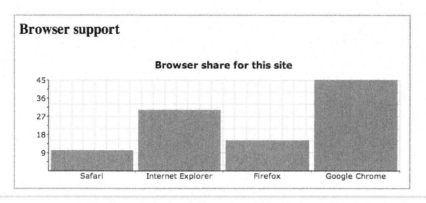

Figure 20—Our graph rendered on the canvas

```
html5_canvas/javascripts/graph.js
var canvas = document.getElementById('browsers');
if (canvas.getContext){
  canvasGraph();
}
```

With that, our graph is ready (but won't work for people using browsers that don't support the <canvas> tag).

Falling Back

When building this solution, we already covered fallbacks for accessibility and lack of JavaScript, but our graph won't display in Internet Explorer 8 because it doesn't have canvas support.

ExplorerCanvas (which we talked about in *Falling Back*, on page 118) and RGraph work really well together. We just need to include excanvas.js in our <head> section, and our graphs will automatically work in Internet Explorer 8. However, if you're working with Internet Explorer 7 or older, you'll have to use an alternative solution.

However, since ExplorerCanvas needs to be loaded in the <head> section, there can sometimes be race conditions where things are loaded in the wrong order. In our case, ExplorerCanvas has to make modifications to the DOM and it doesn't always do those modifications as quickly as we need it to. There are two ways to avoid this. First, we could use the configuration we used in *Falling Back*, on page 118, to force ExplorerCanvas to see our canvas element. Second, we could use jQuery's $(document).ready() method to invoke the canvasGraph() function. This ensures that the document really is ready to be manipulated by our scripts. We're already using jQuery anyway, so let's change our code slightly, like this:

`html5_canvas/javascripts/graph.js`

```
➤ $(document).ready(function(){
    var canvas = document.getElementById('browsers');
    if (canvas.getContext){
      canvasGraph();
    }
➤ });
```

Now everything works in Internet Explorer 8, as well!

Using the canvas has an additional benefit—it got us to start thinking about a fallback solution from the beginning, rather than trying to wedge something in later. That's really good for accessibility. This is one of the most accessible and versatile methods available for graphing data. You can easily create the visual representation as well as a text-based alternative. This way, everyone can understand the important data you're sharing.

Now let's look at a completely different way to draw things in the browser.

Tip 19

Creating Vector Graphics with SVG

We're not limited to drawing graphics on the canvas. HTML5 documents support Scalable Vector Graphics, or SVG. Instead of using JavaScript to plot lines and draw shapes, we define lines, curves, circles, rectangles, and polygons using XML. Graphics in SVG are true vector graphics, meaning that instead of being made up of pixels like raster graphics, they use math to define the lines. That means we can easily resize vector graphics without blurriness or loss of quality, unlike the raster graphics of the Canvas.

To learn about SVG, we'll use SVG's XML syntax to redraw the AwesomeCo logo we drew before.

First we create a simple HTML skeleton with an <svg> element on the page:

```
html5_svg/index.html
<!DOCTYPE html>
<html lang='en'>
  <head>
    <meta charset="utf-8">
    <title>AwesomeCo Logo Test</title>
  </head>
  <body>
    <script type="image/svg+xml">
      <svg id="awesomeco_logo" width="900" height="80">
      </svg>
    </script>
  </body>
</html>
```

We define the <svg> tag within a <script> tag with the content type of image/svg+xml. This will ensure that the SVG content is skipped when browsers parse the HTML elements of the page. Within the <svg> tag we also specify the height and width of the SVG element. The XML that defines the image we're going to create goes between the opening and closing <svg> tags.

Drawing Lines

Let's start by drawing the main line of the logo that the text rests on. When we did this using the canvas, we used a path, but SVG supports something called a <polyline>, which is designed to create lines with angles. We can whip up the main line, including the angled part, with this code:

```
html5_svg/index.html
<polyline id="line"
          points="0,40 30,0 60,40 285,40"
          style="fill:none;stroke:rgb(255,0,0);stroke-width:2">
</polyline>
```

Just like with the canvas, we start out on a coordinate system with x=0 and y=0 in the upper-left corner. To plot our line with <polyline>, we specify a set of points. We start at 0 pixels across and 40 pixels down. Then we move to 30 pixels across and 0 pixels down to create the first part of the line. From there we go over to 60 pixels across and 40 pixels down, and then finally over to 285 pixels across and 40 pixels down.

We also set the style attribute, setting the stroke of the line to a thickness and a color. When we're done, the plotted line looks like this:

From here we can add the text.

Adding Text

We use the <text> tag to define text we want to place. We specify the font family, font size, font style, and font weight using attributes with the same names (but with hyphens between the words).

Within the <text> tag, we place a <tspan> element that creates the actual block of text. We specify its position using the x and y attributes, and we place the text we want to display within the opening and closing <tspan> tags. To get our text rendered the way we want it, we code it like this:

```
html5_svg/index.html
<text id="AwesomeCo"
      fill="rgb(255,0,0)"
      font-family="Arial" font-size="40"
      font-style="italic" font-weight="normal">
    <tspan x="60" y="36" fill="rgb(255,0,0)">AwesomeCo</tspan>
  </text>
```

The text appears properly placed within our logo:

Now we can move on to creating the smaller square and rectangle.

Adding Shapes

SVG has definitions for circles, ellipses, and even irregular polygons. We need a square, and we'll use the <rect> tag for that. To create a square, we specify the starting coordinates and the width and height.

```
html5_svg/index.html
<rect id="square"
      x="20" y="20" height="20" width="20"
      style="fill:rgb(255,0,0)"></rect>
```

We define the stroke and fill just like we did with <polyline>, by specifying it with the style attribute. Our logo is shaping up:

All we have left is the small white triangle.

Freehand Drawing with Paths

We could use the <polygon> tag to define a triangle, but instead we'll use a path like we did when we drew the original triangle on the <canvas> version of this logo. The approach is actually quite similar, except we have to specify all of the movements and points as a single array of coordinates separated by spaces rather than a series of steps. It's similar to how we defined the <polyline> earlier.

We use the d attribute to define how to draw the line. We start by defining the starting point of our line, and then we draw each point on our line. Since we're doing a triangle, we're going to end up where we started so we can connect the last point to the first point. Here's the code:

```
html5_svg/index.html
<path id="Triangle"
      d="M20,40 L30,20 L40,40 Z M20,40"
      fill="rgb(255,255,255)"></path>
```

We use M to move the origin. We use L to specify a point on the line, and we use Z to close the path, which means we've connected the starting point to the endpoint so that its contents can be filled. Just think of it like a game of "connect the dots." You move the pen to the first dot, then you draw a line to the next one, and so on.

And when we're done, our finished logo looks like this:

AwesomeCo

SVG files don't have to be embedded into the document like we did here. You can make them external files and even load them as background images in CSS, provided that the browser supports it.

Drawing with SVG is similar to drawing on the canvas, but we also have the ability to define these images in separate files and link them in to our document. This gives us some greater flexibility. However, they're not as programmable as canvas-based graphics are. SVG-based graphics might be better choices for logos and nondynamic content, while canvas graphics might be better for games. Now that you've seen both, you can explore each further to find out what works for you.

Falling Back

Browsers that don't support SVG graphics natively can use any number of fallback solutions. The simplest one to implement is SVG Web,[4] which provides partial support for SVG 1.1. SVG Web uses Flash to render the vector graphics.

To make it work, we download SVG Web and place the svg.js and svg.swf files in the javascripts folder. We then link svg.js to our web page with a <script> tag in the <head> of our document, like this:

html5_svg/index.html
```
<script src="javascripts/svg.js" data-path="javascripts"></script>
```

and we've got fallback support.

6.1   The Future

Now that you know a little about how the canvas works, you can start thinking of other ways you might use it. You could use it to create a game using libraries like Impact or Crafty,[5,6] or create a user interface for a media player, or build a better image gallery. All you need to start painting is a little bit of JavaScript and a little bit of imagination. And as support ramps up, speed and features will improve.

But it doesn't stop with 2D graphics. The canvas specification supports 3D graphics as well, and browser manufacturers are implementing hardware

---

4.   https://code.google.com/p/svgweb/
5.   http://impactjs.com/
6.   http://craftyjs.com/

acceleration. The canvas will make it possible to create intriguing user interfaces and engaging games using only JavaScript. Dig into the excellent Three.js library to see what amazing things you can create.[7]

As for SVG, libraries like Raphaël make it easy to create amazing visualizations and graphics that work in all browsers.[8] And best of all, tools like Adobe Illustrator let you export your vector graphics as SVG files you can bring into your web projects. As support for SVG improves, it'll be even easier to create images that can scale with the size of the device. In a world where many users move between small mobile screens and large desktop screens, it's great to have graphics that can scale up and down without losing quality.

---

7. http://threejs.org/
8. http://raphaeljs.com

Embedding Audio and Video

Audio and video are integral parts of the modern Internet. Podcasts, audio previews, and even how-to videos are everywhere, and until a few years ago, they've only been truly usable via browser plug-ins like Flash. HTML5 introduces new methods to embed audio and video files into a page. In this chapter we'll explore a few methods we can use to not only embed audio and video content, but also to ensure that it is available to people using older browsers and to people with disabilities.

We'll discuss the following HTML5 features:

<audio> [<audio src="drums.mp3"></audio>]
> Plays audio natively in the browser. *[C4, F3.6, S3.2, IE9, O10.1, iOS3, A2]*

<video> [<video src="tutorial.m4v"></video>]
> Plays video natively in the browser. *[C4, F3.6, S3.2, IE9, O10.5, iOS3, A2]*

<source> [<source src="video/h264/01_blur.mp4" type='video/mp4'>]
> Specifies the source audio or video file. Used for multiple formats. *[C4, F3.6, S3.2, IE9, O10.5, iOS3, A2]*

<track>
> Supplies subtitles, captions, or chapter points for video. *[C18, S6.1, IE10]*

Before we do that, we need to talk about the history of audio and video on the Web. After all, to understand where we're going, we have to understand where we've been.

7.1 A Bit of History

People have been trying to use audio and video on web pages for a long time. It started with people embedding MIDI or MP3 files on their home pages and using the <embed> tag to reference the file, like this:

```
<embed src="awesome.mp3" autostart="true"
    loop="true" controller="true"></embed>
```

The <embed> tag never became a standard, so people started using the <object> tag instead, which is an accepted World Wide Web Consortium standard. To support older browsers that don't understand the <object> tag, you'd often see an <embed> tag nested within the <object> tag, like this:

```
<object>
<param name="src" value="simpsons.mp3">
<param name="autoplay" value="false">
<param name="controller" value="true">
<embed src="awesome.mp3" autostart="false"
    loop="false" controller="true"></embed>
</object>
```

Not every browser could stream the content this way, though, and not every server was configured properly to serve it correctly. Things got even more complicated when video on the Web became more popular. We went through lots of iterations of audio and video content on the Web, from RealPlayer to Windows Media to QuickTime. Every company had a video strategy, and it seemed like every site used a different method and format for encoding video on the Web. That was inconvenient for developers and content producers, but it was an absolute nightmare for the common user.

Macromedia (now Adobe) realized early on that its Flash Player could be the perfect vehicle for delivering audio and video content across platforms. Flash was available and enabled on close to 97 percent of desktop web browsers. Once content producers discovered they could encode once and play anywhere, thousands of sites turned to Flash streaming for both audio and video.

Then in 2007 Apple decided not to support Flash on the iPhone and iPod Touch (and later the iPad). Because of the popularity of the iOS platform, many of the most popular content providers, including YouTube, responded by making available video streams that would play right in Safari on iOS. These videos, using the H.264 codec, were also playable via the normal Flash Player, which allowed content providers to still encode once while targeting multiple platforms.

The creators of the HTML5 specification believe that the browser should support audio and video natively rather than relying on a plug-in that requires a lot of boilerplate HTML. Browsers should treat audio and video as first-class citizens in terms of web content, just like still images. But before we look at how to embed audio and video on pages, let's talk about formats.

7.2   Containers and Codecs

When we talk about video on the Web, we talk in terms of containers and codecs. You might think of a video you get off your digital camera as an AVI or an MPEG file, but that's an oversimplification. A *container* is like an envelope that holds audio streams, video streams, and sometimes additional metadata such as subtitles. These audio and video streams need to be encoded, and that's where *codecs* come in. Video and audio can be encoded in hundreds of different ways, but when it comes to HTML5 video, only a few matter.

Video Codecs

When you watch a video, your video player has to decode it. Unfortunately, the player you're using might not be able to decode the video you want to watch because the video was encoded using a format your player can't read. Some players use software to decode video, which can be slower or more CPU-intensive but can often play a wider range of formats. Other players use hardware decoders and are thus limited in what they can play. You need to know about three video formats if you want to start using the HTML5 <video> tag in your work today: H.264, Theora, and VP8. Each format is a little different, and unfortunately for us, browsers each support different formats.

Video Codecs and Supported Browsers

H.264
   [C3, F21 (Windows 7+), S4, IE9, iOS]

Theora
   [F3.5, C4, O10]

VP8
   [C5, F4, S6 and IE9 (if codec installed), O10.7]

H.264

H.264 is a high-quality codec that was created by the MPEG group, and standardized in 2003. To support low-definition or low-bandwidth devices such as mobile phones while also handling video for high-definition devices, the H.264 specification is split into various profiles. These profiles share a set of common features, but higher-end profiles offer additional options that improve quality. For example, the iPhone and Flash Player can both play videos encoded with H.264, but the original iPhone supported only the lower-quality "baseline" profile, while Flash Player supports higher-quality streams.

It's possible to encode a video one time and embed multiple profiles so that it looks nice on various platforms.

H.264 is a de facto standard because of support from Microsoft and Apple, which are licensees. On top of that, Google's YouTube converted its videos to the H.264 codec so they could play on the iPhone, and Adobe's Flash Player supports it, as well. However, it's not an open technology. It is patented, and its use is subject to licensing terms. Content producers must pay a royalty to encode videos using H.264, but these royalties do not apply to content that is made freely available to end users.[1]

Proponents of free software are concerned that eventually the rights holders may begin demanding high royalties from content producers. That concern has led to the creation and promotion of alternative codecs.

Theora

Theora is a royalty-free codec developed by the Xiph.org Foundation. Although content producers can use Theora to create videos of similar quality to those made with H.264, device manufacturers have been slow to adopt it. Firefox, Chrome, and Opera will play videos encoded with Theora on any platform without additional software, but Internet Explorer, Safari, and the iOS devices will not. Apple and Microsoft were wary of "submarine patents," a term used to describe patents for which the patent application purposely delays the publication and issuance of the patent to lay low while others implement the technology. When the time is right, the patent applicant "emerges" and begins demanding royalties from an unsuspecting market. Because of this, Theora has fallen out of favor and is being replaced by the VP8 format.

VP8

Google's VP8 is an open codec with quality similar to H.264's. It is supported by Mozilla, Chrome, and Opera. Safari 6 and Internet Explorer 9 support VP8 as long as the user has installed a codec already. It's also supported in Adobe's Flash Player, making it an interesting alternative. It is not supported on Safari on iOS devices, which means that although this codec is free to use, content producers wanting to deliver video content to iPhones or iPads still need to use the H.264 codec. In addition, VP8 may infringe on patents related to the H.264 codec.[2]

---

1. http://www.reelseo.com/mpeg-la-announces-avc-h264-free-license-lifetime/
2. http://www.fosspatents.com/2013/03/nokia-comments-on-vp8-patent.html

Audio Codecs

As if competing standards for video weren't complicating matters enough, we also have to be concerned with competing standards for audio.

Audio Codecs and Supported Browsers

AAC
  [S4, C3, iOS]

MP3
  [C3, S4, IE9, iOS]

Vorbis (OGG)
  [F3, C4, O10]

Advanced Audio Coding (AAC)

This is the audio format that Apple uses in its iTunes Store. It is designed to have better audio quality than MP3s for around the same file size, and it offers multiple audio profiles, similar to H.264. Also like H.264, it's not a free codec and does have associated licensing fees.

All Apple products play AAC files. So do Adobe's Flash Player and the open source VLC player.

MP3

The MP3 format, although extremely common, isn't supported in Firefox and Opera because it's patent-encumbered. It is supported in Safari and Chrome.

Vorbis (OGG)

This open source royalty-free format is supported by Firefox, Opera, and Chrome. You'll find it used with the Theora and VP8 video codecs, as well. Vorbis files have very good audio quality but are not widely supported by hardware music players.

Video codecs and audio codecs need to be packaged together for distribution and playback. Let's talk about video containers.

Containers and Codecs, Working Together

A container is a metadata file that identifies and interleaves audio or video files. A container doesn't have any detail about how the information it contains is encoded. Essentially, a container "wraps" audio and video streams. Containers can often hold any combination of encoded media, but we'll see these three combinations when it comes to working with video on the Web:

- The OGG container, with Theora video and Vorbis audio, which will work in Firefox, Chrome, and Opera.

- The MP4 container, with H.264 video and AAC audio, which will work in Safari and Chrome, as well as Internet Explorer 9 and up. It will also play through Adobe Flash Player and on iPhones, iPods, and iPads.

- The WebM container, using VP8 video and Vorbis audio, which will work in Firefox, Chrome, Opera, and Adobe Flash Player.

Given that Google andMozilla are moving ahead with VP8 and WebM, we'll eliminate Theora from the mix eventually, but we're still looking at encoding our videos at least twice—once using H.264 for Safari, iOS, and Internet Explorer 9 and up, and then again in VP8 for Firefox and Opera, since both of those browsers refuse to play H.264.[3]

Browser	Container	Video	Audio
Internet Explorer 9+	MP4	H.264	AAC or MP3
Safari and Safari on iOS	MP4	H.264	AAC
Firefox, Chrome, Opera, and the Android browser	WebM	VP8	Vorbis

That's a lot to take in, but now that you're familiar with the history and the limitations, let's dig into implementation, starting with audio.

---

3. http://lists.whatwg.org/pipermail/whatwg-whatwg.org/2009-June/020620.html

Tip 20

Working with Audio

AwesomeCo is developing a site to showcase royalty-free audio loops for use in screencasts, and it would like to see a mockup page of a single loop collection. When we're done, we'll have a list of the audio loops and a visitor will be able to quickly audition each one. We don't have to worry about finding audio loops for this project, because the client's sound engineer has already provided us with the samples we'll need in both MP3 and OGG formats. You can find a small bit of information on how to encode your own audio files in Appendix 3, *Encoding Audio and Video for the Web*, on page 273.

Building the Basic List

The audio engineer has provided us with four samples: drums, organ, bass, and guitar. We need to describe each one of these samples using HTML markup. Here's the markup for the drums loop:

```
html5_audio/audio.html
<article class="sample">
  <header><h2>Drums</h2></header>
  <audio id="drums" controls>
    <source src="sounds/ogg/drums.ogg" type="audio/ogg">
    <source src="sounds/mp3/drums.mp3" type="audio/mpeg">
    <a href="sounds/mp3/drums.mp3">Download drums.mp3</a>
  </audio>
</article>
```

We define the <audio> tag first and tell it that we want to have some controls displayed. Within the <audio> tag, we define multiple <source> tags, one for the MP3 version and another for the OGG versions. The type attribute describes the type of audio, and if we supply it, the browser doesn't need to go to the server to ask what format the video is; it can look at its supported types and check very quickly. If it can't play the first file it finds, it'll try the next, until there are no more <source> tags to try.

Finally, we display a link to allow the visitor to download the MP3 file directly. This will show up if the browser doesn't support the <audio> tag.

This basic bit of code will work in Chrome, Safari, and Firefox. Let's put it inside an HTML5 template with the three other sound samples.

html5_audio/audio.html
```
    <article class="sample">
      <header><h2>Drums</h2></header>
      <audio id="drums" controls>
        <source src="sounds/ogg/drums.ogg" type="audio/ogg">
        <source src="sounds/mp3/drums.mp3" type="audio/mpeg">
        <a href="sounds/mp3/drums.mp3">Download drums.mp3</a>
      </audio>
    </article>

    <article class="sample">
      <header><h2>Guitar</h2></header>
      <audio id="guitar" controls>
        <source src="sounds/ogg/guitar.ogg" type="audio/ogg">
        <source src="sounds/mp3/guitar.mp3" type="audio/mpeg">
        <a href="sounds/mp3/guitar.mp3">Download guitar.mp3</a>
      </audio>
    </article>

    <article class="sample">
      <header><h2>Organ</h2></header>
      <audio id="organ" controls>
        <source src="sounds/ogg/organ.ogg" type="audio/ogg">
        <source src="sounds/mp3/organ.mp3" type="audio/mpeg">
        <a href="sounds/mp3/organ.mp3">Download organ.mp3</a>
      </audio>
    </article>

    <article class="sample">
      <header><h2>Bass</h2></header>
      <audio id="bass" controls>
        <source src="sounds/ogg/bass.ogg" type="audio/ogg">
        <source src="sounds/mp3/bass.mp3" type="audio/mpeg">
        <a href="sounds/mp3/bass.mp3">Download bass.mp3</a>
      </audio>
    </article>
  </body>
</html>
```

When we open the page in an HTML5-compatible browser, each entry in the list will have its own audio player, like in Figure 21, *The audio players in Chrome*, on page 139.

The browser itself handles the playback of the audio when you press the Play button.

When we open the page in Internet Explorer, the download links show since the browser doesn't understand the audio element. This makes for a decent fallback solution, but let's see whether we can do better.

Samples:

Drums

Guitar

Organ

Bass

Figure 21—The audio players in Chrome

Falling Back

Audio fallback support is built into the element itself. We've defined multiple sources for our audio using the <source> tag and have provided links to download the audio files. If the browser cannot render the <audio> element, it will display the link we've placed inside the field. We could even go a step further and use Flash as a fallback after we define our sources.

However, this might not be the best approach. You may encounter a browser that supports the <audio> tag but doesn't support the formats you've supplied. For example, you may decide it's not worth your time to provide audio in multiple formats. Additionally, the HTML5 specification indicates that the fallback support for <audio> is not to be used to place content that would be read by screen readers.

The simplest solution is to move the download link outside the <audio> tag and use JavaScript to hide it, like this:

```
html5_audio/advanced_audio.html
<article class="sample">
  <header><h2>Drums</h2></header>
  <audio id="drums" controls>
    <source src="sounds/ogg/drums.ogg" type="audio/ogg">
    <source src="sounds/mp3/drums.mp3" type="audio/mpeg">
  </audio>
  <a href="sounds/mp3/drums.mp3">Download drums.mp3</a>
</article>
```

Fallbacks with audio are relatively easy, and some of your users may appreciate the ability to easily download the file, so you might consider not hiding the links at all.

If you want to do something more advanced, you need to detect support for audio. You can do basic detection by creating a new audio element in JavaScript and checking whether it responds to the canPlayType() method, like this:

```
var canPlayAudioFiles = !!(document.createElement('audio').canPlayType);
```

If you want to detect support for a certain type of audio file, you'd then use the canPlayType() method on the audio element:

```
var audio = document.createElement('audio');
if(audio.canPlayType('audio/ogg')){
  // plays ogg files
}
```

The canPlayType() method doesn't return Boolean values. Instead of true or false values, you'll get one of the following string values back:

- "probably", meaning it'll most likely work.

- "maybe", meaning it might work.

- "", an empty string, which is considered "falsey." That means that although it's not a Boolean false, JavaScript won't see it as true.

Modernizr has a little better support for checking audio availability. It wraps canPlayType(), creating some nice convenience methods:

```
if(Modernizr.audio.ogg){
  // plays ogg files
}

if(Modernizr.audio.mp3){
  // plays MP3 files
}
```

However, Modernizr still uses the HTML5 specification's return values for testing audio formats playable by a browser.

Playing audio in the browser natively is just the beginning. Browsers are starting to support the HTML5 JavaScript application programming interfaces (APIs) for audio and video, which you can read about in *Explore the Media Content JavaScript API*, on page 149.

Now that you know how to make audio work natively, let's look at how we do the same with video.

Tip 21

Embedding Video

AwesomeCo wants to showcase its new series of training videos on its website, and it wants the videos to be viewable on as many devices as possible, especially on the iPad. As a trial, we've been provided two videos in the "Photoshop Tips" series, which we'll use to build a prototype. Thankfully, we've been given the video files in H.264, Theora, and VP8 formats, so we can focus on creating the page. (If you want to learn more about encoding your own video files, check out Appendix 3, *Encoding Audio and Video for the Web*, on page 273.)

The <video> tag works exactly like the <audio> tag. We just need to provide our sources, and Chrome, Firefox, Safari, Safari on iOS, and Internet Explorer 9 display the video without any additional plug-ins. The markup for our first video file, 01_blur, looks like this:

```
html5_video/native.html
<article>
  <header>
    <h2>Saturate with Blur</h2>
  </header>
  <video id="video_blur" preload="auto" controls
        width="640" height="480">
    <source src="video/h264/01_blur.mp4"    type='video/mp4'>
    <source src="video/theora/01_blur.ogv" type='video/ogg'>
    <source src="video/webm/01_blur.webm"   type='video/webm'>
    <p>Your browser does not support the video tag.</p>
  </video>
</article>
```

We define the <video> tag and tell it that we want it to show playback controls. We use the preload attribute to tell browsers to attempt to load the video in the background, and we implicitly tell it that it should not play automatically by *not* including the autoplay attribute.

Within the <video> tag, we define each video source with the <source> tag, and we specify its type. The browser will play the file type it understands, but we have to provide the proper format for that browser. If we only provided the MP4 format, then browsers that support the <video> tag but don't support MP4 files would just show the user a blank video player.

To ensure that web servers know how to handle our video files, we need to add the proper MIME types to our server. This varies by platform, but if we were using Apache, we'd create a new .htaccess file in the same folder as our new web page that defines the MIME types for the videos, like this:

```
html5_video/.htaccess
AddType video/ogg  .ogv
AddType video/mp4  .mp4
AddType video/webm .webm
```

If you're serving videos from Amazon S3, you can set the content-type header for each video. And if you're using Microsoft's Internet Information Server, you just use its interface to edit the MIME types for your site.

Once we upload these files to our web server and configure the MIME types, our videos will play in a wide variety of browsers, and our users will see a video player similar to the one shown in the following figure.

We still can't reach users of Internet Explorer 8 and older. We'll need to use Flash to make that work.

Figure 22—Our video displayed using Chrome's native HTML5 video player

Falling Back

To properly support a Flash-based fallback and still use HTML5 video, we place the Flash object code within the <video> tag. The site Video for Everybody outlines this process in detail,[4] but there's a much easier way to get videos to work across platforms without writing a ton of markup.

The Video.js library makes it incredibly easy to support video on all platforms, using the information within the <video> tag to build a suitable Flash fallback for browsers that don't support HTML video. Here's how we make it work.[5]

First, we add the Video.js library and style sheet to our existing page. Video.js provides a content-delivery network we can use, so we don't have to download the libraries ourselves. We just need to add this code to the <head> section of our page:

html5_video/videojs_index.html

```
<link href="http://vjs.zencdn.net/4.0/video-js.css" rel="stylesheet">
<script src="http://vjs.zencdn.net/4.0/video.js"></script>
```

Then we change the <video> tag by adding some attributes:

```
<video id="video_blur" preload="auto" controls
       width="640" height="480"
       class="video-js vjs-default-skin"
       data-setup="{}">
```

We use the class attribute to tell Video.js that it should use this video, and it should use the player skin we specify. The data-setup attribute is a custom one that contains configuration options represented as JavaScript Object Notation (JSON) data. We don't need any special options, so we simply pass a blank object.

When we bring up our page in Internet Explorer 8, our video plays and we don't need to encode to *another* format or load our own Flash-based player. Our Internet Explorer friends will see something like Figure 23, *Our video in Internet Explorer using Video.js*, on page 144. It's important to note that Flash's security settings may prevent you from seeing the video unless you're serving the HTML and the video from a web server. Using a file: URL may not work.

Of course, we still have to come up with a solution for people who don't have native video support *and* don't have Flash installed. We'll let people download our video content by adding another section with download links (see the following code).

---

4. http://camendesign.com/code/video_for_everybody
5. http://www.videojs.com/

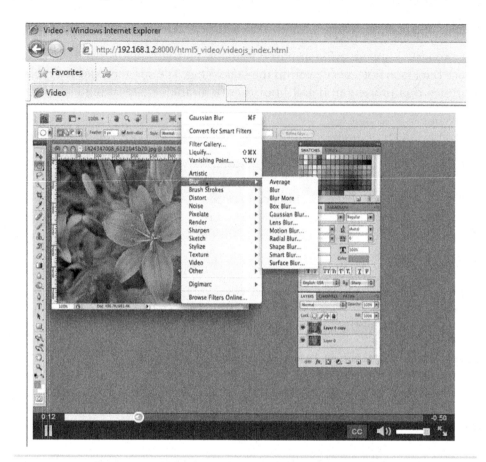

Figure 23—Our video in Internet Explorer using Video.js

```
html5_video/videojs_index.html
<section class="downloads">
  <header>
    <h3>Downloads</h3>
  </header>
  <ul>
    <li><a href="video/h264/01_blur.mp4">
      H264, playable on most platforms</a></li>
    <li><a href="video/theora/01_blur.ogv">OGG format</a></li>
    <li><a href="video/webm/01_blur.webm">WebM format</a></li>
  </ul>
</section>
```

We could use Modernizr to detect video support like we saw in Tip 20, *Working with Audio*, on page 137. But in many cases it makes more sense to let people download these videos for offline use so they can watch them later on a tablet or other device. Hiding the links might save screen real estate, but it won't prevent savvy people from downloading the videos directly, so don't hide links as a security measure.

Forcing Flash for Certain Clients

By default, Video.js uses Flash as a fallback for browsers that don't understand the video element. In some cases you may want to force Flash for certain browsers even if they do support HTML5 video. Keep in mind that if a user's browser supports the <video> tag, it's not going to use the Flash fallback, so you have to include the video format supported by the browser, or the Flash fallback will never fire. If you have lots of videos already in the MP4 format, you may not want to convert all of those videos. Flash will play MP4 files just fine.

By using a simple combination of feature detection and Video.js's configuration options, we can tell Video.js it should use Flash if the browser doesn't support MP4.

After each <video> tag, we place this code, which tests to see if the browser supports MP4 files:

```
html5_video/mp4only_index.html
<script>
  var videoElement = document.createElement("video");
  if(videoElement.canPlayType){
    if (videoElement.canPlayType("video/mp4") === ""){
      videojs("video_blur", {"techOrder": ["flash","html5"]});
    };
  }
</script>
```

We create a video element and then see what it supports using canPlayType(). If the canPlayType() method returns an empty string, then we don't have support and we then use the videojs object provided by the Video.js library to configure the options for the video player.

The videojs object takes the id of the <video> tag as its first argument, followed by the hash of options that configure how the player will work.

With this in place, Firefox, which doesn't support MP4 files natively, will fall back to Flash. It's worth noting that this isn't an optimal solution; you should encode the videos for the browsers you support. But if you don't have the ability or resources to do that, this is a good compromise.

Video is a wonderful way to share ideas and information, but what do we do for people who can't see the video or hear the audio? Read on to find out!

Tip 22

Making Videos Accessible

None of the fallback solutions we've discussed work well for users with disabilities. In fact, the HTML5 specification explicitly points that out. A hearing-impaired person won't find any value in being able to download the audio file, and a visually impaired person won't have much use for a video file that's viewable outside of the browser. When you provide content to our users, you should provide usable alternatives whenever possible. Video and audio files should have transcripts that people can view. If you produce your own content, transcripts are easy to make if you plan them from the start because they can come right from the script. Let's add a simple transcript right below our video:

```
html5_video/videojs_index.html
<section class="transcript">
  <h2>Transcript</h2>
  <p>
    We'll drag the existing layer to the new button on the bottom of
    the Layers palette to create a new copy.
  </p>
  <p>
    Next we'll go to the Filter menu and choose Gaussian Blur.
    We'll change the blur amount just enough so that we lose a little
    bit of the detail of the image.
  </p>
  <p>
    Now we'll double-click on the layer to edit the layer and
    change the blending mode to Overlay. We can then adjust the
    amount of the effect by changing the opacity slider.
  </p>
  <p>Now we have a slightly enhanced image.</p>
</section>
```

You can hide the transcript or link to it from the main video page. As long as you make it easy to find and easy to follow, it's going to be really helpful. If a transcript isn't possible, consider a summary that highlights the important parts of the video. Anything is better than nothing.

Adding Captions

Transcripts are great, but we can do something even better. HTML5 supports video captioning and subtitles through the new <track> tag. This isn't widely supported natively, but the Video.js library supports it nicely. To use it, we create a text file of captions and cue points using a format called Web Video Text Tracks, or *Web VTT*. Web VTT is supported in Internet Explorer 10, Chrome, Opera, and Safari. Let's try it out with one of our videos.

First we create a captions folder within our video. Then we create the file 01_blur.vtt in that folder. This file has the cue points and the text for the caption that should be played at that point. Building these up takes time, so here's a finished version:

```
html5_video/video/captions/01_blur.vtt
WEBVTT

00:00.000 --> 00:08.906
We'll drag the existing layer to the New button on the
bottom of the layers panel to create a new copy.

00:08.906 --> 00:14.167
Now we'll go to the Filter menu and choose Gaussian Blur.

00:14.167 --> 00:22.907
We'll change the blur amount just enough so we lose a
little detail of the image.

00:22.907 --> 00:33.670
Now we'll double-click on the layer to edit the layer.

00:33.670 --> 00:41.928
And we'll change the blending mode to overlay. This allows
the original layer underneath to show through.

00:41.928 --> 00:48.812
We can then adjust the amount of the effect by changing
the opacity.

00:48.812 --> 00:57.507
And now we have a slightly enhanced image.
```

This file links up the captions to parts of the video. We define a time range and then place the text for the caption underneath each range. We can have multiline captions as long as we don't leave any blank lines. To make this work with the video, we add a <track> tag inside of the <video> tag that points to this file:

```
html5_video/videojs_index.html
<track kind="captions" src="video/captions/01_blur.vtt"
       srclang="en-us" label="English" />
```

We specify that it's a caption and that it's in English. We could create captions for other languages, as well, and store those in separate files. But for this example it's good enough, and we can see the result in the following figure.

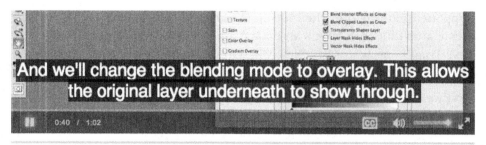

Figure 24—Captions as displayed by Video.js

It's a lot of work to build up caption files for your videos, but it makes things much easier for the hearing impaired. It's also nice for situations in which your viewers don't have audio, like in an office environment or a library. Best of all, thanks to Video.js, you have a great fallback solution that you can start using right now.

Limitations of HTML5 Video

HTML5 video has a few obstacles to overcome before it's usable everywhere.

First, HTML5 video has no provisions for streaming the video files. Users have become accustomed to being able to seek to a specific part of a video. Flash-based video players excel at this because of the amount of effort Adobe has put into Flash as a video-delivery platform. To seek with HTML5 video, the file must be downloaded completely on browsers. This may change in time.

Second, there's no way to manage rights. Sites such as Hulu that want to prevent piracy of their content can't rely on HTML5 video. Flash remains a viable solution for these situations.

Finally, and most importantly, the process of encoding videos is costly and time-consuming. The need to encode in multiple formats makes HTML5 video much less attractive. For that reason, you see many sites supplying video in the patent-encumbered H.264 format so that it can be played on the widest range of devices using a combination of the HTML5 video tag and Flash.

These issues aren't going to derail HTML5, but they are things to be aware of before we can use HTML5 video to replace Flash as a video-delivery vehicle.

7.3 The Future

First-class audio support in the browser opens up a ton of possibilities for developers. JavaScript web applications can easily trigger sound effects and alerts without our having to use Flash to embed the audio. Native video

Explore the Media Content JavaScript API

In this chapter we've briefly touched on the JavaScript APIs for the audio and video elements. The full API can detect the types of audio files the browser can play, and it provides methods to control the playback of the audio elements.

In Tip 20, *Working with Audio*, on page 137, we built a page with multiple sound samples. We could use the JavaScript API to make all the sounds play at (roughly) the same time. Here's a really simplified approach:

```
html5_audio/javascripts/audio.js
var element = $("<p><input type='button' value='Play all'/></p>")
element.click(function(){
  $("audio").each(function(){
    this.play();
  })
});

$("body").append(element);
```

We add a Play All button that, when pressed, cycles through all the audio elements on the page and calls the play() method on each element.

We can do similar things with videos. There are methods to start and pause elements, query the current time, and integrate with the data inside caption or subtitle tracks.

Be sure to look at the possibilities outlined in the specification to see what's possible.[a]

---

a.   http://www.w3.org/TR/html5/embedded-content-0.html#media-elements

support enables us to make video available to devices such as iPhones, but it also provides an open, standard method of interacting with audio and video using JavaScript. Most importantly, we'll be able to treat video and audio clips just like we treat images by marking them up semantically and making them easier to identify.

Web VTT is another area to watch closely. You can use Web VTT for more than just captioning. It supports subtitles for multiple languages, chapters to make navigation easier, and additional metadata about the video. You can even use HTML and JSON and interact with the video using JavaScript, making events fire when cue points are entered and exited. This would be a great way to build interactive computer-based training that incorporates video. Unfortunately, at the time of writing not every browser has incorporated all of the APIs, and by the time they do the specification may have changed. But it's certainly something to think about.

CHAPTER 8

Eye Candy

As web developers, we're always interested in making our user interfaces a little more eye-catching, and CSS3 provides quite a few ways for us to do that. We can use our own custom fonts on our pages. We can create elements with rounded corners and drop shadows. We can use gradients as backgrounds, and we can even rotate elements so things don't look so blocky and boring all the time. We can do all of these things without resorting to Photoshop or other graphics programs, and this chapter will show you how. We'll start off by softening up a form's appearance by rounding some corners. Then we'll construct a prototype banner for an upcoming trade show, and add shadows, rotations, gradients, and opacity. Then we'll talk about how to use CSS3's @font-face feature so we can use nicer fonts on the company blog. We'll wrap up with learning how to use CSS to do some animations.

Specifically, we'll explore the following CSS3 features in this chapter:

border-radius [border-radius: 10px;]
> Rounds corners of elements. *[C4, F3, S3.2, IE9, O10.5]*

RGBa support [background-color: rgba(255,0,0,0.5);]
> Uses RGB color instead of hex codes, along with transparency. *[C4, F3.5, S3.2, IE9, O10.1]*

box-shadow [box-shadow: 10px 10px 5px #333;]
> Creates drop shadows on elements. *[C3, F3.5, S3.2, IE9, O10.5]*

Rotation [transform: rotate(7.5deg);]
> Rotates any element. *[C3, F3.5, S3.2, IE9, O10.5]*

Gradients [linear-gradient(top, #fff, #efefef);]
> Creates gradients for use as images. *[C4, F3.5, S4]*

src: url(http://example.com/awesomeco.ttf); font-weight: bold; }]

> Allows use of specific fonts via CSS. *[C4, F3.5, S3.2, IE5, O10.1]*

Transitions [transition: background 0.3s ease]

> Gradually transition a CSS property from one value to another over time.
> *[C4, F3.5, S4, IE10]*

Animations [animation: shake 0.5s 1;]

> Gradually transition a CSS property from one value to another over time
> using defined keyframe animations. *[C4, F3.5, S4, IE10]*

Tip 23

Rounding Rough Edges

On the Web, everything is a rectangle by default. Form fields, tables, and even sections of web pages all have a blocky, sharp-edged look, so designers have turned to different techniques over the years to add rounded corners to these elements to soften up the interface.

CSS3 has support for easily rounding corners, and Chrome, Firefox, and Safari have supported this for quite a long time. Internet Explorer 9 introduced support as well, so you can easily add this feature to your designs without much worry. Let's see how it's done.

Softening Up a Login Form

We've been asked to create a new login form for the AwesomeCo customer portal and support site. The wireframes and mock-ups we received from the designer show form fields with rounded corners. Let's round those corners using only CSS3 first. Our goal is to create something that looks like the following figure.

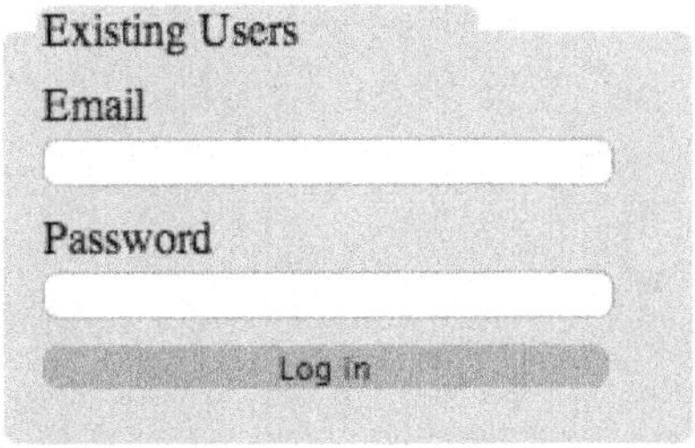

Figure 25—Our form with round corners

For the login form, we'll use some simple HTML.

```
css3_rough_edges/index.html
  </head>
  <body>
    <form class="login" action="/login" method="post">
      <fieldset>
        <legend>Existing Users</legend>
        <ol>
          <li>
```

```
          <label for="email">Email</label>
          <input id="email" type="email" name="email">
        </li>
        <li>
          <label for="password">Password</label>
          <input id="password" type="password"
                 name="password" value="" autocomplete="off"/>
        </li>
        <li><input type="submit" value="Log in"></li>
      </ol>
    </fieldset>
  </form>
 </body>
</html>
```

Let's style the form to give it a less boring look.

css3_rough_edges/stylesheets/style.css

```css
.login{
  width: 250px;
}

.login fieldset{
  background-color: #ddd;
  border: none;
}
.login legend{
  background-color: #ddd;
  padding: 0 64px 0 2px;
}

.login ol{list-style: none;
  margin: 2px;
  padding:0;
}
.login li{
  margin: 0 0 9px 0;
  padding: 0;
}

.login input{
  background-color: #fff;
  border: 1px solid #bbb;
  display:block;
  width: 200px;
}
.login input[type="submit"]{
 background-color: #bbb;
 padding: 0;
 width: 202px;
}
```

These basic styles remove the bullets from the list and ensure that the input fields are all the same size. We also modify the form's <fieldset> and <legend> to create a "tab" for the form. With the basic styling in place, we can turn our attention to rounding the edges of the legend, fields, button, and form.

To round all the input fields on our form, we need a CSS rule like this:

css3_rough_edges/stylesheets/style.css
```
.login input, .login fieldset, .login legend{
  border-radius: 5px;
}
```

Add that to your style.css file, and you have rounded corners.

Falling Back

We have everything working in Firefox, Safari, Chrome, and Internet Explorer 9 and 10, but it doesn't work in Internet Explorer 8. That's ridiculously easy to fix thanks to PIE,[1] which gives us drop-in support for border-radius and a few other features. Download PIE, unzip the archive, and place PIE.htc in the stylesheets folder.

Before we get to rounding the corners, we have a style glitch to fix. Internet Explorer treats legends a little differently, so when we look at our form in IE we don't see the legend as a tab; the legend is placed completely inside of the fieldset. We can add in a small style fix for IE that pushes the fieldset's legend up a few pixels so that it looks the same as it does in Firefox and Chrome. We'll create a new file called stylesheets/ie.css and link to it from our web page with a conditional comment so it loads only in IE 8 or earlier:

css3_rough_edges/index.html
```
<!--[if lte IE 8]>
<link rel="stylesheet" href="stylesheets/ie.css" type="text/css" media="screen">
<![endif]-->
```

Then, in stylesheets/ie.css we'll add the fixes for the legend and fieldset:

css3_rough_edges/stylesheets/ie.css
```
.login {margin-top: 20px;}

.login fieldset legend{
  margin-top: -10px;
  margin-left: 10px;
}
.login fieldset{
  padding-left: 10px;
}
```

---

1. http://css3pie.com/

We just bump the fieldset down 20 pixels and pull the legend up 10 pixels, creating the tab. We also nudge the legend over to the right, but because of Internet Explorer's default styling, we need to add some padding to the fieldset itself. Now it looks similar to the style in other browsers.

Finally, we load PIE by using behavior, a special CSS rule that Internet Explorer understands:

```
css3_rough_edges/stylesheets/ie.css
.login fieldset, .login input, .login legend{
  behavior: url(stylesheets/PIE.htc);
}
```

Note that we saved PIE.htc in the stylesheets folder. The link to PIE.htc in our style sheet must be relative to the HTML page that loads the style sheet, not relative to the style sheet.

Now things look similar on all of the major browsers; you can see the Internet Explorer version in the following figure.

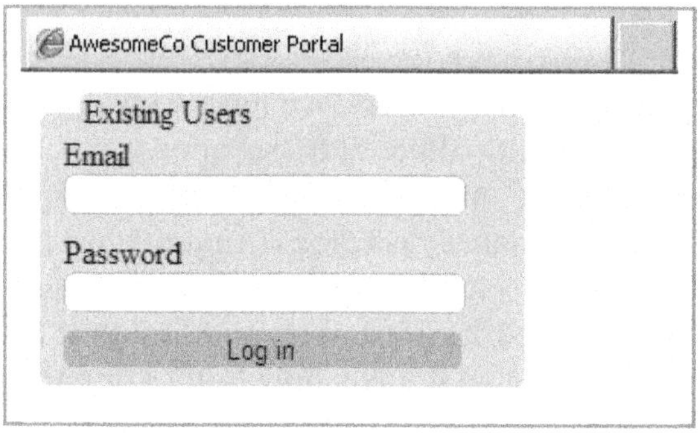

Figure 26—Our form in Internet Explorer

In our example, the client really wanted rounded corners for all browsers. However, you should always keep these kinds of features optional if you can. Although some people may argue that there's a real benefit to softening up the way a form looks, you should first have an idea of how many people use browsers that don't support CSS-based rounding. If your visitors are using Internet Explorer 9 or higher, it's not worth your time to maintain a fallback solution.

Rounded corners add a touch of softness to your interfaces. That said, it's important to be consistent with your implementation and to not overuse this technique, just like any other aspect of design.

Tip 24

Working with Shadows, Gradients, and Transformations

Rounded corners get a lot of attention, but they're just the beginning of what we can do with CSS3. We can add drop shadows to elements to make them stand out from the rest of the content, we can use gradients to make backgrounds look more defined, and we can use transformations to rotate elements. Let's put several of these techniques together to mock up part of a banner for the upcoming AwesomeConf, a trade show and conference that AwesomeCo puts on each year. The graphic designer has sent over a PSD that looks like the following figure, with a tilted name badge and a big slightly transparent white space where some web content will eventually go.

Figure 27—The original concept, which we can re-create using CSS3

We can do the badge, shadow, and even the transparency all in CSS. The only thing we'll need from the graphic designer is the background image of the people.

The Basic Structure

Let's start by marking up the basic structure of the banner in HTML. In a new HTML file, add this code:

css3_banner/index.html
```
<!DOCTYPE html>
<html lang='en'>
  <head>
    <meta charset="utf-8">
    <title>Sample Banner</title>
    <link rel="stylesheet" href="stylesheets/style.css">
    <div id="conference">
```

```
      <section id="badge">
        <h3>Hi, My Name Is</h3>
        <h2>Barney</h2>
      </section>

      <section id="info">
      </section>
    </div>

  </body>
</html>
```

Next let's create stylesheets/style.css and add some basic styling to define the layout for the badge and the main content region.

css3_banner/stylesheets/style.css

```css
#conference{
  background-color: #000;
  background-image: url('../images/awesomeconf.jpg');
  background-position: center;
  height: 240px;
  width: 960px;
}
#badge{
  border: 2px solid blue;
  display: block;
  text-align: center;
  width: 200px;
}
#info{
  display: block;
  height: 160px;
  margin: 20px;
  padding: 20px;
  width: 660px;
}
#badge, #info{
  background-color: #fff;
  float: left;
}
#badge h2{
  color: red;
  margin: 0;
  font-size: 40px;
}
#badge h3{
  background-color: blue;
  color: #fff;
  margin: 0;
}
```

With that in place, we have our badge and content region displayed side by side, as in the following figure.

Figure 28—Our basic banner

Now let's style the badge.

Adding a Gradient

We can add definition to the badge by changing the white background to a subtle gradient that goes from white to light gray. The gradient we define becomes the background image of the element. This gradient will work in Firefox, Safari, and Chrome, but the implementation varies by browser.

Versions of Firefox prior to 15 use the -moz-linear-gradient method, in which we specify the starting point of the gradient, followed by the starting color, and, finally, the ending color. WebKit-based browsers use the same rule, but switch out the -moz- prefix to -webkit-.

The standard way of doing gradients is with linear-gradient,[2] which looks almost the same but uses to bottom instead of top for the direction. We can use to bottom, to right, to left, to top, or a specific angle, such as 45deg.

To make the effect we're looking for work in the widest variety of browsers, we add this to our style sheet:

```
css3_banner/stylesheets/style.css
#badge{
  background-image: -webkit-linear-gradient(top, #fff, #eee);
  background-image:    -moz-linear-gradient(top, #fff, #eee);
  background-image:          linear-gradient(to bottom, #fff, #eee);
}
```

That does it for our needs, but we can do radial gradients too, and we can specify more color stops in the gradient. Our example uses a starting color

---

2. http://dev.w3.org/csswg/css3-images/#linear-gradients

and an ending color, but we can specify more colors than that if we want more control over the gradient. But let's shift gears and work with shadows.

Adding a Shadow to the Badge

We can easily make the badge appear to be sitting above the banner by adding a drop shadow. In the old days we'd do this shadow in Photoshop by adding it to the image or by inserting it as a background image. However, the CSS3 box-shadow property lets us quickly define a shadow on our elements.[3]

We'll apply this rule to our style sheet to give the badge a shadow. We add this within the #banner selector, right below the gradient we previously defined:

css3_banner/stylesheets/style.css
```
box-shadow: 5px 5px 5px 0px #333;
```

The box-shadow property has a total of six parameters, although we're using only five. The first is the horizontal offset. A positive number means the shadow will fall to the right of the object; a negative number means it'll fall to the left. The second parameter is the vertical offset. With the vertical offset, positive numbers make the shadow appear below the box, whereas negative values make the shadow appear above the element. The third parameter is the blur radius. A value of 0 gives a sharp value, and a higher value makes the shadow blurrier. The fourth parameter is the spread distance, or the width of the shadow. The final parameter we specified defines the shadow's color.

The sixth available parameter (inset), if specified, puts the shadow *inside* of the box, creating an inner shadow instead of the default outer shadow.

Notice that in our example we didn't use any vendor prefixes. Internet Explorer 10, as well as the most recent versions of Chrome, Firefox, Safari, and Opera, support this without any prefixes. However, if you find you need to support iOS 3, Android 2.1, or browsers released earlier than 2011, you can use the same rule but with the -moz- and -webkit- prefixes.

You should experiment with these values to get a feel for how they work and to find values that look appropriate to you. When working with shadows, take a moment to investigate how shadows work in the physical world. Grab a flashlight and shine it on objects, or go outside and observe how the sun casts shadows on objects. Proper use of perspective is important, because creating inconsistent shadows can make your interface more confusing, especially if you apply shadows to multiple elements incorrectly. The easiest approach you can take is to use the same settings for each shadow you create.

---

3.   http://www.w3.org/TR/css3-background/#the-box-shadow

Shadows on Text

In addition to adding styles on elements, you can easily apply shadows to your text. It works just like box-shadow.

h1{text-shadow: 2px 2px 2px 0px #bbbbbb;}

You specify the x- and y-coordinate offsets, the amount of the blur, the spread, and the color of the shadow.

This is the same approach we use to apply a drop shadow to an element. Shadows on text create a neat effect, but they can make text harder to read if you make the shadow too strong. Be sure your content is readable, above all else.

Rotating the Badge

We use CSS3 transformations to rotate, scale, and skew elements, much like you can with vector-graphics programs such as Flash, Illustrator, or Inkscape.[4] This can help make elements stand out more and is another way to make a web page not look so boxy. Let's rotate the badge just a bit so it breaks out of the straight edge of the banner. Again, we're putting this within the #banner selector:

```
css3_banner/stylesheets/style.css
-webkit-transform: rotate(-7.5deg);
   -moz-transform: rotate(-7.5deg);
    -ms-transform: rotate(-7.5deg);
     -o-transform: rotate(-7.5deg);
        transform: rotate(-7.5deg);
```

Rotation with CSS3 is pretty simple. If we provide the degree of rotation, the rendering just works. All the elements contained within the element we rotate are rotated as well. However, this time we can't get away with the standard rule. We have to apply all of the vendor prefixes to get this to work everywhere.

Rotating is just as easy as rounding corners, but don't overuse it. The goal of interface design is to make the interface usable. If you rotate elements that hold a lot of content, ensure that your viewers can read the content without turning their heads too far in one direction!

Precise Transformations with Matrix

Rotation is just one of the ways we can transform elements. We can scale, skew, and even do 3D transformations. Even cooler, we can use the matrix() function on transform to do more-controlled transformations of elements. To

---

4.   http://www.w3.org/TR/css3-2d-transforms/#transform-property

do that we specify cosines and sines of the angle we want. For example, let's say we want to specify our badge rotation using matrix() instead of rotate().

To do this, we need to take the angle we used, (–7.5 degrees) and calculate the cosine, the negative value of sine, the sine, and the cosine again. In other words, we do a linear transformation using a 2×2 matrix, like this:

```
-webkit-transform: matrix(0.99144,-0.13052,0.13052,0.99144,0,0);
   -moz-transform: matrix(0.99144,-0.13052,0.13052,0.99144,0px,0px);
    -ms-transform: matrix(0.99144,-0.13052,0.13052,0.99144,0,0);
     -o-transform: matrix(0.99144,-0.13052,0.13052,0.99144,0,0);
        transform: matrix(0.99144,-0.13052,0.13052,0.99144,0,0);
```

Complicated? Yes, and more so when you look at the previous example closely. Remember that our original angle was *negative* 7.5 degrees. So, for our *negative* sine, we need a positive value, and our sine gets a *negative value*.

But this is cool because it means that we can do warping, skewing, rotation, and any other transformation by specifying the right values. This is incredibly powerful once you get the hang of it. If you want to see how more of this is done, check out http://peterned.home.xs4all.nl/matrices/.

Math is hard. Let's make transparent backgrounds instead.

Transparent Backgrounds

Graphic designers have used semitransparent layers behind text for quite some time, and that process usually involves either making a complete image in Photoshop or layering a transparent PNG on top of another element with CSS. CSS3 lets us define background colors with a new syntax that supports transparency.

When you first learn about web development, you learn to define your colors using hexadecimal color codes. You define the amount of red, green, and blue using pairs of numbers. 00 is "all off" or "none," and FF is "all on." So, the color red would be FF0000 or "all on for red, all off for blue, and all off for green."

CSS3 introduces the rgb and rgba functions. The rgb function works like the hexadecimal counterpart, but you use values from 0 to 255 for each color. You'd define the color red as rgb(255,0,0).

The rgba function works the same way as the rgb() function, but it takes a fourth parameter to define the amount of opacity, from 0 to 1. If you use 0, you'll see no color at all, because it's completely transparent. To make the white box semitransparent, we'll add this style rule to the info box:

css3_banner/stylesheets/style.css
```
#info{
  background-color: rgba(255,255,255,0.95);
}
```

When working with transparency values like this, your users' contrast settings can sometimes impact the resulting appearance, so experiment with the value and check on multiple displays to ensure you get a consistent result.

While we're working with the info section of our banner, let's round the corners.

css3_banner/stylesheets/style.css
```
#info{
  background-color: rgba(255,255,255,0.95);
➤ border-radius: 12px;
}
```

With that, our banner looks pretty good in Safari, Firefox, and Chrome. Now let's implement a style sheet for Internet Explorer.

Falling Back

The techniques we've used in this section work fine in Internet Explorer 10 and other modern browsers, but they're not going to work in Internet Explorer 8 and 9. We can emulate them somewhat with Microsoft's DirectX filters, but the filters tend to be CPU intensive, interfere with other functionality, and end up making for a horrible user interface. You're better off not using a fallback solution for this. Remember that the things we did in this section are presentational. When we created the initial style sheet, we made sure to apply background colors so that text would be readable. Browsers that cannot understand the CSS3 syntax can still display the content in a readable manner.

Of course, if you're the curious sort and want to explore on your own, you can look at the file css3_banner/stylesheets/ie.css in the book's code download to see an attempt to make things work in Internet Explorer 8 and earlier. But be warned—it's far from perfect, and the syntax for the fallback solutions is quite complex. Worst of all, the end result is disappointing.

You could, instead, use a conditional style sheet to apply a PNG background to the container element. But ask yourself if it's worth the duplication of effort.

Transformations, gradients, and shadows are nice, but people come to web pages to read the content. The right font can make all the difference, and CSS3 gives us more control over the fonts we can use. Let's see how.

Working with Fonts

Typography is important to user experience. The book you're reading right now has fonts that were carefully selected by people who understand how the right fonts and the right spacing can make it much easier for readers. These concepts are just as important to understand on the Web.

The fonts we choose for conveying our message to our readers impact how our readers interpret that message. Here's a font that's perfectly appropriate for a loud heavy-metal band:

Metal Band

But that might not work out so well for the cover of this book:

HTML5 and CSS3

As you can see, choosing a font that matches your message is really important. The problem with fonts on the Web is that we web developers have been limited to a handful of fonts, commonly known as "web-safe" fonts. These are the fonts that are prevalent across most users' operating systems.

To get around that, we've historically used images for our fonts and either directly added them to our page's markup or used other methods, like CSS background images or sIFR,[5] which renders fonts using Flash. CSS3's Fonts module offers a much nicer approach.

---

5. http://www.mikeindustries.com/blog/sifr

AwesomeCo's director of marketing has decided that the company should decide on a font for both print and the Web. You've been asked to investigate a font called Garogier, a simple, thin font that is free for commercial use. As a trial run, we'll apply this font to the blog example we created in Tip 1, *Redefining a Blog Using Semantic Markup*, on page 15. That way, everyone can see the font in action. Let's look at how we specify and use fonts with pure CSS.

@font-face

The @font-face directive was introduced as part of the CSS2 specification and was implemented in Internet Explorer 5.[6] However, Microsoft's implementation used a font format called Embedded OpenType (EOT), and most fonts today are in TrueType or OpenType format, which all modern browsers support quite well.

Font Formats

Fonts are available in a variety of formats, and the browsers you're targeting will determine what format you'll need to serve to your visitors.

Font Type	Supported Browsers
Web Open Font (WOFF)	*[F3.6, C5, S5.1, IE9, O11.1, iOS5]*
TrueType (TTF)	*[F3.5, C4, S3, O10, iOS4.2, A2.2]*
OpenType (OTF)	*[F3.5, C4, S3, O10, iOS4.2, A2.2]*
Embedded OpenType (EOT)	*[IE5–8]*
Scalable Vector Graphics (SVG)	*[iOS]*

Microsoft, Opera, and Mozilla jointly created the Web Open Font format, which allows lossless compression and better licensing options for font-makers.

To hit all of these browsers, we have to make our fonts available in multiple formats. Let's see how we do that.

Changing Our Font

The font we're looking at is available at Font Squirrel in TrueType, WOFF, SVG, and EOT formats, which will work perfectly.[7]

Using the font involves two steps—defining the font and attaching the font to elements. In the style sheet for the blog, add this code:

---

6. http://www.w3.org/TR/css3-fonts/
7. You can grab it from http://www.fontsquirrel.com/fonts/Garogier and in the book's downloadable code.

Fonts and Rights

Some fonts aren't free. As with stock photography or other copyrighted material, you are expected to comply with the rights and licenses of the material you use on your website. If you purchase a font, you're usually within your rights to use it in your logo and images on your pages. These are called *usage rights*. However, the @font-face approach brings a different kind of licensing into play—redistribution rights.

When you embed a font on your page, your users will have to download that font, meaning your site is now distributing the font to others. You need to be absolutely positive the fonts you're using on your pages allow for this type of usage.

Adobe's Typekit has a large library of licensed fonts available, with tools and code that make it easy to bring these fonts into your website.[a] Typekit isn't a free service, but it's quite affordable if you need to use a specific font.

Google provides the Google Font API,[b] which is similar to Typekit but contains only open source fonts.

Both of these services use JavaScript to load the fonts, so you'll need to ensure that your content is easy to read for users without JavaScript.

As long as you remember to treat fonts like any other asset, you shouldn't run into problems.

---

a.   http://www.typekit.com/
b.   http://code.google.com/apis/webfonts/

css3_fonts/stylesheets/style.css

```css
@font-face {
  font-family: 'GarogierRegular';
  src: url('fonts/garogier_unhinted-webfont.eot?#iefix')
         format('embedded-opentype'),
     url('fonts/garogier_unhinted-webfont.woff') format('woff'),
     url('fonts/garogier_unhinted-webfont.ttf') format('truetype'),
     url('fonts/garogier_unhinted-webfont.svg#garogierregular') format('svg');
  font-weight: normal;
  font-style: normal;
}
```

We're defining the font family first, giving it a name, and then supplying the font sources. We'll put the Embedded OpenType version first so that Internet Explorer 8 sees it right away, and then we'll provide the other sources. A user's browser is going to just keep trying sources until it finds one that works.

The ?#iefix' prefix on the .eot file fixes a nasty parsing bug in Internet Explorer 8. Without that markup, IE 8 would generate 404 errors as it tried to parse

Joe asks:

How Do I Convert My Own Fonts?

If you have developed your own font or have purchased the rights to a font and need to make it available in multiple formats, you can use the website Font Squirrel to convert the font and provide you with a style sheet with the @font-face code you'll need.[a] Be sure your font's license allows this type of usage, though.

_____

a.   http://www.fontsquirrel.com/fontface/generator

the rest of the rules. The question mark makes IE 8 think everything after the EOT is query parameters, and it's essentially ignored.

This code assumes we've placed all of the fonts in stylesheets/fonts. The links to the fonts are relative to the location of the style sheet, not the HTML page that calls the style sheet. That makes sense, because the style sheet will be called from different HTML pages in a real-world site.

Now that we've defined the font family, we can use it in our style sheet. We'll change our original font style so it looks like this:

css3_fonts/stylesheets/style.css
```
body{
  font-family: "GarogierRegular";
}
```

With that small change, our page's text displays in the new font, as shown in Figure 29, *The blog with the new font applied*, on page 168.

Applying a font is relatively easy in modern browsers, but we need to consider browsers that don't support this yet.

Falling Back

We've already provided fallbacks for various versions of Internet Explorer and other browsers, but we still need to ensure our pages are readable in browsers that lack support for the @font-face feature or are for some reason unable to download our font.

We provided alternate versions of the Garogier font, but when we applied the font, we didn't specify any fallback fonts. That means if the browser doesn't support display of our Garogier font, it's going to use the browser's default font. That isn't ideal.

AwesomeCo Blog!

Latest Posts   Archives   Contributors   Contact Us

How Many Should We Put You Down For?

Posted by Brian on October 1st, 2013 at 2:39PM

The first big rule in sales is that if the person leaves empty-handed,
they're likely not going to come back. That's why you have to be
somewhat aggressive when you're working with a customer, but you
have to make sure you don't overdo it and scare them away.

Figure 29—The blog with the new font applied

Font stacks are lists of fonts ordered by priority. You specify the font you most want your users to see, and then specify fonts that are suitable fallbacks. When creating a font stack, take the extra time to find truly suitable fallback fonts. Letter spacing, stroke width, and general appearance should be similar. The website Unit Interactive has an excellent article on this.[8]

Let's alter our font like this:

```
css3_fonts/stylesheets/style.css
font-family: "GarogierRegular", Georgia,
             "Palatino", "Palatino Linotype",
             "Times", "Times New Roman", serif;
```

We're providing a wide array of fallbacks here, which should help us maintain a similar appearance in various circumstances. It's not perfect in all cases, but it's better than relying on the default font, which can sometimes be quite hard to read.

Fonts can go a long way toward making your page more attractive and easier to read. Experiment with your own work. There's a large number of fonts, both free and commercial, waiting for you.

Now let's look at how we can use CSS to create animations.

---

8.   http://unitinteractive.com/blog/2008/06/26/better-css-font-stacks/

Tip 26

Making Things Move with Transitions and Animations

CSS3 provides two methods for performing animations: *transitions* and *animations*. They're similar in how they work, but serve two distinct purposes. Transitions let us state that we want a property to gradually change from one value to another. Animations let us get more specific, defining keyframes for complex animations.

We've been asked to "spice up" the login form we did back in Tip 23, *Rounding Rough Edges*, on page 153. The product manager wants to see the form fields fade to a different color when the user gives them focus, and he wants the form to "shake" when the user enters the wrong username and password. We can use simple transitions for the form fields, and animations for the form.

Creating Fades with CSS Transitions

In Tip 9, *In-Place Editing with contenteditable*, on page 59, we wrote some CSS that changed the background color of an element when the element had focus:

```
li>span[contenteditable=true]:focus{
  background-color: #ffa;
  border: 1px shaded #000;
}
```

The change happens abruptly, with the new background color and border replacing the old ones. But with CSS transitions, we can make it happen over a period of time. All we have to do is define how we want the transition to work, how long it should take, and what properties should be affected.

We can use the following properties to define transitions:

- transition-property defines the CSS property that should be transitioned.

- transition-duration specifies how long the transition should take.

- transition-delay lets us define how long to wait before starting the transition.

- transition-timing-function specifies how the intermediate values of the transition are specified.

Understanding Timing Functions

Remember in algebra when the teacher had you graph equations and you wondered if you'd ever have to use that for anything?

The transition-timing-function property describes how transitions happen over time in relation to the duration of the animation. We specify this timing function using a cubic Bézier curve, which is defined by four control points on a graph. Each point has an x-axis value and a y-axis value, from 0 to 1. The first and last control points are usually set to (0.0, 0.0) and (1.0, 1.0), and the two middle points determine the shape of the curve. This is how we define acceleration curves for animations, and if you've done animation before, you may have heard the term *easing*.

Several built-in easing functions are defined in the specification:

- linear
- ease-in
- ease-out
- ease-in-out
- ease

If you want the animation to be a constant speed, you'd use linear. If you want the animation to start slow and speed up, you'd use ease-in. If you want it to start slow, speed up, and end slow, you'd use ease-out.

Each of these functions defines a cubic Bézier curve, and while they may be good enough for many cases, knowing how they work will make it possible for you to define your own with the cubic-bezier function, which you do by defining the four points on a graph. Let's look at a few of these functions.

A linear curve has its control points set to the two end points, which creates a straight line at a 45-degree angle. The four points for a linear curve are ((0.0, 0.0), (0.0,0.0), (1.0, 1.0), (1.0, 1.0)), and it looks like this:

A more complex curve, with points ((0.0, 0.0), (0.42,0.0), (1.0, 1.0), (1.0, 1.0)), called an *ease-in* curve, looks like this:

This time, only the second point has changed, which is what causes the bottom-left part of the line to curve. Thus, the animation starts out slow, and then speeds up till the end.

Compare that to the *ease-out* curve, which defines an animation that starts out constant and slows down at the end, using a curve that looks like this:

The points for this curve would be ((0.0, 0.0), (0.0,0.0), (0.58, 1.0), (1.0, 1.0)).

The *ease-in-out* curve has a curve at the bottom and at the top, like this:

The points for this curve are ((0.0, 0.0), (0.42,0.0), (0.58, 1.0), (1.0, 1.0)), and the animation will speed up at the start and slow down at the end.

The *ease* curve is similar to the *ease-in-out* curve, but the animation starts slightly faster than it ends.

If you provide the four control points to the cubic-bezier() function, you can define your own timing function:

```
css3_animation/examples/style.css
.bounce{
  transition-property: left;
  transition-timing-function: cubic-bezier(0.1, -0.6, 0.2, 0);
  transition-duration: 1s;
}
.bounce:hover{
 left: 200px;
}
```

This timing function gives us a little bounce effect at the start, thanks to the negative value for the first control point. The starting point is still at (0.0, 0.0), so we get a little bounce.

If you want to learn more about making these curves, you can check out a great script that shows examples and helps you see the coordinates: http://www.netzgesta.de/dev/cubic-bezier-timing-function.html.

Creating Our Transitions

When we select a field, we want the color to transition. To do that, we define the transition properties on the form elements. Think of this as the beginning of the transition. It tells the browser to watch these properties for changes, and defines how they should be animated when they change.

```
input[type="email"], input[type="password"]{
  transition-timing-function: linear;
  transition-property: background, border;
  transition-duration: 0.3s;
}
```

This is the standard way to define transitions, but if you want things to work in all of the browsers, you'll need to define these transitions again using the vendor prefixes like -webkit- and -moz- like we've done with other CSS properties. That's going to get a little lengthy. Thankfully there's a shorthand notation for this, which is the recommended way to define transitions:

```
css3_animation/stylesheets/style.css
.login input[type="email"], .login input[type="password"]{
  -webkit-transition: background 0.3s linear
                      border 0.3s linear;
     -moz-transition: background 0.3s linear,
                      border 0.3s linear;
       -o-transition: background 0.3s linear,
                      border 0.3s linear;
          transition: background 0.3s linear,
                      border 0.3s linear;
}
```

This shorthand transition property lets us supply the CSS property to transition, the duration, and the timing function. We can specify multiple properties, durations, and timing functions by separating them with commas.

And of course, if you want to support older versions of Firefox and Opera, you'll need to define them again with the -moz- and -o- prefixes, respectively. For brevity, we'll leave those out.

We've defined the transitions, and so when we add effects using :focus, like this:

css3_animation/stylesheets/style.css
```
.login input[type="email"]:focus, .login input[type="password"]:focus{
  background-color: #ffe;
  border: 1px solid #0e0;
}
```

the browser transitions the background and the border smoothly.

Transitions provide a simple way to animate CSS properties from one value to another, but they're not the only way to make animations.

Making the Box Shake with CSS Animations

Transitions are great when we need to move from one point to another, or transition a property from one state to the next. But creating a shake or rumble effect, where the region shakes from side to side, requires something more powerful. With CSS Animations,[9] we can define *keyframes* of animation. A shake is nothing more than moving the box to the left and to the right a few times.

Let's define the shake animation. In stylesheets/style.css, we define the keyframes like this, using @keyframes:

css3_animation/stylesheets/style.css
```
@keyframes shake{
  0%{left:0;}
  20%{left:-2%;}
  40%{left:2%;}
  60%{left:-2%;}
  80%{left:2%;}
  100%{left:0;}
}
```

This is the standard, and works on Internet Explorer 10 and the most recent versions of Firefox and Chrome. But if you want Safari to work, you need to define the keyframes again using a browser prefix, just like with transitions.

---

9. http://www.w3.org/TR/css3-animations/

```
css3_animation/stylesheets/style.css
@-webkit-keyframes shake{
  0%{left:0;}
  20%{left:-2%;}
  40%{left:2%;}
  60%{left:-2%;}
  80%{left:2%;}
  100%{left:0;}
}
```

Remember to add in the -moz- and -opera- prefixes as well if you want to support those browsers.

Now that we have the keyframes for the animation defined, we can apply the animation to a CSS rule. We need to trigger the shake effect only when the user submits the form and gets the username and password wrong. So, we'll use jQuery to capture the form submission and make an Ajax call. Then we'll add a shake class to the form, which will trigger the animation. Let's start by defining the shake rule in our style sheet, like this:

```
.shake{
  animation-name: shake;
  animation-duration: 0.5s;
  animation-delay: 0;
  animation-iteration-count: 1;
  animation-timing-function: linear;
}
```

This markup looks very similar to the way we define transitions. We have control over the animation, the timing function, the duration, the delay, and the iteration count.

That's a lot of typing, especially since we also need to add the vendor prefixes to these rules. Let's reduce that to the shorthand notation:

```
css3_animation/stylesheets/style.css
.shake{
  -webkit-animation: shake 0.5s 1;
     -moz-animation: shake 0.5s 1;
          animation: shake 0.5s 1;
}
```

That takes care of the CSS part. Now we just need to apply the style when the form submission fails. First let's make a function that does the Ajax request. In javascripts/form.js, add this new method:

```
css3_animation/javascripts/form.js
var processLogin = function(form, event){
  event.preventDefault();
  var request = $.ajax({
```

```
    url: "/login",
    type: "POST",
    data: form.serialize(),
    dataType: "json"
  });
  request.done = function(){
    // Do what you do when the login works.
  };
  return(request);
};
```

This function has two parameters; a jQuery object containing the form that should be submitted, and the event. We prevent the event's default behavior, and then we build the Ajax request, passing the serialized form as the data.

We're using jQuery's support for *promises* to define what happens when we have a successful response from the server. Promises let us write asynchronous code without resorting to nested callbacks.

jQuery's $.ajax() method returns an object that implements the Promise interface. Instead of defining the success() callback inside of the $.ajax() method, we can define done() and fail() callbacks on the object returned from $.ajax(). Those callbacks will get executed once the Ajax request is completed, or immediately if the request has already completed. This lets us define callbacks on promises programmatically, even in other parts of our program. It also lets us separate our code into smaller chunks instead of one big ball of unmanageable callbacks. You should read Trevor Burnham's book *Async JavaScript: Build More Responsive Apps with Less Code [Bur12]* to learn about promises in greater detail.

We've already defined the done() callback inside of this processLogin() function. To make the form shake when the login fails, we need to create two event listeners. The first listener handles the form submit event and calls the processLogin() function we just wrote. That function returns the request, and since request implements the Promise interface, we can now define the fail() callback, where we apply the shake class to the form.

css3_animation/javascripts/form.js
```
var addFormSubmitWithCSSAnimation = function(){
  $(".login").submit(function(event){
    var form = $(this);
    request = processLogin(form, event);
    request.fail(function(){
      form.addClass("shake");
    });
  });
};
```

We need to remove the shake class once the animation is done, so that the animation occurs on subsequent form submissions. The animationEnd() event lets us run code when the animation is done, so we need to define an event handler for that. Unfortunately, we have vendor prefixes for these events as well, so we have to cover our bases.

```
css3_animation/javascripts/form.js
var addAnimationEndListener = function(){
  $(".login").on
    ("webkitAnimationEnd oanimationend msAnimationEnd animationend",
      function(event){
        $(this).removeClass("shake");
  });
};
```

Finally, we call the methods that add the listeners:

```
css3_animation/javascripts/form.js
addFormSubmitWithCSSAnimation();
addAnimationEndListener();
```

And now when we click the Submit button, our request fails and the form shakes. We could've done this JavaScript code in one large function, but by breaking it up and using promises, we've made it much easier to add support for browsers that don't support animations.

Falling Back

The best way to make these transitions and animations work is with a jQuery fallback. We'll need both jQuery and the jQuery Color plug-in, and since we'll need entirely different behaviors for those browsers, we'll use Modernizr to detect support and invoke the appropriate code.

First we add Modernizr to the <head> section of the page, using the same version we used in *Detecting Features with Modernizr*, on page 47, which includes the load() function.

```
css3_animation/index.html
<script src="javascripts/modernizr.js"></script>
```

Then we download the jQuery Color plug-in and place it in the javascripts folder. We need this plug-in to do animations on colors.[10]

Now let's get into the actual fallbacks.

---

10. http://code.jquery.com/color/jquery.color-2.1.2.min.js

Handling Transitions with jQuery

When we select a text box, we want the same fade effect, and we can achieve that with jQuery's animate() method. We have to use two events, though; when the field gets focus we want it to fade to yellow, and when it loses focus we want it to go back to white. Here's how we do it:

css3_animation/javascripts/form.js
```
var addTransitionFallbackListeners = function(){
  $(".login input[type=email], .login input[type=password]").focus(function(){
    $(this).animate({
        backgroundColor: "#ffe"
    }, 300 );
  });
  $(".login input[type=email], .login input[type=password]").blur(function(){
    $(this).animate({
        backgroundColor: "#fff"
    }, 300 );
  });
};
```

We define these callbacks inside of a function and then we use Modernizr to detect support for transitions, load the jQuery color plug-in if the browser doesn't support transitions, and then call the function that defines the callbacks:

css3_animation/javascripts/form.js
```
Modernizr.load(
  {
    test: Modernizr.csstransitions,
    nope: "javascripts/jquery.color-2.1.2.min.js",
    callback: function(url, result){
      if (!result){
        addTransitionFallbackListeners();
      }
    }
  }
);
```

And with that we have the transitions working. It's pretty easy to add support for transitions thanks to jQuery. Now on to the animations.

Handling the Animations with jQuery

We can make the form shake using jQuery's animate() function. In javascripts/form.js we define a new function called addFormSubmitWithFallback() that handles the form submission, calls our existing processLogin() method, and defines a fail() callback —just like we did before, except this time we use jQuery to animate the box.

```
css3_animation/javascripts/form.js
var addFormSubmitWithFallback = function(){
  $(".login").submit(function(event){
    var form = $(this);
    request = processLogin(form, event);
    request.fail(function(){
        form.animate({left: "-2%"}, 100)
          .animate({left: "2%"}, 100)
          .animate({left: "-2%"}, 100)
          .animate({left: "2%"}, 100)
          .animate({left: "0%"}, 100);
    });
  });
};
```

Finally, we use Modernizr to detect animation support. If the browser supports animations, we use our original approach. If it doesn't support animations, we call the fallback approach, which still calls the original form-processing code we wrote, but this time uses the fail() callback to attach the animation.

```
css3_animation/javascripts/form.js
if(Modernizr.cssanimations){
    addFormSubmitWithCSSAnimation();
    addAnimationEndListener();
}else{
    addFormSubmitWithFallback();
}
```

There's a little code duplication, but by moving most of the common functionality into a another function, we kept it manageable. Plus we got to learn about promises a bit as we built this out.

Take a second to reflect on what we did and think about whether it's necessary. Like the rest of the topics in this chapter, it might not be worth your time, or even necessary, to create a fallback solution. If the box doesn't shake for 15 percent of your users, do you care? Just because you can add a fallback solution doesn't mean you should—unless, of course, your next paycheck depends on it.

8.1 The Future

In this chapter, we explored a few ways CSS3 replaces traditional web-development techniques, but we only scratched the surface. The specification includes 3D transformations, support for multiple border images, reflection, and even filter effects on images.

The CSS3 modules, when completed, will make it much easier for us to create richer, better, and more inviting interface elements for our users while separating the presentation from the behavior. Things that you used to do with jQuery can be done entirely in CSS now, from creating simple menus to making complex accordion controls. Keep an eye on the specifications and continue exploring.

Part III

Beyond Markup

We've talked about HTML5 and CSS3 markup, but now let's turn our attention to some of the technologies and features associated with HTML5. These features let us communicate across domains and create solutions that allow our users to work offline. We can manipulate the browser history, create more interactive interfaces, and make persistent connections to servers.

Some of these features were spun off from the HTML5 specification. Others were never part of the specification at all, but browser-makers and developers have associated these with HTML5 because the specification is being implemented alongside other features. In either case, they're valuable tools that let us build better user experiences.

Saving Data on the Client

Remember when cookies were awesome? Neither do I. Cookies have been rather painful to deal with since they came on the scene, but we put up with the hassle because they've been the only reliable way to store information on the clients' machines.

To use cookies, we have to name them and set their expiration. This involves a bunch of JavaScript code we wrap in a function so we never have to think about how it actually works, kind of like this:

```
html5_localstorage/setcookie.js
// via http://www.javascripter.net/faq/settinga.htm
function SetCookie(cookieName,cookieValue,nDays) {
  var today = new Date();
  var expire = new Date();
  if (nDays==null || nDays==0) nDays=1;
  expire.setTime(today.getTime() + 3600000*24*nDays);

  document.cookie = cookieName+"="+escape(cookieValue)
                  + ";expires="+expire.toGMTString();
}
```

Aside from the hard-to-remember syntax, there are also the security concerns. Some sites use cookies to track users' surfing behavior, so users disable cookies in some fashion or delete them frequently.

HTML5 introduces new options for storing data on the client: Web Storage (using either localStorage or sessionStorage),[1] IndexedDB,[2] and Web SQL Databases.[3] These new methods are incredibly powerful and reasonably secure. Best of all, they're implemented today by several browsers, including

---

1.   http://www.w3.org/TR/webstorage/
2.   http://www.w3.org/TR/IndexedDB
3.   http://www.w3.org/TR/webdatabase/

Safari on iOS and Android 2.0's web browser. Technically, they're not all part of the HTML5 specification anymore, as they've been spun off into their own specifications.

Although these new mechanisms can't replace cookies intended to be shared between the client and the server—like in the case of web frameworks that use the cookies to maintain state across requests—they can be employed to store data that only users care about, such as visual settings or preferences. They also come in handy for building mobile applications that can run in the browser but are not constantly connected to the Internet. Many web applications currently call back to a server to save user data, but with these new storage mechanisms, an Internet connection is no longer an absolute necessity. User data could be stored locally and backed up or synchronized when necessary.

When you combine these methods with HTML5's new offline features, right in the browser you can build complete database applications that work on a wide variety of platforms, from desktops to tablets and smartphones. In this chapter, you'll learn how to use these techniques to persist user settings and create a simple notes database.

We'll delve into the following features:

localStorage

Stores data in key/value pairs, tied to a domain, and persists across browser sessions. *[C5, F3.5, S4, IE8, O10.5, iOS3.2, A2.1]*

sessionStorage

Stores data in key/value pairs, tied to a domain, and is erased when a browser session ends. *[C5, F3.5, S4, IE8, O10.5, iOS3.2, A2.1]*

IndexedDB

An in-browser object store that persists across sessions. *[C25, F10, IE10]*

Web SQL Databases

Fully relational databases with support for creating tables, inserts, updates, deletes, and selects, with transactions. Tied to a domain and persistent across sessions. No longer an active specification. *[C5, S3.2, O10.5, iOS3.2, A2]*

Offline Web Applications

Defines files to be cached for offline use, allowing applications to run without an Internet connection. *[C4, F3.5, S4, O10.6, iOS3.2, A2]*

Tip 27

Saving Preferences with Web Storage

The Web Storage mechanism provides a simple method for developers to persist data on the client's machine using a name/value store built into the web browser. With a very small amount of JavaScript, storing and retrieving simple strings of data is a breeze. It's one of the most widely available storage application programming interfaces (APIs), implemented in Internet Explorer 8 and the old versions of iOS and Android browsers.

Data stored in Web Storage's localStorage system persists between browser sessions and can't be read by other websites, because it's restricted to the domain you're currently visiting. Just watch out when you're developing things locally. If you're working on a local server, like localhost, for example, you can easily get your variables mixed up and will have to constantly tell the browser to clear the storage out.

AwesomeCo is in the process of developing a new customer-service portal and wants users to be able to change the text size, background, and text color of the site. Let's implement that using Web Storage so that when we save the changes, they persist from one browser session to the next. When we're done, we'll end up with a prototype that looks like the following figure.

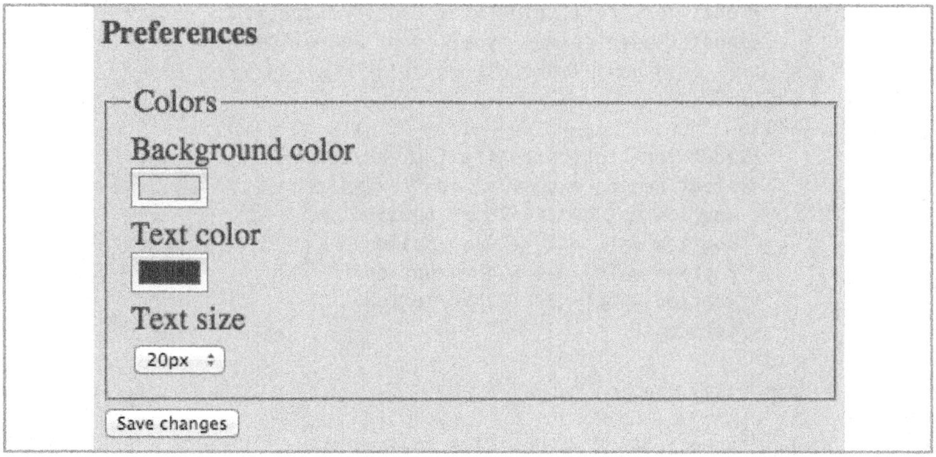

Figure 30—Our Preferences page

Building the Preferences Form

Let's craft a form using some semantic HTML5 markup and some of the new form controls you learned about in Chapter 3, *Creating User-Friendly Web Forms*, on page 37. We want to let the user change the foreground color, the background color, and the font size.

```
html5_localstorage/index.html
<!DOCTYPE html>
<html lang="en-US">
  <head>
    <meta charset="utf-8">
    <title>Preferences</title>
    <link rel="stylesheet" href="stylesheets/style.css">
    <script src="javascripts/modernizr.js"></script>
  </head>
  <body>
    <div id="container">
      <p><strong>Preferences</strong></p>
      <form id="preferences" action="save_prefs"
            method="post" accept-charset="utf-8">
        <fieldset id="colors" class="">
          <legend>Colors</legend>
          <ol>
            <li>
              <label for="background_color">Background color</label>
              <input class="color" type="color" name="background_color"
                     value="" id="background_color">
            </li>
            <li>
              <label for="text_color">Text color</label>
              <input class="color" type="color" name="text_color"
                     value="" id="text_color">
            </li>
            <li>
              <label for="text_size">Text size</label>
              <select name="text_size" id="text_size">
                <option value="16">16px</option>
                <option value="20">20px</option>
                <option value="24">24px</option>
                <option value="32">32px</option>
              </select>
            </li>
          </ol>
        </fieldset>

        <input type="submit" value="Save changes">
      </form>
    </div>
  </body>
</html>
```

We'll use HTML color codes for the colors, and we'll use the HTML5 color type for the fields. We'll also add a tiny bit of CSS to style the form:

html5_localstorage/stylesheets/style.css

```css
form ol{
  list-style: none;
  margin: 0;
  padding: 0;
}

form li{
  margin: 0;
  padding: 0;
}

form li label{ display:block; }
```

This is enough to get the prototype ready. Now let's persist the changes we make on the form.

Saving and Loading the Settings

To work with the localStorage system, we use JavaScript to access the window.localStorage() object. Setting a name and value pair is as simple as this:

html5_localstorage/javascripts/storage.js

```javascript
localStorage.setItem("background_color", $("#background_color").val());
```

Grabbing a value back out is just as easy:

html5_localstorage/javascripts/storage.js

```javascript
var bgcolor = localStorage.getItem("background_color");
```

Let's create a method for saving all the settings from the form. Create the file javascripts/storage.js and add this code:

html5_localstorage/javascripts/storage.js

```javascript
var save_settings = function(){
  localStorage.setItem("background_color", $("#background_color").val());
  localStorage.setItem("text_color", $("#text_color").val());
  localStorage.setItem("text_size", $("#text_size").val());
  apply_preferences_to_page();
};
```

This method pulls the values out of the form fields and puts them into the keys in localStorage.

Next, let's build a similar method that will load the data from the localStorage system and place it into the form fields.

```
html5_localstorage/javascripts/storage.js
var load_settings = function(){
  var bgcolor = localStorage.getItem("background_color");
  var text_color = localStorage.getItem("text_color");
  var text_size = localStorage.getItem("text_size");

  $("#background_color").val(bgcolor);
  $("#text_color").val(text_color);
  $("#text_size").val(text_size);

  apply_preferences_to_page();
};
```

This method also calls a method that will apply the settings to the page itself, which we'll write next.

Applying the Settings

Now that we can retrieve the settings from localStorage, we need to apply them to the page. The preferences we're working with are all related to CSS in some way, so we'll use jQuery to modify the element's styles.

```
html5_localstorage/javascripts/storage.js
var apply_preferences_to_page = function(){
  $("body").css("backgroundColor", $("#background_color").val());
  $("body").css("color", $("#text_color").val());
  $("body").css("fontSize", $("#text_size").val() + "px");
};
```

Finally, we kick all this off at the bottom of the script.

```
html5_localstorage/javascripts/storage.js
load_settings();

$('form#preferences').submit(function(event){
  event.preventDefault();
  save_settings();
});
```

The only thing we have left to do is load our script and jQuery when the HTML page loads. Add these two lines right above the closing <body> tag:

```
html5_localstorage/index.html
<script src="http://ajax.googleapis.com/ajax/libs/jquery/1.9.1/jquery.min.js">
</script>
<script src="javascripts/storage.js"></script>
```

And now the settings persist between browser sessions.

sessionStorage

We can use localStorage for things that we want to persist even after our users close their web browsers, but sometimes we need a way to store some information while the browser is open and throw it away once the session is over. That's where sessionStorage comes into play. It works the same way as localStorage, but the contents of the sessionStorage are cleared out once the browser session ends. Instead of grabbing the localStorage object, you grab the sessionStorage object.

```
sessionStorage.setItem('name', 'Brian Hogan');
var name = sessionStorage.getItem('name');
```

This is a lot more convenient than a cookie-based approach.

Falling Back

The localStorage method works on all modern browsers and a few older ones, so we don't need a client-side fallback solution. However, there's no way to share the data we store in localStorage with the server or another computer, so if users make settings changes at home, those changes won't be available on the users' work computers. Additionally, it's not going to work if users disable JavaScript. So, a good fallback solution would be to persist these settings to a server. For an application like this, we could save the settings to the server when the user presses the Submit button, linking the settings with a user record. We'd craft the form so that it submits directly to the server, and we'd alter the page so that if there are no client-side settings, the server-side settings would be used. Unfortunately, writing a server-side solution is beyond the scope of this book.

Web Storage is a simple approach for storing small bits of data, but it has performance limitations on mobile devices and isn't a good fit for lots of data. Let's look at how we can store more complex data structures client-side.

Tip 28

Storing Data in a Client-Side Database Using IndexedDB

The localStorage and sessionStorage methods give us an easy way to store simple name/value pairs on the client's computer, but sometimes we need more than that. The HTML5 specification initially introduced the ability to store data in relational databases. The storage part has since been spun off into a separate specification called Web SQL Database.[4]

If you have even a basic background in writing SQL statements, you'll feel right at home in no time. Unfortunately, that specification is all but abandoned in favor of IndexedDB, an object database that is incredibly powerful, though a little more complex to use. Let's explore IndexedDB as we build a simple client-side web application. Before we begin, you should know that this tip involves writing a lot of JavaScript code and is a bit lengthy, but the ability to create a flexible way to store data on the client machine is worth the effort.

AwesomeCo wants to equip its sales team with a simple application to collect notes while on the road. This application will need to let users create new notes, as well as update and delete existing ones.

The Notes Interface

The interface for the notes application consists of a left sidebar that will have a list of the notes already taken, and a form on the right side with a title field and a larger text area for a new note. Look at the following figure to see what we're building.

Figure 31—Our notes application

---

4.   http://dev.w3.org/html5/webdatabase/

To start, we need to code up the interface.

html5_indexedDB/index.html

```html
<!DOCTYPE html>
<html>
  <head>
    <meta charset="utf-8">
    <title>AwesomeNotes</title>
    <link rel="stylesheet" href="stylesheets/style.css">
    <script src="javascripts/IndexedDBShim.min.js"></script>
  </head>
  <body>
    <div id="container">
      <section id="sidebar">
        <input type="button" id="new_button" value="New note">
        <input type="button" id="delete_all_button" value="Delete all">
        <ul aria-live="polite" id="notes">
        </ul>
      </section>
      <section id="main" aria-live="polite">
        <form>
          <ol>
            <li>
              <label for="title">Title</label>
              <input type="text" id="title">
            </li>
            <li>
              <label for="note">Note</label>
              <textarea id="note"></textarea>
            </li>
            <li>
              <input type="submit" id="save_button" value="Save">
              <input type="submit" id="delete_button" value="Delete">
            </li>
          </ol>
        </form>
      </section>
    </div>
  </body>
</html>
```

We define the sidebar and main regions using <section> tags, and we give IDs to each of the important user-interface controls, like the Save button. This will make it easier for us to locate elements so that we can attach event listeners.

We'll also need a style sheet so that we can make this look more like the figure. style.css looks like this:

html5_indexedDB/stylesheets/style.css
```css
#container{
  margin: 0 auto;
  width: 80%;
}
#sidebar, #main{
  display: block;
  float: left;
}

#main{ width: 80%; }

#sidebar{ width: 20%;}

form ol{
  list-style: none;
  margin: 0;
  padding: 0;
}

form li, #sidebar li{
  margin: 0;
  padding: 0;
}

form li label{ display:block; }

#note, #title{
  border: 1px solid #000;
  font-size: 20px;
  width: 100%;
}


#sidebar ul{
  list-style: none;
  padding: 0;
};

#sidebar li{ cursor: hand; cursor: pointer; }

#title{ height: 20px; }

#note{ height: 80px; }
```

This style sheet turns off the bullet points, sizes the text areas, and lays things out in two columns. With the interface done, we can build the JavaScript we need to make this work.

Creating and Connecting to the Database

Create the file javascripts/notes.js. We'll put all of our application logic in this file. Be sure to link it to the bottom of index.html, right above the <body> tag along with jQuery, which we'll use for event handling and easy Document Object Model manipulation.

```
html5_indexedDB/index.html
<script
  src="http://ajax.googleapis.com/ajax/libs/jquery/1.9.1/jquery.min.js">
</script>
<script src="javascripts/notes.js"></script>
```

Inside javascripts/notes.js, we need to set up a few variables for our application.

```
html5_indexedDB/javascripts/notes.js
// Database reference
var db = null;
window.indexedDB = window.indexedDB || window.mozIndexedDB ||
                   window.webkitIndexedDB ||window.msIndexedDB;
```

We're declaring the db variable at the top of our script. Doing this makes it available to the rest of the methods we'll create. It puts the variable into the global scope, and that's not always a good idea. For this example, we're keeping the JavaScript code as simple as possible.

Then we define the window.indexedDB variable because, unfortunately, different browsers have different names for this object. Lucky for us, although they have different names, they work pretty much the same way, so we can create one variable and reference it.

Let's create a simple function that handles connecting to the database:

```
html5_indexedDB/javascripts/notes.js
var connectToDB = function(){
  var version = 1;
  var request = window.indexedDB.open("awesomenotes", version);
  request.onsuccess = function(event) {
    db = event.target.result;
    fetchNotes();
  };
  request.onerror = function(event){
    alert(event.debug[1].message);
  }
};
```

This uses the open() method on indexedDB to create the connection. We specify a schema version when we connect, and we get a request object back. The request object has a success() callback that fires when the connection is established, and an error() method that fires when the connection doesn't work.

In the success() callback, we call the fetchNotes() method, which we'll build later. This method will go through the database and load the notes into the sidebar. But before we can do anything with the database, we have to create it.

Creating the Notes Table

Our notes table needs three fields:

Field	Description
id	The note's unique identification
title	The title of the note, for easy reference
Note	The note itself

To create this table, we hook into a callback on the request object we created in the connectToDB() method we just defined. The callback, onupgradeneeded(), fires when the schema version number changes. In our case, our connectToDB() method specifies a version and connects to a database that doesn't exist yet. The browser then fires the onupgradeneeded() callback because it knows we'll need to create a table. Add this code to the connectToDB():

```
html5_indexedDB/javascripts/notes.js
var connectToDB = function(){
  var version = 1;
  var request = window.indexedDB.open("awesomenotes", version);

➤ request.onupgradeneeded = function(event) {
➤   alert("unupgradeneeded fired");
➤   var db = event.target.result;
➤   db.createObjectStore("notes", { keyPath: "id", autoIncrement: true });
➤ };
  request.onsuccess = function(event) {
    db = event.target.result;
    fetchNotes();
  };
  request.onerror = function(event){
    alert(event.debug[1].message);
  }
};
```

The createObjectStore() method defines the database table we'll use. We pass in the name of the table, followed by a hash of options. In our case, we're declaring that we want each record to have a unique, autoincrementing key called id.

In the future, if we change the version to something else, the onupgradeneeded() callback will fire again. This gives us an easy way to update schemas on the user's machine.

Now that we have our table, we can make this application actually do something.

Loading Notes

When the application loads, we want to connect to the database, create the table if it doesn't already exist, and then fetch any existing notes from the database. Our connectToDB() method takes care of connecting and creating the database, and on a successful connection, it calls fetchNotes(), which we need to write next.

The fetchNotes() method will fetch all of the notes from the database. We define it like this:

```
html5_indexedDB/javascripts/notes.js
var fetchNotes = function(){
  var keyRange, request, result, store, transaction;

  transaction = db.transaction(["notes"], "readwrite");
  store = transaction.objectStore("notes");

  // Get everything in the store;
  keyRange = IDBKeyRange.lowerBound(0);
  request = store.openCursor(keyRange);

  request.onsuccess = function(event) {
    result = event.target.result;
    if(result){
      addToNotesList(result.key, result.value);
      result.continue();
    }
  };

  request.onerror = function(event) {
    alert("Unable to fetch records.");
  };
};
```

This method grabs the results from the database using a *cursor*. If a result is found, we call a method, addNoteToList(), which will add the note to the sidebar. This process repeats for every record in the database thanks to the call to result.continue(), which gets the next record, which invokes the onsuccess() callback again. It's a little bit of event recursion instead of a loop.

We need both the key and the data for the result. The key is the id field we defined as the keypath, and the data is a JavaScript object containing the note's title and body. We pass both of those to addNoteToList() to add the note to the sidebar. We define addNoteToList() like this:

```
html5_indexedDB/javascripts/notes.js
var addToNotesList = function(key, data){
  var item = $("<li>");
  var notes = $("#notes");

  item.attr("data-id", key);
  item.html(data.title);
  notes.append(item);
};
```

We're embedding the ID of the record into a custom data attribute on the element. We'll use that ID to locate the record to load when the user clicks the list item. We then add the new list item we create to the unordered list in our interface, with the ID of notes.

We're using jQuery's attr() method to set the custom data attribute that holds the ID. jQuery's data() method can interact with custom data attributes,[5] but the data() method has side effects when setting and retrieving HTML5 data-values. Values retrieved by the data() method will be coerced to a data type automatically, and using data() to set values saves the value to the jQuery object rather than into the element's data- attribute. So, for simplicity and consistency, we'll avoid jQuery's data() method in this app.

Now we need to add code to load that item into the form when we select a note from this list.

Fetching a Specific Record

We could add a click event to each list item, but a more practical and performant approach is to watch any clicks on the unordered list and then determine which one was clicked. This way, when we add new entries to the list (like when we add a new note), we don't have to add the click event to the new DOM element we add to the list.

Add this event handler to javascripts/notes.js:

```
html5_indexedDB/javascripts/notes.js
$("#notes").click(function(event){
  var element = $(event.target);
  if (element.is('li')) {
    getNote(element.attr("data-id"));
  }
});
```

---

5.   http://api.jquery.com/data/

This fires off the getNote() method, which takes in the ID and gets the single note from the database. We define getNote() like this:

```
html5_indexedDB/javascripts/notes.js
var getNote = function(id){
  var request, store, transaction;
  id = parseInt(id);

  transaction = db.transaction(["notes"]);
  store = transaction.objectStore("notes");

  request = store.get(id);

  request.onsuccess = function(event) {
    showNote(request.result);
  };

  request.onerror = function(error){
    alert("Unable to fetch record " + id);
  };
}
```

This method looks a lot like the previous fetchNotes() method. We get a request object by calling get() on the store, passing it the ID. When the request is successful we display the note on the form by calling showNote(), which we define like this:

```
html5_indexedDB/javascripts/notes.js
var showNote = function(data){
  var note = $("#note");
  var title = $("#title");

  title.val(data.title);
  title.attr("data-id", data.id);
  note.val(data.note);
  $("#delete_button").show();
}
```

This method also activates the Delete button and embeds the ID of the record into a custom data attribute so that updates can easily be handled. Our Save button will check for the existence of the ID. If it exists, we'll update the record. If it's missing, we'll assume this is a new record. Let's write that bit of logic next.

Creating, Updating, and Deleting Records

Our system retrieves records and displays them, but we need to make it possible to put notes into the system. Let's start by activating the New button, which clears the form out when clicked so a user can create a new note after having edited an existing one. We first add an event handler when the New button is clicked:

html5_indexedDB/javascripts/notes.js

```
$("#new_button").click(function(event){
  newNote();
});
```

Inside the handler we clear out the data-id attribute of the title field and remove the values from the forms. We'll also hide the Delete button from the interface.

html5_indexedDB/javascripts/notes.js

```
var newNote = function(){
  var note = $("#note");
  var title = $("#title");

  $("#delete_button").hide();
  title.removeAttr("data-id");
  title.val("");
  note.val("");
}
```

When a user clicks the Save button, we want to trigger code to either insert a new record or update the existing one. We'll use the same pattern as we did before—we'll start with the event handler for the Save button:

html5_indexedDB/javascripts/notes.js

```
$("#save_button").click(function(event){
  var id, note, title;

  event.preventDefault();
  note = $("#note");
  title = $("#title");
  id = title.attr("data-id");

  if(id){
    updateNote(id, title.val(), note.val());
  }else{
    insertNote(title.val(), note.val());
  }
});
```

This method checks the data-id attribute of the form's Title field. If it has no ID, the form assumes we're inserting a new record and invokes the insertNote() method, which we define next:

html5_indexedDB/javascripts/notes.js

```
var insertNote = function(title, note){
  var data, key

  data = {
```

```
    "title": title,
    "note": note,
  };

  var transaction = db.transaction(["notes"], "readwrite");
  var store = transaction.objectStore("notes");
  var request = store.put(data);

  request.onsuccess = function(event) {
    key = request.result;
    addToNotesList(key, data);
    newNote();
  };
};
```

The insertNote() method adds the record into the database and uses the key property of the result to get the ID for the record that was just created. Remember, we set this to an autoincrementing field, so when we create a new record, the database gives us a new unique ID for the record. Then we invoke our addToNotesList() method to add the note to our list on the side of the page, passing the key and the rest of the data. It also calls the newForm() method to clear out the form.

Next we need to handle updates. The updateNote() method looks just like the rest of the methods we've added so far:

```
html5_indexedDB/javascripts/notes.js
var updateNote = function(id, title, note){
  var data, request, store, transaction;
  id = parseInt(id);
  data = {
    "title": title,
    "note": note,
    "id" : id
  };

  transaction = db.transaction(["notes"], "readwrite");
  store = transaction.objectStore("notes");
  request = store.put(data);

  request.onsuccess = function(event) {
    $("#notes>li[data-id=" + id + "]").html(title);
  };
};
```

When the record update is successful, we update the title of the note in our list of notes by using jQuery to find the element in the sidebar whose data-id attribute matches the value of the ID we just updated.

Deleting records is almost the same. We need a handler for the delete event:

```
html5_indexedDB/javascripts/notes.js
$("#delete_button").click(function(event){
  var title = $("#title");
  event.preventDefault();
  deleteNote(title.attr("data-id"));
});
```

Then we need the delete() method itself, which removes the record not only from the database, but also from the list of notes in the sidebar.

```
html5_indexedDB/javascripts/notes.js
var deleteNote = function(id){
  var request, store, transaction;

  id = parseInt(id);

  transaction = db.transaction(["notes"], "readwrite");
  store = transaction.objectStore("notes");
  request = store.delete(id);

  request.onsuccess = function(event) {
    $("#notes>li[data-id=" + id + "]").remove();
    newNote();
  };
};
```

This also calls newForm() to clear out the form so we can create a new record without accidentally duplicating the one we just deleted.

Finally, we need to handle clearing out all of the records. We add a click handler to the Delete All button, like this:

```
html5_indexedDB/javascripts/notes.js
$("#delete_all_button").click(function(event){
  clearNotes();
});
```

and have it invoke the clearNotes() method, which removes every record from our database. The clearNotes() method looks like this, and follows the same pattern we've seen all along:

```
html5_indexedDB/javascripts/notes.js
var clearNotes = function(id){
  var request, store, transaction;

  transaction = db.transaction(["notes"], "readwrite");
  store = transaction.objectStore("notes");
  request = store.clear();
```

```
  request.onsuccess = function(event) {
    $("#notes").empty();
  };

  request.onerror = function(event){
    alert("Unable to clear things out.");
  }
};
```

With that last change, our notes application is complete. To kick everything off, we call the connectToDB() method and load the records from our database. We also need to call the newForm() method so that the form is ready to be used. This way, the Delete button is hidden too.

html5_indexedDB/javascripts/notes.js
```
connectToDB();
newNote();
```

That's all there is to it. We have to be careful with this app, though. Since the data is all stored on the client, it could be easily erased if the user clears out his cache and his local data stores, just like with cookies. It also doesn't follow the user from computer to computer. To solve those problems, we'd need to build in a mechanism to synchronize this data with a server, and that's beyond the scope of this book.

Our application works on Internet Explorer 10 and desktop machines running Chrome and Firefox. However, Safari, the mobile Android browsers, and Safari on iOS don't support IndexedDB. They support the deprecated (but widely used) Web SQL Databases standard instead. Internet Explorer 8 and 9 don't support either Web SQL Databases or IndexedDB. Let's look at how we handle these situations.

Falling Back

The simplest solution would be to convince users of an app like this to upgrade their browsers to something that supports IndexedDB, like Internet Explorer 10, or, if that's not possible because of operating-system limitations, the latest version of Chrome. That's not an unheard-of practice, especially if using an alternative browser allows you to build an internal application.

Of course, we're developers and we don't always get to make those calls. But we can use IndexedDBShim to make our app work in browsers that support the Web SQL Databases specification,[6] meaning we can easily make this notes app work on mobile devices like iPhones, iPads, and Android tablets, since

---

6.   http://nparashuram.com/IndexedDBShim/

those browsers do support Web SQL Databases. To use IndexedDBShim, we download the minified version and load it in the <head> section of the page:

html5_indexedDB/index.html
```
<script src="javascripts/IndexedDBShim.min.js"></script>
```

It has to be in the <head> section of the page or its features might not be available right away in Safari, causing things to break wildly. You could use Modernizr to load this library only when needed, but that raises the question of whether it makes sense to load another library just to load one that does its own detection anyway. If you're going to use Modernizr for something else, then it absolutely makes sense to use it to load all libraries on demand.

With this fallback in place, when we load this app in Safari or other browsers that support Web SQL databases, things just work. This fallback solution isn't perfect, so you'll want to test it carefully, but it is a workable and widely supported solution for browsers that support Web SQL.

Unfortunately, there is no fallback for IndexedDB for Internet Explorer 8 and 9. Users of those browsers will be left out of the fun.

We can store data on the client's browser, but we can also create apps that work without an active Internet connection. Let's explore offline applications.

Web SQL Databases—Awesome but Stalled

The Web SQL Databases draft specification defines an API that lets developers use a database in the browser; the database is based on SQLite, the popular open source database that's often used on the iOS and Android platforms. This API is implemented in Safari, Safari on iOS, the Android browsers, and Chrome, and is extremely easy to use if you understand how to write SQL statements.

Unfortunately, because the Web SQL Databases specification focused on only a single implementation, the standards committee decided it shouldn't move forward unless someone brought forth a competing implementation. Mozilla and Microsoft decided to move ahead with IndexedDB instead, and Google added IndexedDB to recent versions of Chrome.

However, if you'd like to see how Web SQL databases work, you can find an implementation of this notes application using Web SQL databases in the html5_websql folder within the downloadable source code for this book. This specification could be extremely useful if you're developing applications on platforms that use this technology, even if the specification itself is stalled.

Tip 29

Working Offline

With HTML5's Offline Web Applications support,[7] we can use HTML and related technologies to build applications that can still function while disconnected from the Internet. This is especially useful for developing applications for mobile devices that may drop connections, or for simply building an app that you want to run completely offline.

This technique works in Firefox, Chrome, and Safari, as well as on the iOS and Android 2.0 devices, but there's no fallback solution that will work to provide offline support for Internet Explorer.

AwesomeCo just bought its sales team some iPads, and would like to make the notes application we developed in Tip 28, *Storing Data in a Client-Side Database Using IndexedDB*, on page 190, work offline. Thanks to the HTML5 application cache manifest file, that will be a simple task. Let's see how it works.

Defining an Application Cache with the Manifest

Our notes app has a lot of dependencies. When we download the main HTML page, the browser has to go and get some CSS files and some JavaScript files. We can create a manifest file that contains a list of all the web application's client-side files that need to exist in the client browser's cache in order to work offline. When the user visits the page for the first time, all the files in the manifest will be downloaded. *Every* file that the application will reference needs to be listed in the manifest for things to work properly. The only exception is that the file that includes the manifest doesn't need to be listed; it is cached implicitly.

Let's build a manifest for our notes app so we can use it offline. Create a file called notes.appcache. Its contents should look like this:

html5_offline/notes.appcache
```
CACHE MANIFEST
# v = 1.0.0
stylesheets/style.css
javascripts/notes.js
javascripts/IndexedDBShim.min.js
```

---

7. http://www.w3.org/TR/html5/browsers.html#offline

```
javascripts/jquery-1.9.1.min.js
```

When we change our code, we need to modify the manifest so the browser knows to fetch the new versions of our code. It's not enough to update the manifest's timestamp; we have to actually change the contents of the file; that's what the version comment in this file is for.

Also, we've been letting Google host jQuery for us, but that won't work if we want our application to work offline, so we need to download jQuery and modify our <script> tag to load jQuery from our javascripts folder.

html5_offline/index.html
```
<script src="javascripts/jquery-1.9.1.min.js"></script>
<script src="javascripts/notes.js"></script>
```

Next we need to link the manifest file to our HTML document by changing the <html> tag to this:

html5_offline/index.html
```
<html manifest="notes.appcache">
```

That's all. If you enable the console in Chrome, you can see the manifest at work, as in the next figure.

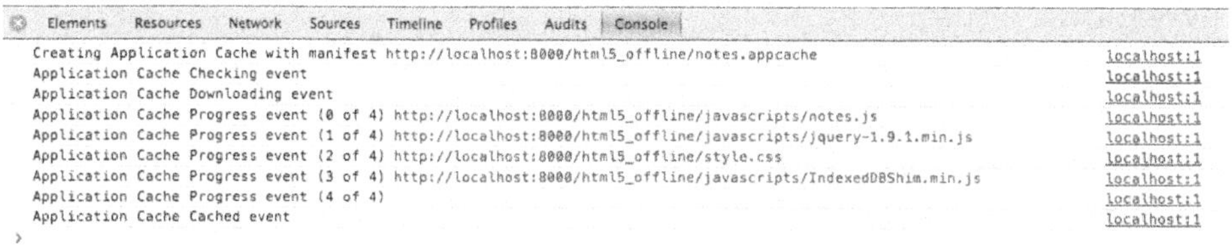

Figure 32—Console output showing cached files

Once all the files are cached, a user can disconnect from the Internet and the application will still work. There's just one little catch—the manifest file has to be served by a web server because the manifest must be served using the text/cache-manifest MIME type, or the browser won't use it. The Node.js-based server in this book's source code handles this for you for testing purposes, but if you're using Apache, you can set the MIME type in a .htaccess like this:

html5_offline/.htaccess
```
AddType text/cache-manifest .appcache
```

After we request our notes application the first time, the files listed in the manifest get downloaded and cached. We can then disconnect from the network and use this application offline as many times as we want.

Be sure to investigate the specification. The manifest file has more complex options you can use. For example, you can specify that certain things should not be cached and should never be accessed offline, which is useful for ignoring certain dynamic files.

Manifest and Caching

When you're working with your application in development mode, you want to disable any caching on your web server. By default, many web servers cache files by setting headers that tell browsers not to fetch a new copy of a file for a given time. This can trip you up while you're adding things to your manifest file.

If you use Apache, you can disable caching by adding this to your .htaccess file:

```
html5_offline/.htaccess
ExpiresActive On
ExpiresDefault "access"
```

This disables caching on the entire directory, so it's not something you want to do in production. But it ensures that your browser will always request a new version of your manifest file.

If you change a file listed in your manifest, you'll want to modify the manifest file, too, by changing the version-number comment we added.

Detecting Network Connectivity

The application we wrote works offline, but what if we want to detect an active network connection and synchronize the local data to a server? We can do that.

First, by using the navigator.onLine property, we can determine if we are currently online.

```
html5_offline/offlinetest.html
if (navigator.onLine) {
  alert('online')
} else {
  alert('offline');
}
```

This works in Safari, Firefox, and Chrome and is easy to use, but it's just a simple check for network connectivity. With this, we know the current status of the connection. We also have events we can listen for so we can handle dropped connections:

```
html5_offline/offlinetest.html
window.addEventListener("offline", function(e) {
  alert("offline");
}, false);

window.addEventListener("online", function(e) {
  alert("online");
}, false);
```

Using this approach, we could detect when we lose connectivity, display a message, and then synchronize everything back up when the connection becomes active again.

Since synchronizing the data in our app would require some back-end coding, this is as far as we'll go in this book. But you have the tools you need to investigate further.

9.1 The Future

Features like Web Storage and IndexedDB give developers the ability and flexibility to build applications in the browser that don't have to be connected to a web server. Applications like the ones we worked on run on iPad and Android devices, as well, and when we combine them with the HTML5 manifest file, we can build offline rich applications using familiar tools instead of proprietary platforms. As additional browsers enable support, developers will be able to leverage them more, creating applications that run on multiple platforms and devices, that store data locally, and that can sync up when connected.

Creating Interactive Web Applications

Beyond the new markup, styles, and multimedia capabilities of HTML5 and CSS3 lie incredibly powerful application programming interfaces (APIs) for making richer, more powerful web applications. We've already touched on how to store data on the client's machine, but we can go even farther. In this chapter we'll spend a little time working with the HTML5 History API, and then we'll make pages on different servers talk with the Cross-Document Messaging API, Then we'll look at Web Sockets and Geolocation, two very powerful APIs that can help you make even more interactive applications. We'll wrap up by exploring HTML5's Drag and Drop API support.

Many of these APIs started out as part of the HTML5 specification and were eventually spun off into their own projects. Others were never part of HTML5 proper, but have become so associated with HTML5 that sometimes it's hard for developers to really tell the difference. But by combining what you've already learned with these new features, you'll be able to provide better experiences for your users. Let's start with a look at the History API.

We'll use the following APIs in this chapter:

History
> Manages the browser history. *[C5, F3, S4, IE8, O10.1 iOS3.2, A2]*

Cross-Document Messaging
> Sends messages between windows and <iframe>s with content loaded on different domains. *[C5, F4, S5, iOS4.1, A2]*

Web Sockets
> Creates a stateful connection between a browser and a server. *[C5, F6, S5, IE10, O12.1, iOS6]*

Geolocation

Gets latitude and longitude from the client's browser. *[C5, F3.5, S5, O10.6, iOS3.2, A2.1]*

Drag and Drop

Provides for drag-and-drop interaction. *[C4, F3.5, S3.1, IE6 (partial), IE10 (full), O12]*

Tip 30

Preserving History

The HTML5 specification introduces an API to manage browser history.[1] With it, we can add entries into the history, replace entries, and even store data, which we can retrieve when we revisit the page. This is great for single-page applications where things update dynamically but you still want to allow the user to use the Back button.

In Tip 15, *Creating an Accessible Updatable Region*, on page 98, we built a prototype for AwesomeCo's new home page that switched out the main content when we clicked one of the navigation tabs. One drawback with the approach we used is that there's no support for the browser's Back button. If we click a tab, pressing the Back button in the browser takes us to the previous web page we visited, rather than the previous tab. Let's use the History API to fix the example code we built in that tip.

Storing the Current State

When a visitor brings up a new web page, the browser adds that page to its history. When a user brings up a new tab, we need to add that new tab to the history ourselves. The current home-page prototype already has the code for switching tabs. We just need to add code to store the tab the user selects. Create a new method called addTabToHistory():

html5_history/javascripts/application.js

```
Line 1  var addTabToHistory = function(target){
     2    var tab = target.attr("href");
     3    var stateObject = {tab: tab};
     4    window.history.pushState(stateObject, "", tab);
     5  }
```

This function takes in the tab the user clicked on. We use the href attribute's value to add a history state to the browser using pushState(), which takes three arguments. The first argument is an object that we'll be able to interact with later. We'll use this object to store the ID of the tab we want to display when our user navigates back to this point. For example, when the user clicks the Services tab, we'll store "#services" in the state object, under a property called tab.

---

1.   http://www.w3.org/TR/html5/browsers.html#history

The second argument is a title that we can use to identify the state in our history. It has nothing to do with the page's <title> element; it's just a way to identify the entry in the browser's history. Most browsers don't do anything with this, so we'll give it an empty string value.

The third argument is the URL that should display in the title bar. This can be anything we want. We'll use the tab's ID again here because it'll add a hash to the URL. If we were working with a back-end server and doing some Ajax, it might make more sense to give a relative URL like /about or /services. That way, when a user goes directly to the URL, the back end could respond appropriately. Since we don't have any static pages like that, we can't just tinker with the URL and have it work.

To activate this new code, we place a call to the addTabToHistory() method inside the click handler for the links, passing in the tab the user clicked on:

```
html5_history/javascripts/application.js
$("nav ul").click(function(event){
  var target = $(event.target);
  if(target.is("a")){
    event.preventDefault();
    if ( $(target.attr("href")).attr("aria-hidden")){
      addTabToHistory(target);
      activateTab(target.attr("href"));
    };
  };
});
```

Although our current code adds a history state, we still have to write the code to handle what happens when the user presses the Back button.

Retrieving the Previous State

When the user clicks the Back button, the window.onpopstate() event gets fired. We use this hook to display the tab we stored in the state object.

```
html5_history/javascripts/application.js
var configurePopState = function(){
  window.onpopstate = function(event) {
    if(event.state){
      var tab = (event.state["tab"]);
      activateTab(tab);
    }
  };
};
```

All we have to do is grab the tab out of the object we stored in history and pass it to our activateTab() function. Hurray for code reuse!

Setting the Default State

We have a couple of issues to resolve. When we first bring up our page, our history state is going to be null, so we'll need to set it ourselves. Also, the URL changes whenever we click a tab, but if we press Reload, the Welcome tab shows up instead of the tab we want. So, on page load we check the URL, see what tab should be open, and set it.

```
html5_history/javascripts/application.js
var activateDefaultTab = function(){
  tab = window.location.hash || "#welcome";
  activateTab(tab);
  window.history.replaceState( {tab: tab}, "", tab);
};
```

If there's no value for location.hash, we give it the default value. We then use history.replaceState() to set the tab. This works like pushState(), but instead of adding a new entry, it replaces the current one.

Now, to keep things nicely organized, let's create an init() function that calls these new methods and the original configureTabSelection():

```
html5_history/javascripts/application.js
➤ var init = function(){
    configureTabSelection();
➤   configurePopState();
➤   activateDefaultTab();
➤ };
```

Then we just need to call init() to start things off.

```
html5_history/javascripts/application.js
init();
```

When we bring up the page, we can cycle through our tabs and easily use the Back button to return to previously visited tabs—thanks to the History API.

Falling Back

This works in Chrome, Firefox, Safari, and Internet Explorer 9 and higher. The best solution out there for legacy browsers is History.js,[2] which creates a cross-browser layer to make this functionality work. However, it's not a drop-in replacement. To use it, you include the library and then modify your code to use it instead of the browser's history object. Thankfully, it follows the specification very closely, and eliminates the need for you to check for history

---

2.   https://github.com/browserstate/history.js/

support. But because it does require rewriting the code, we're not going to go through that process. I'll leave that up to you.

However, we should still prevent errors from occurring on older browsers, so we'll use Modernizr to detect for history support. Add Modernizr to the HTML page:

html5_history/fallback/index.html
```
<script src="javascripts/modernizr.js"></script>
```

Then use Modernizr.history to wrap calls to the window.history object.

html5_history/fallback/javascripts/application.js
```
    $("nav ul").click(function(event){
      var target = $(event.target);
      if(target.is("a")){
        event.preventDefault();
        if ( $(target.attr("href")).attr("aria-hidden")){
➤         if(Modernizr.history){
            addTabToHistory(target);
➤         }
          activateTab(target.attr("href"));
        };
      };
    });
  var init = function(){
    configureTabSelection();
➤   if(Modernizr.history){
      configurePopState();
      activateDefaultTab();
➤   }
  };
```

If you decide to implement History.js, you could use Modernizr.load() to load different versions of your code based on whether you need a fallback.

Next let's explore how to exchange information between two sites on different domains.

Tip 31

Talking across Domains

Client-side web applications have traditionally been restricted from talking directly to scripts on other domains—a restriction designed to protect users. This is known as the same-origin policy,[3] and while it protects users, it makes our work more difficult if we have legitimate reasons to make two separate sites communicate. There are numerous clever ways around this restriction, including the use of server-side proxies and URL hacks. But now there's a better way.

Cross-Document Messaging, or *Web Messaging*,[4] is an API that makes it possible for scripts hosted on different domains to pass messages back and forth. For example, we can have a form on http://support.awesomecompany.com post content to another window or <iframe> whose content is hosted on http://www.awesomecompany.com. For our current project, we need to do just that.

AwesomeCo's new support site will have a contact form, and the support manager wants to list all the support contacts and their email addresses next to the contact form, like in the following figure.

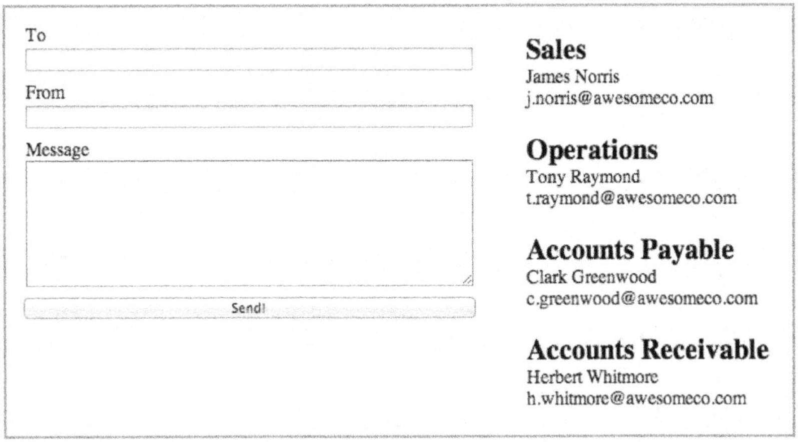

Figure 33—Our completed support site

3.   https://developer.mozilla.org/en/Same_origin_policy_for_JavaScript.

4.   http://www.w3.org/TR/webmessaging/#web-messaging

The support contacts will eventually come from a content-management system on another server, so for this prototype we'll embed the contact list alongside the form using an <iframe>. The catch is that the support manager would love it if we could let users click a name from the contact list and have the email automatically added to our form.

We can do this quite easily, but you'll need to use two web servers to properly test everything on your own setup. The examples we're working on here don't function in every browser unless we serve the pages from a server. At the very least, you'll need to have the contact-list application on one port and the support site on another port so you can prove that cross-document messaging really does work. The downloadable example code for the book has a simple script you can use to fire up web servers for this recipe. It requires Node.js, but you can refer back to *Node.js and the Example Server*, on page xv, for details on how to set that up and start this server. For this recipe, the example code will use the URLs and ports of this server:

- The contact list will be served from *localhost:4000*.

- The support page list will be served from *localhost:3000*.

If you're going to follow along and place your files on separate servers that you control, just change the URLs in the code.

The Contact List

We'll create the contact list first. This is the file that will be embedded in the support site's <iframe> and will send messages to the support site. Our basic markup will look like this:

```
html5_cross_document/contactlist/index.html
<!DOCTYPE html>
<html lang="en-US">
  <head>
    <meta charset="utf-8">
    <title>Contact List</title>
    <link rel="stylesheet" href="stylesheets/style.css" >
  </head>
  <body>
    <ul id="contacts">
      <li>
        <h2>Sales</h2>
        <p class="name">James Norris</p>
        <p class="email">j.norris@awesomeco.com</p>
      </li>
      <li>
        <h2>Operations</h2>
        <p class="name">Tony Raymond</p>
```

```
      <p class="email">t.raymond@awesomeco.com</p>
    </li>
    <li>
      <h2>Accounts Payable</h2>
      <p class="name">Clark Greenwood</p>
      <p class="email">c.greenwood@awesomeco.com</p>
    </li>
    <li>
      <h2>Accounts Receivable</h2>
      <p class="name">Herbert Whitmore</p>
      <p class="email">h.whitmore@awesomeco.com</p>
    </li>
  </ul>
  </body>
</html>
```

On that page, we'll also load both the jQuery library and our own custom application.js file right above the closing <body> tag:

`html5_cross_document/contactlist/index.html`
```
<script
   src="http://ajax.googleapis.com/ajax/libs/jquery/1.9.1/jquery.min.js">
</script>

<script src="javascripts/application.js"></script>
```

The style sheet for the contact list looks like this:

`html5_cross_document/contactlist/stylesheets/style.css`
```
ul{
  list-style: none;
}

ul h2, ul p{margin: 0;}

ul > li{margin-bottom: 20px;}
```

It takes just a couple of small tweaks to make the list look a little cleaner.

Posting the Message

When a user clicks an entry in our contact list, we'll grab the email from the list item and post a message back to the parent window. The postMessage() method takes two parameters: the message itself and the target window's origin. Remember, the contact list is being served from *http://localhost:4000*, but it's going to be *included* in an <iframe> by a page served from *http://localhost:3000*. So that's the URL we'll send messages back to.

Here's how the entire event handler looks:

```
html5_cross_document/contactlist/javascripts/application.js
$("#contacts li").click(function(event){
  var email, origin;
  email = $(this).find(".email").html();
  origin = "http://localhost:3000/index.html";
  if(window.postMessage){
    window.parent.postMessage(email, origin);
  }
});
```

You'll need to change the origin if you're following along with your own servers, since it needs to match the URL of the parent window for security reasons.

Now we need to implement the page that will hold this frame and receive its messages.

The Support Site

The support site's structure is going to look very similar, but to keep things separate, we should work in a different folder, especially since this site will need to be placed on a different web server. Make sure you include links to a style sheet, jQuery, and a new application.js file. Our support page needs a contact form and an <iframe> that points to our contact list. We'll do something like this:

```
html5_cross_document/supportpage/index.html
  <div id="form">
    <form id="supportform">
      <fieldset>
        <ol>
          <li>
            <label for="to">To</label>
            <input type="email" name="to" id="to">
          </li>
          <li>
            <label for="from">From</label>
            <input type="text" name="from" id="from">
          </li>
          <li>
            <label for="message">Message</label>
            <textarea name="message" id="message"></textarea>
          </li>
        </ol>
        <input type="submit" value="Send!">
      </fieldset>
    </form>
  </div>
<div id="contacts">
  <iframe src="http://localhost:4000/index.html"></iframe>
</div>
```

We style it up with this CSS that we add to stylesheets/style.css:

html5_cross_document/supportpage/stylesheets/style.css

```css
#form{
  width: 400px;
  float: left;
}

#contacts{
  width: 200px;
  float: left;
}

#contacts iframe{
  border: none;
  height: 400px;
}

fieldset{
  width: 400px;
  border: none;
}

fieldset legend{
  background-color: #ddd;
  padding: 0 64px 0 2px;
}

fieldset>ol{
  list-style: none;
  padding: 0;
  margin: 2px;
}

fieldset>ol>li{
  margin: 0 0 9px 0;
  padding: 0;
}

/* Make inputs go to their own line */
fieldset input, fieldset textarea{
  display:block;
  width: 380px;
}
fieldset input[type=submit]{
  width: 390px;
}
fieldset textarea{
  height: 100px;
}
```

This places the form and the <iframe> side by side and adds basic styles to the form fields.

Receiving the Messages

The onmessage() event fires whenever the current window receives a message. The message comes back as a property of the event. We'll register this event using jQuery's on() method so it works the same in all browsers.

```
html5_cross_document/supportpage/javascripts/application.js
$(window).on("message",function(event){
  $("#to").val(event.originalEvent.data);
});
```

jQuery's on() method wraps the event and doesn't expose every property. We can get what we need by accessing it through the event's originalEvent property instead.

If you open the support site in Firefox, Chrome, Safari, or Internet Explorer 8 or higher, you'll see that it works extremely well. There's no need for a fallback solution. Be sure to run the web-server script in the example code and visit *http://localhost:3000* to see this in action if you get stuck.

The ability to make two separate pages or applications communicate like this opens up a lot of possibilities for making more modular applications.

Limitations in Internet Explorer 8 and 9

While Internet Explorer 8 and 9 both support Cross-Document Messaging, the postMessage() function can handle only strings. It can't handle objects. In addition, messaging works only between frames and iframes. The jQuery PostMessage plug-in might be useful, as it does allow object serialization.[5]

Now that we know how to send messages between websites, let's look at how we can do two-way communication with our users.

---

5. http://benalman.com/projects/jquery-postmessage-plugin/

Tip 32

Chatting with Web Sockets

Web developers have been pursuing real-time interaction with users for many years, but most of the implementations have involved using JavaScript to periodically hit the remote server to check for changes. HTTP is a stateless protocol, so a web browser makes a connection to a server, gets a response, and disconnects. Doing any kind of real-time work over a stateless protocol can be quite rough. The HTML5 specification introduced web sockets, which let the browser make a stateful connection to a remote server.[6] We can use web sockets to build all kinds of great applications. One of the best ways to get a feel for how they work is to write a chat client—which, coincidentally, AwesomeCo wants for its support site.

AwesomeCo wants to create a simple web-based chat interface on its support site that will let geographically dispersed members of the support staff communicate internally. See the following figure.

AwesomeCo Help!

Nickname GuestUser   Change

connecting....
Connected to the server

Message   Send

Figure 34—Our chat interface

---

6. Web sockets have been spun off into their own specification, which you can find at http://www.w3.org/TR/websockets/.

We'll use web sockets to implement the web interface for the chat server. Users can connect and send a message to the server. Every connected user will see the message. A visitor can assign himself a nickname by sending a message such as "/nick brian," mimicking the IRC chat protocol. We won't be writing the actual server for this, because that has, thankfully, already been written by another developer. The example code's web server fires up a chat server, so we can test our code with that.

The Chat Interface

We're looking to build a very simple chat interface that looks like Figure 34, *Our chat interface*, on page 219, with a form to change the user's nickname, a large area where the messages will appear, and, finally, a form to post a message to the chat.

In a new HTML5 page, we'll add the markup for the chat interface, which consists of two forms and a div that will contain the chat messages.

html5_websockets/index.html

```html
<!DOCTYPE html>
<html>
  <head>
    <meta charset="utf-8">
    <title>My Chat Server</title>
    <link rel="stylesheet" href="stylesheets/style.css">
  </head>
  <body>
    <div id="chat_wrapper">
      <h2>AwesomeCo Help!</h2>
      <form id="nick_form" action="#" method="post">
        <p>
          <label>Nickname
            <input id="nickname" type="text" value="GuestUser"/>
          </label>
          <input type="submit" value="Change">
        </p>
      </form>
      <div id="chat">connecting....</div>
      <form id="chat_form" action="#" method="post">
        <p>
          <label>Message
            <input id="message" type="text" />
          </label>
          <input type="submit" value="Send">
        </p>
      </form>
    </div>
  </body>
</html>
```

We'll also need to add links to jQuery and a JavaScript file that will contain our code to communicate with our web-sockets server. These can go right above the closing <body> tag.

html5_websockets/index.html

```
<script
   src="http://ajax.googleapis.com/ajax/libs/jquery/1.9.1/jquery.min.js">
</script>
<script src='javascripts/chat.js'></script>
```

Our style sheet, which we create in stylesheets/style.css, contains these style definitions:

html5_websockets/stylesheets/style.css

```
Line 1  #chat_wrapper{
          background-color: #ddd;
          height: 440px;
          padding: 10px;
    5     width: 320px;
        }

        #chat_wrapper h2{ margin: 0; }

   10   #chat{
          background-color: #fff;
          height: 300px;
          overflow: auto;
          padding: 10px;
   15     width: 300px;
        }
```

On line 13, we set the overflow property on the chat message area so that its height is fixed and any text that doesn't fit should be hidden, viewable with scroll bars.

With our interface in place, we can get to work on the JavaScript that will make the interface talk with our chat server.

Talking to the Server

No matter what web-sockets server we're working with, we'll use the same pattern over and over. We'll make a connection to the server, and then we'll listen for these events from the server and respond appropriately:

Event	Description
onopen()	Fires when the connection with the server has been established
onmessage()	Fires when the connection with the server sends a message
onclose()	Fires when the connection with the server has been lost or closed

In our javascripts/chat.js file, we first need to connect to our web-sockets server, like this:

```
html5_websockets/javascripts/chat.js
var setupChat = function(){
 // change this to the IP address of the websocket server
 var webSocket = new WebSocket('ws://192.168.1.2:9394/');
};
```

We're placing all of these event handlers inside a function called setupChat(). This will keep it a little more organized and let us control when we attach the events, instead of having them run immediately. We'll eventually need to detect for socket support in the browser and load a fallback, so we don't want these events firing until we're ready.

When we connect to the server, we should let the user know. We define the onopen() method like this, inside the setupChat() function:

```
html5_websockets/javascripts/chat.js
webSocket.onopen = function(event){
  $('#chat').append('<br>Connected to the server');
};
```

When the browser opens the connection to the server, we put a message in the chat window. Next, we need to display the messages sent to the chat server. We do that by defining the onmessage() method like this, again inside of the setupChat() function:

```
html5_websockets/javascripts/chat.js
Line 1  webSocket.onmessage = function(event){
     2    $('#chat').append("<br>" + event.data);
     3    $('#chat').animate({scrollTop: $('#chat').height()});
     4  };
```

The message from the server comes back to us via the event object's data property. We just add it to our chat window. We'll prepend a break so each response falls on its own line, but you could mark this up any way you want. On line 3, we use jQuery to make the chat window scroll so we can see the new message at the bottom.

Next we'll handle disconnections. The onclose() method fires whenever the connection is closed.

```
html5_websockets/javascripts/chat.js
webSocket.onclose = function(event){
  $("#chat").append('<br>Connection closed');
};
```

Now we just need to hook up the text area for the chat form so we can send our messages to the chat server. This handler also goes in the setupChat() function:

html5_websockets/javascripts/chat.js
```
$("form#chat_form").submit(function(e){
  e.preventDefault();
  var textfield = $("#message");
  webSocket.send(textfield.val());
  textfield.val("");
});
```

We hook into the form submission, grab the value of the form field, and send it to the chat server using the send() method.

We implement the nickname-changing feature the same way, except we prefix the message we're sending with "/nick. " The chat server will see that and change the user's name.

html5_websockets/javascripts/chat.js
```
$("form#nick_form").submit(function(e){
  e.preventDefault();
  var textfield = $("#nickname");
  webSocket.send("/nick " + textfield.val());
});
```

Finally, we can call the setupChat() function, so all of these events get called.

html5_websockets/javascripts/chat.js
```
setupChat();
```

In a more complex app, it'd be much better to break the setupChat() method into individual methods that each do their own thing. But this works and proves the concept we're exploring.

That's all there is to it. Safari, Firefox, and Chrome users can immediately participate in real-time chats using this client. Of course, we still need to support browsers without native Web Sockets support. We'll do that using Flash.

Falling Back

Browsers may not all have support for making socket connections, but Adobe Flash has had it for quite some time. We can use Flash to act as our socket communication layer, and thanks to the web-socket-js library,[7] implementing a Flash fallback is a piece of cake.

---

7. http://github.com/gimite/web-socket-js/

We can download a copy of the web-socket-js library[8] and place it within our project. We'll use Modernizr again to detect for support and load in the JavaScript files on our page. First, we add Modernizr to our page, using the customized version that includes the load() function like we used in *Detecting Features with Modernizr*, on page 47:

html5_websockets/index.html
```
<script src='javascripts/modernizr.js'></script>
```

Then in javascripts/chat.js we use Modernizr.load() to load and configure the fallback:

html5_websockets/javascripts/chat.js
```
Modernizr.load(
  {
    test: Modernizr.websockets,
    nope:
      {
        "swfobject" : "web-socket-js/swfobject.js",
        "websocket" : "web-socket-js/web_socket.js"
      },
    callback: function(url, result, key){
      if (!result){
        if(key === "swfobject"){
          WEB_SOCKET_SWF_LOCATION = "web-socket-js/WebSocketMain.swf";
          WEB_SOCKET_DEBUG = true;
        }
      }
    },
    complete: function(){
      setupChat();
    }
  }
);
```

When our browser doesn't support sockets, the library gets loaded, but we also need to set a variable that specifies the location of the WebSocketMain file, so we do that in the callback(), but only when socket support isn't available.

We're loading two separate scripts here, and the callback() gets fired once for each script that gets loaded. Modernizr lets us tag each script with a key. It passes the key to the callback. This way we can tell which script was loaded. In this example we're using the key to identify when the web-socket script was loaded so we can set the variables the fallback requires.

Regardless of whether the browser supports sockets, we always have to run the setupChat() method so the chat application starts. To do that, we move the

8.　https://github.com/gimite/web-socket-js/archive/master.zip

setupChat() method into the complete() callback. The complete() callback runs at the very end of the loading process, regardless of the outcome of the test. It's the perfect place for code that we always have to run.

With that in place, our chat application will work in all major browsers, provided that the server hosting your chat server also serves a Flash Socket Policy file.

Flash Socket Policy What?

For security purposes, Flash Player will communicate via sockets only with servers that allow connections to Flash Player. Flash Player attempts to retrieve a simple XML file called the Flash Socket Policy file on port 843, and then on the same port your server uses. The player sends a request containing this data:

```
<policy-file-request/>
```

It expects the server to return a response like this:

```
<cross-domain-policy>
    <allow-access-from domain="*" to-ports="*" />
</cross-domain-policy>
```

This is a very generic policy file that allows everyone to connect to this service. You'd want to specify the policy to be more restrictive if you were working with more sensitive data. Just remember that you have to serve this file from the same IP address as your Web Sockets server, on either the same port or port 843. It's best if you can serve it from port 843, because Flash Player always sends a request there first.

The sample web server in the example code for this book contains a simple Flash Socket Policy server, so you can try this code out. See *Node.js and the Example Server*, on page xv, for instructions on setting up Node.js and the sample servers for this book. Once the server is running, you should be able to play with the completed chat server at *http://localhost:8000/html5_web-sockets/index.html*. For extra fun, connect to it from Internet Explorer 8 and Chrome, as in Figure 35, *Cross-browser chatting*, on page 226.

If you're using virtual machines for testing, make sure you use the IP address of the computer running the server, as localhost won't work.

We can't go through it in detail here, but know that you should explore the code for the chat server, too. You'll find it in the example code in lib/chat.js.

Chat servers are just the beginning. With Web Sockets, we finally have a robust yet simple way to push data to our visitors' browsers in real time.

Next we'll use the web browser to determine our latitude and longitude.

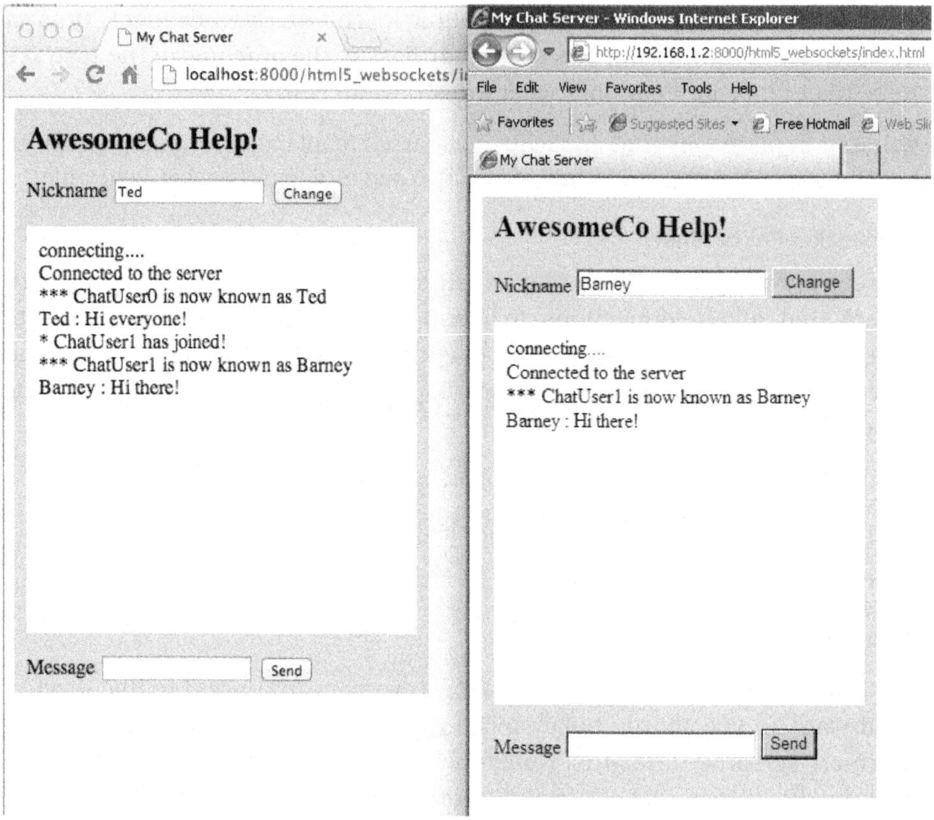

Figure 35—Cross-browser chatting

Tip 33

Finding Yourself: Geolocation

Geolocation is a technique for discovering where people are, based on their computers' location. Of course, "computer" really can mean smartphone, tablet, or other portable device as well as a desktop or laptop computer. Geolocation determines a person's whereabouts by looking at her computer's IP address, MAC address, Wi-Fi hotspot location, or even GPS coordinates if available. Although it's not strictly part of the HTML5 specification (and never was), Geolocation is often associated with HTML5 because it came on the scene at the same time. Like Web Storage, it's a very useful technology that is already implemented in Firefox, Safari, and Chrome. Let's see how we can use it.

Locating Awesomeness

We've been asked to create a contact page for the AwesomeCo website, and the CIO has asked whether we can show people's location on a map along with the various AwesomeCo support centers. He'd love to see a prototype, so we'll get one up and running quickly.

We'll use Google's Static Map API for this because it doesn't require an API key and we're going to generate a very simple map. When we're done, we'll have something that looks like Figure 36, *Our current location is marked on the map with a Y*, on page 228.

AwesomeCo service centers are located in Portland, Oregon; Chicago, Illinois; and Providence, Rhode Island. Google's Static Map API makes it really easy to plot these points on a map. All we have to do is construct an img tag and pass the addresses in the URL, like this:

```
html5_geolocation/index.html
<img id="map" alt="Map of AwesomeCo Service Center locations"
src="http://maps.google.com/maps/api/staticmap?
&amp;size=900x300
&amp;sensor=false
&amp;maptype=roadmap
&amp;markers=color:green|label:A|1+Davol+square,+Providence,+RI+02906-3810
&amp;markers=color:green|label:B|22+Southwest+3rd+Avenue,Portland,+OR
&amp;markers=color:green|label:C|77+West+Wacker+Drive+Chicago+IL">
```

Figure 36—Our current location is marked on the map with a *Y*.

We define the size of the image, and then we tell the Maps API that we did not use any sensor device, such as a client-side geolocation, with the information we're passing to this map. Then we define each marker on the map by giving it a label and an address. We could use comma-separated pairs of coordinates for these markers if we had them, but an address is easier for our demonstration.

How to Be Found

We need to plot our visitor's current location on this map, and we'll do that by providing latitude and longitude for a new marker. We can ask the browser to grab our visitor's latitude and longitude, like this:

```
html5_geolocation/javascripts/geolocation.js
var getLatitudeAndLongitude = function(){
  navigator.geolocation.getCurrentPosition(function(position) {
   showLocation(position.coords.latitude, position.coords.longitude);
  });
};
```

This method prompts the user to provide us with her coordinates. If the visitor allows us to use her location information, we call the showLocation() method.

The showLocation() method takes the latitude and longitude and reconstructs the image, replacing the existing image source with the new one. Here's how we implement that method:

```
html5_geolocation/javascripts/geolocation.js
Line 1  var showLocation = function(lat, lng){
2         var fragment = "&markers=color:red|color:red|label:Y|" + lat + "," + lng;
3         var image = $("#map");
4         var source = image.attr("src") + fragment;
5         source = source.replace("sensor=false", "sensor=true");
6         image.attr("src", source);
7       };
```

Rather than duplicate the entire image source code, we'll append our location's latitude and longitude to the existing image's source. Before we assign the modified image source back to the document, we need to change the sensor parameter from false to true. We do that on line 5 with the replace() method.

Finally, we call the getLatitudeAndLongitude() method we defined, which kicks everything off.

```
html5_geolocation/javascripts/geolocation.js
getLatitudeAndLongitude();
```

When we bring up the page in our browser, we see our location, marked with a *Y*, among the other locations.

Falling Back

As it stands, visitors without Geolocation support will still see the map with the locations of the AwesomeCo support centers, but they'll get a JavaScript error since there's no Geolocation object available. We need to detect support for Geolocation before we attempt to get the visitor's location. We can use Modernizr for that, but where do we get latitude and longitude if we can't get it from the browser?

Google's Ajax API does location lookup, so it's a great fallback solution.[9]

Our fallback looks like this:

```
html5_geolocation/javascripts/geolocation.js
Line 1  var getLatitudeAndLongitudeWithFallback = function(){
2         if ((typeof google === 'object') &&
3             google.loader && google.loader.ClientLocation) {
4               showLocation(google.loader.ClientLocation.latitude,
5                           google.loader.ClientLocation.longitude);
6         }else{
7           var message = $("<p>Couldn't find your address.</p>");
8           message.insertAfter("#map");
9         }
10      };
```

---

9. http://code.google.com/apis/ajax/documentation/#ClientLocation

We use Google's ClientLocation() method on line 3 to get a visitor's location and invoke our showLocation() method to plot the location on our map.

Then we tell Modernizr to test for Geolocation. If we have support, we'll call our original method. If we don't have support, we'll use a simplified version of Modernizr.load() to load Google's library and then call our function to plot the coordinates.

`html5_geolocation/javascripts/geolocation.js`
```
if(Modernizr.geolocation){
  getLatitudeAndLongitude();
}else{
  Modernizr.load({
    load: "http://www.google.com/jsapi",
    callback: function(){
        getLatitudeAndLongitudeWithFallback();
    }
  });
}
```

Unfortunately, Google can't geolocate every IP address out there, so we may still not be able to plot the user on our map; we account for that by placing a message underneath our image on line 7. Our fallback solution isn't fool-proof, but it does give us a greater chance of locating our visitor.

Without a reliable method of getting coordinates from the client, we need to come up with a way for the user to provide us with an address, but that's an exercise I'll leave up to you.

Next, let's take a look at HTML5's built-in support for dragging and dropping elements.

Tip 34

Getting It All Sorted Out with Drag and Drop

Since the introduction of the mouse, we've been trained to drag elements around on the screen. For many years, we've relied on JavaScript and Document Object Model solutions to bring drag-and-drop capabilities to the browser. The HTML5 specification gives us a native and more performant way to make elements draggable, although the implementation is a bit complex.

AwesomeCo's management team has an idea for a piece of software where users can enter ideas on virtual notecards and then reorder them on the screen. We get to build the basic user interface for this, and it's is a great opportunity for us to experiment with native Drag and Drop. When we're done, we'll have something that looks like the following figure.

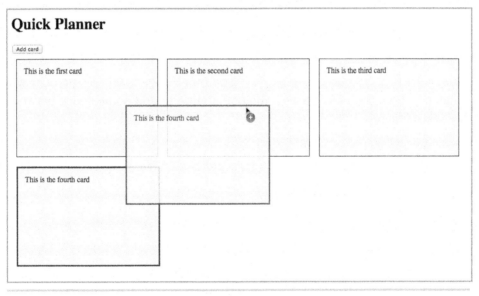

Figure 37—The card-sorting application lets us drag cards around.

Creating the Basic Interface

Let's start off the interface for this application with a basic HTML5 skeleton that includes a link to a style sheet called stylesheets/style.css, a button to add a card, and a region on the screen where the cards will be inserted and sorted.

```
html5_dragdrop/index.html
<!DOCTYPE html>
<html lang='en'>
  <head>
    <meta charset="utf-8">
    <title>AwesomeCards</title>
    <link rel="stylesheet" href="stylesheets/style.css">
  </head>
  <body>
    <h1>Quick Planner</h1>
    <input type="button" id="addcard" value="Add card">

    <div id="cards">
    </div>

  </body>
</html>
```

Next we'll create the CSS for this application in stylesheets/style.css. We'll create each card with JavaScript when we click on the Add Card button, and the markup for the card will look like this:

```
<div class="card" draggable="true" id="card1">
  <div class="editor" contenteditable="true"></div>
</div>
```

Each card is a <div> inside of a <div>. The inner <div> is where the user will be able to type the note, so we'll include styling to add some space between the two elements.

```
html5_dragdrop/stylesheets/style.css
.card{
  background-color: #ffc;
  border: 1px solid #000;
  float: left;
  height: 200px;
  margin: 10px;
  width: 300px;
}

.editor{
  border: none;
  margin: 5%;
  width: 90%;
  height: 80%;
}

.editor:focus{ background-color: #ffe; }
.card:active{ border: 3px solid #333; }
```

We're using the :active pseudoclass to change the border on the card when the user clicks and holds on the element.

Adding Cards to the Interface

First we need to write the code that adds a new card when we click on the Add Card button. We do this with a little bit of jQuery, which we'll wrap in its own function:

```
html5_dragdrop/javascripts/cards.js
addCardClickHandler = function(){
  window.currentCardIndex = window.currentCardIndex || 0;
  $("#addcard").click(function(event){
    event.preventDefault();

    var card = $("<div></div>")
      .attr("id", "card" + (window.currentCardIndex++))
      .attr("class", "card")
      .attr("draggable", true);

    var editor = $("<div></div>")
      .attr("contenteditable", true)
      .attr("class", "editor");

    card.append(editor);
    card.appendTo($("#cards"));
  });
};
```

When we add a card, we need to give it a unique ID. We could come up with an elaborate mechanism to do that, but we'll just use a simple counter. On line 2, we reference a variable called _currentCardIndex on the window object. The first time we call this function, the variable will be initialized to 0. We're declaring it on the window object so that subsequent calls to this function will be able to see the value. Remember, the window object is available globally. In a more complex scenario, we might create our own Application object and store values in that object to avoid polluting the global space.

Then we create the new element for the card. We have an outer div element that represents the card, and an inner div element that has the contenteditable attribute set. This is the card's text. We use the jQuery function to create the card element, and then, on line 7, we set the ID by incrementing the _currentCardIndex by one.

Finally, we apply a class of card to the element, set its draggable attribute, and append the card to the cards region. At this point we can click the Add Card button, and new index cards get added to the user interface. Since we set the contenteditable attribute, we can click on each one and set its text.

Making the Cards Sortable

Before we write the code to make the cards sortable, let's go over how it's going to work. When we drag one card over another card, the card we dragged will be inserted after the card we drag it over. To do that, we'll pass the ID of the card we're dragging to the element we're dropping the card on. When the card is dropped, we'll use jQuery to locate the original element by its ID and move it into the proper position.

The Drag and Drop specification supports the following events:

Event	Description
ondragstart	Fires when the user starts dragging the object
ondragend	Fires when the user stops dragging the object *for any reason*
ondragenter	Fires when a draggable element is moved into a drop listener
ondragover	Fires when the user drags an element over a drop listener
ondragleave	Fires when the user drags an element out of a drop listener
ondrop	Fires when the user drops an element into a drop listener
ondrag	Fires when the user drags an element anywhere; fires constantly but can give x- and y-coordinates of the mouse cursor

We'll need to worry about only a couple of these as we build out our code for this project.

We'll start by creating a new function called createDragAndDropEvents(), which will hold all of the event handlers we need for drag-and-drop functionality. The first thing we'll do with this method is use jQuery to grab the cards region of the page. This is the region where the cards are being inserted.

html5_dragdrop/javascripts/cards.js
```
var createDragAndDropEvents = function(){
  var cards = $("#cards");
};
```

Within this method we'll define our events. When the user starts dragging a card, the ondragstart() method will fire. We'll need create an event handler for that, and inside of that handler we'll grab the card's ID and store it in the dataTransfer object. This object holds the data that's being dragged from one element to another. We use the setData() method for that.

To do all of this, we want to watch the ondragstart() event on each card. Adding event handlers to each card creates a lot of handlers, which could impact performance, so we use jQuery to create delegated events. We create the event on the cards region of the page, but tell jQuery to delegate the event to an individual card. This event will get registered for new cards the user adds later, too.

Inside the createDragAndDropEvents() function, add this code to create the event handler and store the card's ID:

html5_dragdrop/javascripts/cards.js

```
Line 1  cards.on("dragstart", ".card", function(event){
    2    event.originalEvent.dataTransfer.setData('text', this.id);
    3  });
```

The setData() method requires both the data type and the data we want to send. Since we're sending only the element's ID, we're using plain text for the data type. setData() can accept any MIME type as its first argument, but for maximum compatibility with older browsers, we're using the keyword text here, which the HTML5 specification supports and maps to the MIME type of text/plain. At the time of publication, Internet Explorer 10 is the only modern browser that doesn't understand MIME types here.

When we drop the card on top of another card, we want the card we dropped to be placed right after the card we drop it on. We do that with the ondrop() event, which we'll create in the same fashion as the ondragstart() event:

html5_dragdrop/javascripts/cards.js

```
Line 1  cards.on("drop",".card", function(event){
    2    event.preventDefault();
    3    var id = event.originalEvent.dataTransfer.getData('text');
    4    var originalCard = $("#" + id);
    5    originalCard.insertAfter(this);
    6    return(false);
    7  });
```

From the dataTransfer object we fetch the ID of the element we dropped, and we use getData() to specify the data type. We create a new jQuery element with that and then use insertAfter() to place it after the current element. Remember, each card is both draggable and a drop target.

The getData() method is available only in the drop() event. For security reasons, the specification doesn't allow any of the other drag-and-drop events to get access to the stored data. The drop() event is the only time the browser can be sure that the user didn't cancel the event.

To ensure that dragging and dropping works correctly, we need to prevent the dragover event from firing, because by default the browser *prevents* us from dropping elements onto other elements.[10] So, we add the following code to our createDragAndDropEvents() function so we can drop cards onto other cards:

```
html5_dragdrop/javascripts/cards.js
cards.on("dragover", ".card", function(event){
  event.preventDefault();
  return(false);
});
```

That does it for the main functionality, but we've hit a limitation with the way Drag and Drop and contenteditable work. Elements that are draggable are not editable. To get around that, we'll need to remove the draggable attribute from the card element when the editor gets focus, and add it back when the editor loses focus. jQuery's parent() method makes it really easy to grab the card element.

```
html5_dragdrop/javascripts/cards.js
cards.on("focus",".editor" , function(event){
  $(this).parent().removeAttr('draggable');
});

cards.on("blur",".editor", function(event){
  $(this).parent().attr('draggable', true);
});
```

Finally, we fire off our two functions to add the events.

```
html5_dragdrop/javascripts/cards.js
  createDragAndDropEvents();
addCardClickHandler();
```

We can add cards, edit them, and drag them around to sort them. Of course, this solution doesn't work everywhere.

Falling Back

Modernizr can't help with detection. Internet Explorer 8 supports Drag and Drop, but it doesn't support it on anything other than text selection, links, and images. Thus, although Modernizr correctly detects Drag and Drop support, it's not *complete* support in this case. So, we'll detect for support by seeing if the <div> element supports the draggable attribute. If it doesn't, then we'll make things sortable using jQuery UI's sortable() method.[11]

---

10. https://developer.mozilla.org/en-US/docs/Web/Reference/Events/dragover
11. http://jqueryui.com/sortable/

```
if ('draggable' in document.createElement('div')) {
   createDragAndDropEvents();
}else{
  Modernizr.load(
    {
      load: "http://code.jquery.com/ui/1.10.3/jquery-ui.js",
      callback: function(result, url, key){
        $('#cards').sortable();
      }
    }
  );
}

addCardClickHandler();
```

On line 1 we detect support for the draggable element on <div> tags. If it's supported, we fire off the createDragAndDropEvents() method. If it's not supported, we use Modernizr.load() to bring in jQuery UI.

Once jQuery UI is loaded, we use the sortable() method it provides to turn our cards region into a sortable region. All of the child elements become sortable. Take a close look at line 8. That's *one line* of code to do what we did with native Drag and Drop support. Of course, that's one line of code that *we* had to add; we still had to bring in an external library.

jQuery UI has tons of great stuff in it, from date-picker widgets to complex animations. It's a huge library, and you might not need everything it includes. In this example we loaded jQuery UI from a content-delivery network. But in production, you should create a customized download and include only the components you need. The jQuery UI website has a tool to help you do that.[12]

Even with a fallback, we have one last thing to worry about: accessibility. The specification doesn't say anything about how to handle people who can't use a mouse. If we implemented drag-and-drop functionality on our interfaces, we'd need to develop a secondary method that didn't require JavaScript or a mouse to work, and that method would depend on what we're trying to do. This card sorter we built is completely unusable by a person without sight— because we didn't plan for accessibility from the start. We could make our code more accessible by adding an order field to each card and letting the user type in a number, and then having a button the user can press to reorder the cards. That interface might even be nice for sighted users who simply don't like the idea of dragging elements around.

---

12. http://jqueryui.com/download/

As a general rule, when thinking about implementing technologies, don't look for fallbacks only for people who are on old web browsers. Think about how you can provide a great experience to all users who want to get the most out of the product or service you've created.

10.1 The Future

The techniques we talked about in this chapter, although not all part of HTML5 proper, represent the future of web development. We'll be pushing many more things to the client side. Better history management makes Ajax and client-side applications much more intuitive and responsive for users. Sites like GitHub and Flickr take advantage of the History API right now while using fallbacks to ensure things work where full support isn't available. Web Sockets can replace periodic polling of remote services for the display of real-time data. Now that the protocol has stabilized, you can expect to see Web Sockets becoming even more popular when creating real-time web applications, especially now that Internet Explorer 10 supports this feature.

Cross-Document Messaging lets us merge web applications that usually would never be able to interact, and Geolocation lets us build better location-aware web applications, which become more and more relevant every day with the growing mobile computing market.

Drag and Drop is maturing, too. Using the File API,[13] it's possible to create applications that let users drag files from their desktops onto the browser. Once more browsers support the File API, you can create a drag-and-drop file uploader without requiring Flash or Silverlight.

Explore these APIs and keep an eye on their adoption. You may soon find these to be invaluable tools in your web-development toolbox.

---

13. http://www.w3.org/TR/FileAPI/

Where to Go Next

We've covered a lot in this book, but there are many other related technologies that make web development even more exciting, including 3D-canvas support with WebGL, new ways of defining layouts with the Flexible Box model, and the ability to make Ajax requests without worrying about the same-origin policy. If that's not enough, we can process data in the background, push messages from the server to the client, and apply filter effects to elements as if we were using a graphics program.

Although the specifications may be a bit in flux and they may not be supported everywhere, the tools covered in this chapter can be valuable in the right situations. Here's what we'll look at:

Flexible Box model
    Creates better layouts with CSS. *[C26, F22, S4, O10.6]*

Cross-Origin Resource Sharing
    Makes Ajax requests across domains. *[C4, F3.5, S4, IE10, O12.0, iOS3.2, A2.1]*

Web Workers
    Process intensive or long-running tasks in a background thread. *[C4, F3.5, S4, IE10, O12.1, iOS5, A2.1]*

Server-Sent Events
    Allows one-way messaging from the server to connected clients. *[C6, F6, S5, O11, iOS4]*

CSS Filter Effects [filter: blur(10px)]
    Allows effects like blur, grayscale, sepia tones, drop shadows, and more to be applied to elements. *[C18, S6, O15, iOS 6]*

3D Canvas with WebGL[1]

Creates 3D objects on the canvas. *[C8, F4, S5.1, O12]*

We'll start by looking at a much better way to define layouts with CSS.

11.1 Defining Layouts with the Flexible Box Model

One of the most difficult parts of using CSS for layouts is learning how to wrangle "floats and clears," two CSS properties that make it possible to get those web layouts we're all so used to seeing, without resorting to tables.

But really, we're abusing floats and clears, and we need a better way. That's the promise of the Flexible Box model,[2] and although it's not quite ready, it will be soon. With this new model, designing complex layouts that work on all devices is much, much easier.

Let's use the Flexible Box model to make the standard "sidebar on the left, content on the right" layout we've seen thousands of times. We'll start with basic markup in an HTML page:

```
where_next/flexbox/index.html
<!DOCTYPE html>
<html>
  <head>
    <meta charset="utf-8">
    <title>Home</title>
    <link rel="stylesheet" href="stylesheets/style.css" />
  </head>
  <body>
    <header>
      <h1>AwesomeCo</h1>
    </header>

    <div class="container">

      <section id="main">
        <h1>Some Story</h1>

        <p>
          Lorem ipsum dolor sit amet, consectetur adipisicing elit, sed do
          eiusmod tempor incididunt ut labore et dolore magna aliqua. Ut
          enim ad minim veniam, quis nostrud exercitation ullamco laboris
          nisi ut aliquip ex ea commodo consequat.
        </p>
```

---

1. This may be disabled by default or require the most recent video drivers to work properly.
2. http://www.w3.org/TR/css3-flexbox/

```
    <p>
      Duis aute irure dolor in reprehenderit in voluptate velit esse cillum
      dolore eu fugiat nulla pariatur. Excepteur sint occaecat cupidatat non
      proident, sunt in culpa qui officia deserunt mollit anim id est laborum.
    </p>
  </section>
  <section id="sidebar">
    <ul>
      <li><a href="#">Related Link</a></li>
      <li><a href="#">Related Link</a></li>
      <li><a href="#">Related Link</a></li>
      <li><a href="#">Related Link</a></li>
    </ul>
  </section>

</div>
<footer>
  <p>Copyright © 2013 AwesomeCo</p>
</footer>
</body>
</html>
```

We have the typical HTML5 template, with a link to our style sheet, a <header>, a <footer>, and a meaningless <div> that holds the main region and the sidebar. This <div> is our container, and all of its child elements will be *flex items*. In our style sheet, we define the container like this:

```
where_next/flexbox/stylesheets/style.css
.container{
  display: -webkit-flex;
  display:          flex;
}
```

Then we define the main region's width and we use the flex property on the sidebar, which makes it fill up the rest of the space.

```
where_next/flexbox/stylesheets/style.css
#main{
  width: 80%;
  -webkit-order: 2;
         order: 2;
}

#sidebar{
  -webkit-flex: 1;
         flex: 1;

  -webkit-order: 1;
         order: 1;
}
```

Even cooler is the fact that we can reorder the elements in the document. The main region was defined in the document first, but we can use the order property to rearrange elements on the page, so our output ends up looking like the following figure.

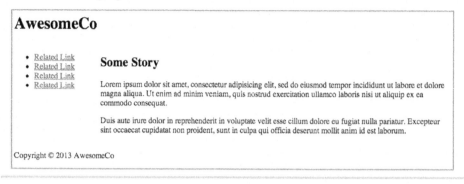

Figure 38—Our sidebar and main region sit where we defined them.

Take a second and think about what that means for responsive web design: you could use this with media queries to easily reorder elements on the page, making the user experience better on phones, with much less developer effort!

Unfortunately, support for this new model is uneven. Internet Explorer 10 and Safari support an old version of the specification, as does iOS. You could use Modernizr to conditionally load style sheets, or you could use Flexie to force the Flexible Box model to work for your site.[3] This might sound strange, but a fair number of sites are using this fallback solution today. You should evaluate this on your own and decide if it's right for your project. It certainly is more attractive than monkeying around with floats and clears.

11.2 Cross-Origin Resource Sharing

The same-origin policy is a security measure that makes it nearly impossible for a page hosted on one domain to make Ajax requests to a page hosted on another. We've found all sorts of ways around the limitations, but cross-origin resource sharing, or CORS, is the standard way of making requests across servers. Best of all, almost every browser supports this, including Internet Explorer 10.

However, to pull it off, the domain you're trying to access has to be configured to accept CORS requests, and you have to configure your code to send those requests. Specifically, the server needs to respond with the following header:

```
Access-Control-Allow-Origin: *
```

---

3. http://flexiejs.com/

That's it. As long as that's set, a modern browser will have no trouble hitting that service and handling requests. It'll send an "Origin" header, and the server will check that header against what it allows. If there's a match, the request goes through.

Since all the work is done on the server, that's as far as we'll go on this topic. But if you visit http://enable-cors.org/, you'll find other valuable information, including how to configure your servers.

11.3 Web Workers

We use JavaScript for all of our client-side coding, but if a task takes a long time, we force the user to wait until the task has finished. Sometimes this even causes the user interface to become unresponsive. Web workers solve this problem by creating a simple way to write concurrent programs, or at least offload long-running tasks to the background.

Web workers are not part of the HTML5 specification, but if you need to do some background processing on the client side you should give web workers a closer look.[4]

Let's look at a trivial example. We'll use web workers to fetch data from YouTube's public application programming interface (API), displaying a thumbnail that, when clicked, plays a video from YouTube. When it's done, it'll look like the following figure.

Figure 39—Videos fetched with web workers

YouTube's public API supports JavaScript Object Notation with Padding (JSONP), which means that instead of making an XmlHttpRequest like we would normally, we append our keywords to the URL for the Search API along with the name of the callback function, and add it to a <script> tag in our

---

4. http://www.whatwg.org/specs/web-workers/current-work/

document. The data from YouTube then gets passed to the callback function we specified. All we have to do is write the callback function to parse the data. It's pretty clever and lets us get around that pesky same-origin policy that browsers have.

Let's build this out. First we'll create a pretty standard HTML page:

`where_next/web_workers/index.html`
```
<!DOCTYPE html>
<html>
  <head>
    <meta charset="utf-8">
    <title>Web Workers</title>
    <style>
      #output > div{float: left; margin-right: 5px;}
    </style>
  </head>
  <body>
    <input type="button" id="button" value="Get Results">
    <div id="output"></div>

    <script
      src="http://ajax.googleapis.com/ajax/libs/jquery/1.9.1/jquery.min.js">
    </script>
    <script src="javascripts/application.js"></script>
  </body>
</html>
```

This page loads up jQuery and a script called scripts/application.js, which will do the basic interaction with the page. We also have a tiny bit of CSS in the <head> section that will arrange the videos in a grid format.

We'll have another file, called javascripts/worker.js, that will do the communication with YouTube. This will be our web worker, and we set it up like this:

`where_next/web_workers/javascripts/application.js`
```
var worker = new Worker("javascripts/worker.js");
```

Any JavaScript file can be launched as a worker, but for the worker to be independent, the worker script can't access the Document Object Model (DOM). That means you can't manipulate elements directly. But you can pass data to the worker and get it back later.

Our main script can send messages to the worker script using postMessage(), like this:

`where_next/web_workers/javascripts/application.js`
```
$("#button").click(function(event){
  worker.postMessage("pragprog");
});
```

In this case we're sending the search term to the worker. The worker can send us messages back, and we can act on those messages if we listen to the worker's onmessage() event:

```
where_next/web_workers/javascripts/application.js
worker.onmessage = function(event){
};

worker.onerror = function(event){
  $("outpout").html("Why do you fail??");
};
```

Every time the worker posts back, this code will fire.

So now let's explore what it takes to make our worker receive and send messages to the main application. First, the worker itself has an onmessage() event we need to listen for. When the main script sends messages to the worker, this code will fire.

```
where_next/web_workers/javascripts/worker.js
var onmessage = function(event) {
  var query = event.data;
  getYoutubeResults(query);
};
```

We pass the search term to our own function called getYoutubeResults(), which will construct the search query for us and send the search request off to YouTube. Usually with JSONP, we have to make the request by adding a <script> tag to the main page. But in a web worker, we don't have access to the DOM, the browser window, or anything like that. But we do have the extremely flexible importScripts() method, which can call local, relative, and remote URLs.

```
where_next/web_workers/javascripts/worker.js
var  getYoutubeResults = function(searchTerm) {
  var callback = "processResults";
  url = "http://gdata.youtube.com/feeds/videos?vq=" + searchTerm +
        "&alt=json-in-script&max-results=5&callback=" + callback;
  importScripts(url);
};
```

This builds up the search URL, passing both the search keyword and the callback function. All we have to do now is write the callback function called processResults().

The response from YouTube will look like this, although with a lot more information:

```
// API callback
processResults({
  "version": "1.0",
  "feed": {
    "title": {
      "$t": "Videos matching: pragprog",
      "type": "text"
    },
    "entry": [{
      "title": {
        "$t": "Using tmux for productive mouse-free programming",
      },
      "media$group": {
        "media$content": [{
            "url": "http://www.youtube.com/v/JXwS7z6Dqic,
            "type": "application/x-shockwave-flash",
            "medium": "video",
            "isDefault": "true"
        }],
        "media$thumbnail": [{
          "url": "http://i.ytimg.com/vi/JXwS7z6Dqic/0.jpg",
          "height": 360,
          "width": 480,
          "time": "00:02:01"
        }]
      }
    }]
  }
});
```

Look at the code for the response carefully—it's calling processResults(), passing it a bunch of data. When our worker receives this response from YouTube, it's going to execute it. We just have to parse the data and send it back to the user interface. We'll pull out just the thumbnail and the video link and put them in a new object, which we send back using postMessage():

where_next/web_workers/javascripts/worker.js

```
var processResults = function(json) {
  var data, result;
  for(var index = 0; index < json.feed.entry.length; index++){
    result = json.feed.entry[index]["media$group"];
    data = {
      thumbnail: result["media$thumbnail"][0]["url"],
      videolink: result["media$content"][0]["url"]
    }
    postMessage(data);
  }
};
```

Finally, back in javascripts/application.js, we fill in the onmessage() event handler and add each result to the page:

```
where_next/web_workers/javascripts/application.js
worker.onmessage = function(event){
➤   var img = $("<img>");
➤   var link = $("<a>");
➤   var result = event.data;
➤   var wrapper;
➤
➤   link.attr("href", result.videolink);
➤   img.attr("src", result.thumbnail);
➤   link.append(img);
➤   wrapper = link.wrap("<div>").parent();
➤   $("#output").append(wrapper);
};

worker.onerror = function(event){
  $("outpout").html("Why do you fail??");
};
```

You might have noticed that the API for web workers works just like the API for cross-domain messaging, which we talked about in Tip 31, *Talking across Domains*, on page 213. We get a message from the worker, and we respond to it. Unfortunately there's no support for web workers in Internet Explorer versions lower than 10. But if you're looking to do some heavier nonblocking client-side work, you'll want to look into this further. In this particular example we could detect for worker support and, if it's not supported, we could call a regular JSONP request with jQuery.

Debugging web workers can be tricky. Since we can't easily access the DOM and we can't use console.log(), our only options are to throw exceptions or to use postMessage() to send data back, then print it to the page in the onmessage() event handler. These methods are a bit kludgy, but they do work.

Web workers are great for situations where you have long-running and often CPU-intensive things you need to do without blocking the main user-interface thread. If your app does some client-side data-crunching, investigate this further.

11.4 Server-Sent Events

Web sockets are cool, but they require a different protocol and are really meant for two-way communication. If you just need to push data to the client from the server, you can use server-sent events, or SSE, which works over regular old HTTP.

To demonstrate this we'll set up a very basic page that will display messages from our server. The web server available in the book's example code already has support for SSE, so we'll focus on the client-side implementation. Create a simple HTML page like this, with a place for the messages to display:

where_next/html5_sse/index.html
```html
<!DOCTYPE html>
<html>
  <head>
    <meta charset="utf-8">
    <title>AwesomeCo Messages</title>
    <link rel="stylesheet" href="stylesheets/style.css">
  </head>
  <body>
    <h2>AwesomeCo Messages</h2>
    <div id="message">connecting....</div>
    <script src='javascripts/streamer.js'></script>
  </body>
</html>
```

We'll also need a place to put our JavaScript code. Create the file javascripts/streamer.js and link it to the HTML file:

where_next/html5_sse/index.html
```html
<script src='javascripts/streamer.js'></script>
```

Now let's get some data displaying on this page.

Listening for Events

In javascripts/streamer.js, we'll create a function called createMessageListeners(), which will define all of the event listeners for server-sent events and will establish the connection to the server's event stream.

where_next/html5_sse/javascripts/streamer.js
```javascript
var createMessageListeners = function(){
  var messageSource = new EventSource("/stream");
}
```

We use the EventSource object to create the connection to the event stream. Depending on the web browser, this source may need to be on the same server as the web page because of the same-origin policy restrictions. CORS support for SSE is not widespread yet.

```javascript
createMessageListeners();
```

Once we establish a connection, the server sends out a continuous stream of messages. The simplest message looks like this:

```
data: We are bringing even more awesomeness to you!
```

That's the word data, followed by a colon, followed by the message text, followed by a blank line—not just a newline character, but a *complete blank line*. A message like this:

```
data: We are bringing even more awesomeness to you!
data: Are you ready to be even more awesome?
```

is a single message with multiple lines. A message like this:

```
data: We are bringing even more awesomeness to you!

data: Are you ready to be even more awesome?
```

is considered two separate messages. You can send plain text, or you can construct JSON, which you could parse on the client. The protocol is really, really simple but very powerful. The server just keeps on sending messages to all connected clients until it stops or the clients disconnect.

To grab a message, we respond to the message event of EventSource and grab the message from event.data, like this:

```
where_next/html5_sse/javascripts/streamer.js
messageSource.addEventListener("message",  function(event){
  document.getElementById("message").innerHTML = event.data;
}, false);
```

That's all it takes. Most of the hard work comes from creating the server and figuring out what you want to do with the messages once you have them.

You can listen to other events, like close, open, or even your own custom events. If the server sends a message like this:

```
event: stockupdate
data: {"stock": "MSFT", "value": "34.01"}
```

on the client, you'd listen for stockupdate events instead of message events, and parse the data out. You can even tell the client how long it should wait to retry by sending this message from the server:

```
retry: 10000
```

This will make the client wait ten seconds between requests instead of its default three seconds.

You can make this work in older browsers that don't support Server-Sent Events. Use Modernizr to detect support and load a simple EventSource polyfill[5] when needed.

---

5.   https://github.com/remy/polyfills/blob/master/EventSource.js

Chapter 11. Where to Go Next • 250

Implementing Your Own Server

To pull this off in a live environment, you'll need to write server-side code that sends continuous messages in this format. The server should send stream responses only if the client requests them with this header:

```
Accept: text/event-stream
```

And the server should make sure to set the response headers to identify that this is a streaming response:

```
Content-Type: text/event-stream;charset=UTF-8
Cache-Control: no-cache
Connection: keep-alive
```

Once you've set up the responses, send the raw text of the messages to all connected clients. And of course, remove any clients that aren't listening anymore.

Take a look at the lib/sse.js file in the book's example code to see a very crude server, or you can build one around node-sse,[6] which handles many of the gory details for you.

11.5 Filter Effects

CSS filter effects let us perform graphics operations on elements as they're inserted into the document.[7] We can do Gaussian blurs, specular lighting, merging, compositing, and many other things that we used to have to turn to graphical editors for.

This specification is pretty far away, and only WebKit-based browsers like Chrome and Safari support some of these filters. Specifically, in WebKit browsers we can use the following filter effects:

blur() blur(10px); Blurs the image, using a blur size in pixels.

grayscale() grayscale(0.5); Removes the color from an image, using values from 0 to 1, where 0 is full color and 1 is grayscale. We can also specify the value as a percentage.

drop-shadow() drop-shadow(5px 5px 5px #333) Gives the image a drop shadow and works just like box-shadow.

sepia() sepia(0.5); Creates that sepia-toned, or old-style brown photo effect, using values from 0 to 1, where 0 is normal and 1 is completely sepia-toned. We can also use percentages.

---

6. https://npmjs.org/package/sse
7. http://www.w3.org/TR/2013/WD-filter-effects-20130523/

brightness() brightness(1.0); Adjusts the brightness of an element's color. 0 is completely dark, 1 is normal, and 10 is maximum brightness. We can use percentages as well, where 100 percent is normal.

contrast() contrast(1.0); Adjusts the contrast, or difference between light and dark values, of an element's color. 0 is no contrast, 1 is normal, and 10 is maximum contrast. We can use percentages here, with 100 percent being normal, and anything over 100 percent resulting in more contrast.

hue-rotate() hue-rotate(90deg) Rotates the element's hue around the color wheel, using either degrees or radians.

saturate() saturate(0.5); Controls the saturation, or the vividness of the image, using values from 0 to 1, where 0 is no saturation and 10 is full saturation. We can also use percentages.

invert() invert(1); Inverts the colors, creating the color-negative effect. We use values from 0 to 1 or 0 percent to 100 percent for this effect. We'll get a gray image at the halfway point.

opacity() opacity(1); Makes an element transparent so we can see the element or colors behind it. We use values from 0 to 1 or 0 percent to 100 percent for this effect. At 0, the element will be completely invisible, and at 1 it will have no transparency.

The neatest thing about all of this is that these properties work with transitions and animations, too. For example, if we wanted images on a page to be grayscale until we hovered over them, we'd only need this tiny bit of CSS:

```
where_next/filters/stylesheets/style.css
img.photo{
  -webkit-filter: grayscale(1);
  -webkit-transition: -webkit-filter 0.5s linear;
}

img.photo:hover{
  -webkit-filter: none;
}
```

This is much simpler than creating separate image files and doing an image swap with JavaScript or CSS background images.

Of course, these aren't available in all the browsers yet, and although there are ways to make them work, it's probably best to avoid them, or use them but not worry about fallbacks. Once filter support stabilizes and these effects show up in other browsers, you can put them to work for you where it makes sense. But like all visual effects, keep these reigned in. Don't "oversaturate" your page with tons of filters that distract from your content.

11.6 WebGL

We talked about the <canvas> tag's 2D context in this book, but there's another specification in progress that describes how to work with 3D objects. The WebGL specification isn't part of HTML5, but Apple, Google, Opera, and Mozilla are part of the working group and have implemented some support in their browsers.[8]

Working with 3D graphics is well beyond the scope of this book, but the site Learning WebGL has some great examples and tutorials.[9]

11.7 Onward!

It's an exciting time to be a developer. This book just barely scrapes the surface of what the future holds. There's so much more to the specifications, and I encourage you to dig deeper. As time goes on, the specifications will change, browsers will gain new abilities, and you'll have even more options at your disposal. I hope you take what you learned here and continue to build and explore, watching the various specifications as you do so.

Now go build something awesome!

---

8.   http://www.khronos.org/registry/webgl/specs/latest/
9.   http://learningwebgl.com/blog/

Features Quick Reference

In the descriptions that follow, browser support is shown in square brackets using a shorthand code and the minimum supported version number. The codes used are *C:* Chrome, *F:* Firefox, *S:* Safari, *IE:* Internet Explorer, *O:* Opera, *iOS:* iOS devices with Safari, and *A:* Android browser.

A1.1 New Elements

Referenced in Tip 1, *Redefining a Blog Using Semantic Markup*, on page 15:

<header>
  Defines a header region of a page or section. *[C5, F3.6, S4, IE8, O10]*

<footer>
  Defines a footer region of a page or section. *[C5, F3.6, S4, IE8, O10]*

<nav>
  Defines a navigation region of a page or section. *[C5, F3.6, S4, IE8, O10]*

<section>
  Defines a logical region of a page or a grouping of content. *[C5, F3.6, S4, IE8, O10]*

<article>
  Defines an article or complete piece of content. *[C5, F3.6, S4, IE8, O10]*

<aside>
  Defines secondary or related content. *[C5, F3.6, S4, IE8, O10]*

Other elements:

Description lists

> Defines a list of names and associated values, like definitions and descriptions. *[All browsers]*

> Referenced in Tip 4, *Defining an FAQ with a Description List*, on page 34

<meter>

> Describes an amount within a range. *[C8, F16, S6, O11]*

> Referenced in Tip 2, *Showing Progress toward a Goal with the meter Element*, on page 26

<progress>

> Control that shows real-time progress toward a goal. *[C8, F6, S6, IE10, O11]*

> Referenced in Tip 2, *Showing Progress toward a Goal with the meter Element*, on page 26.

A1.2 Attributes

Custom data attributes

> Allow the addition of custom attributes to any elements using the data-pattern. *[All browsers support reading these via JavaScript's getAttribute() method.]*

> Referenced in Tip 3, *Creating Pop-Up Windows with Custom Data Attributes*, on page 30

In-place editing support [<p contenteditable>lorem ipsum</p>]

> Support for in-place editing of content via the browser. *[C4, F3.5, S3.2, IE6, O10.1, iOS5, A3]*

> Referenced in Tip 9, *In-Place Editing with contenteditable*, on page 59

A1.3 Forms

Referenced in Tip 5, *Describing Data with New Input Fields*, on page 39:

Email field [<input type="email">]

> Displays a form field for email addresses. *[O10.1, iOS, A3]*

URL field [<input type="url">]

> Displays a form field for URLs. *[O10.1, iOS, A3]*

Range (slider) [<input type="range">]
   Displays a slider control. *[C5, S4, F23, IE10, O10.1]*

Number [<input type="number">]
   Displays a form field for numbers, often as a spinbox. *[C5, S5, O10.1, iOS5, A3]*

Color [<input type="color">]
   Displays a field for specifying colors. *[C5, O11]*

Date fields [<input type="date">]
   Displays a form field for dates. Supports date, month, or week. *[C5, S5, O10.1]*

Dates with times [<input type="datetime">]
   Displays a form field for dates with times. Supports datetime, datetime-local, or time. *[S5, O10.1]*

Search field [<input type="search">]
   Displays a form field for search keywords. *[C5, S4, O10.1, iOS]*

A1.4 Form-Field Attributes

Autofocus support [<input type="text" autofocus>]
   Support for placing the focus on a specific form element. *[C5, S4]*

   Referenced in Tip 6, *Jumping to the First Field with Autofocus*, on page 49

Placeholder support [<input type="email" placeholder="me@example.com">]
   Support for displaying placeholder text inside of a form field. *[C5, F4, S4]*

   Referenced in Tip 7, *Providing Hints with Placeholder Text*, on page 50

Required fields [<input type="email" required>]
   Prevent submission of pages unless the fields are filled in. *[C23, F16, IE10, O12]*

   Referenced in Tip 8, *Validating User Input without JavaScript*, on page 54

Validation via regex [<input pattern="/^(\s||\d+)$/">]*
   Prevents submission of pages unless the field's content matches the pattern. *[C23, F16, IE10, O12]*

   Referenced in Tip 8, *Validating User Input without JavaScript*, on page 54

A1.5 Accessibility

The role attribute [<div role="document">]
   Identifies responsibility of an element to screen readers. *[C3, F3.6, S4, IE8, O9.6]*

Referenced in Tip 14, *Providing Navigation Hints with ARIA Roles*, on page 93

aria-live [<div aria-live="polite">]

Identifies a region that updates automatically, possibly by Ajax. *[F3.6 (Windows), S4, IE8]*

Referenced in Tip 15, *Creating an Accessible Updatable Region*, on page 98

aria-atomic [<div aria-live="polite" aria-atomic="true">]

Identifies whether the entire contents of a live region should be read, or just the elements that changed should be read. *[F3.6 (Windows), S4, IE8]*

Referenced in Tip 15, *Creating an Accessible Updatable Region*, on page 98

<scope> [<th scope="col">Time</th>]

Associates a table header with columns or rows of the table. *[All browsers]*

Referenced in Tip 16, *Improving Table Accessibility*, on page 104

<caption> [<caption>This is a caption</caption>]

Creates a caption for a table. *[All browsers]*

Referenced in Tip 16, *Improving Table Accessibility*, on page 104

aria-describedby [<table aria-describedby="summary">]

Associates a description with an element. *[F3.6 (Windows), S4, IE8]*

Referenced in Tip 16, *Improving Table Accessibility*, on page 104

A1.6 Multimedia

<canvas> [<canvas><p>Alternative content</p></canvas>]

Supports creation of vector-based graphics via JavaScript. *[C4, F3, S3.2, IE9, O10.1, iOS3.2, A2]*

Referenced in Tip 17, *Drawing a Logo on the Canvas*, on page 112, and Tip 18, *Graphing Statistics with RGraph*, on page 120

<svg> [<svg><!-- XML content --></svg>]

Supports creation of vector-based graphics via XML. *[C4, F3, S3.2, IE9, O10.1, iOS3.2, A2]*

Referenced in Tip 19, *Creating Vector Graphics with SVG*, on page 126

<audio> [<audio src="drums.mp3"></audio>]

Plays audio natively in the browser. *[C4, F3.6, S3.2, IE9, O10.1, iOS3, A2]*

Referenced in Tip 20, *Working with Audio*, on page 137

<video> [<video src="tutorial.m4v"></video>]

    Plays video natively in the browser. *[C4, F3.6, S3.2, IE9, O10.5, iOS3, A2]*

Referenced in Tip 21, *Embedding Video*, on page 141

A1.7 CSS3

:nth-of-type [p:nth-of-type(2n+1){color: red;}]

    Finds all *n* elements of a certain type. *[C2, F3.5, S3, IE9, O9.5, iOS]*

Referenced in Tip 10, *Styling Tables with Pseudoclasses*, on page 69

:first-child [p:first-child{color:blue;}]

    Finds the first child element. *[C2, F3.5, S3, IE9, O9.5, iOS3, A2]*

Referenced in Tip 10, *Styling Tables with Pseudoclasses*, on page 69

:nth-child [p:nth-child(2n+1){color: red;}]

    Finds a specific child element counting forward. *[C2, F3.5, S3, IE9, O9.5, iOS3, A2]*

Referenced in Tip 10, *Styling Tables with Pseudoclasses*, on page 69

:last-child [p:last-child{color:blue;}]

    Finds the last child element. *[C2, F3.5, S3, IE9, O9.5, iOS3, A2]*

Referenced in Tip 10, *Styling Tables with Pseudoclasses*, on page 69

:nth-last-child [p:nth-last-child(2){color: red;}]

    Finds a specific child element counting backward. *[C2, F3.5, S3, IE9, O9.5, iOS3, A2]*

Referenced in Tip 10, *Styling Tables with Pseudoclasses*, on page 69

:first-of-type [p:first-of-type{color:blue;}]

    Finds the first element of the given type. *[C2, F3.5, S3, IE9, O9.5, iOS3, A2]*

Referenced in Tip 10, *Styling Tables with Pseudoclasses*, on page 69

:last-of-type [p:last-of-type{color:blue;}]

    Finds the last element of the given type. *[C2, F3.5, S3, IE9, O9.5, iOS3, A2]*

Referenced in Tip 10, *Styling Tables with Pseudoclasses*, on page 69

Column support [*#content{ column-count: 2; column-gap: 20px; column-rule: 1px solid #ddccb5;* }] Divides a content area into multiple columns. *[C2, F3.5, S3, O9.5, iOS3, A2]*

Referenced in Tip 13, *Creating Multicolumn Layouts*, on page 84

:after [*span.weight:after { content: "lbs"; color: #bbb; }*]

Used with content to insert content after the specified element. *[C2, F3.5, S3, IE8, O9.5, iOS3, A2]*

Referenced in Tip 11, *Making Links Printable with :after and content*, on page 78

Media queries [*media="only all and (max-width: 480)"*]

Apply styles based on device settings. *[C3, F3.5, S4, IE9, O10.1, iOS3, A2]*

Referenced in Tip 12, *Building Mobile Interfaces with Media Queries*, on page 81

border-radius [*border-radius: 10px;*]

Rounds corners of elements. *[C4, F3, S3.2, IE9, O10.5]*

Referenced in Tip 23, *Rounding Rough Edges*, on page 153

RGBa support [*background-color: rgba(255,0,0,0.5);*]

Uses RGB color instead of hex codes, along with transparency. *[C4, F3.5, S3.2, IE9, O10.1]*

Referenced in Tip 24, *Working with Shadows, Gradients, and Transformations*, on page 157

box-shadow [*box-shadow: 10px 10px 5px #333;*]

Creates drop shadows on elements. *[C3, F3.5, S3.2, IE9, O10.5]*

Referenced in Tip 24, *Working with Shadows, Gradients, and Transformations*, on page 157

Rotation [*transform: rotate(7.5deg);*]

Rotates any element. *[C3, F3.5, S3.2, IE9, O10.5]*

Referenced in Tip 24, *Working with Shadows, Gradients, and Transformations*, on page 157

Gradients [*linear-gradient(top, #fff, #efefef);*]

Creates gradients for use as images. *[C4, F3.5, S4]*

Referenced in Tip 24, *Working with Shadows, Gradients, and Transformations*, on page 157

src: url(http://example.com/awesomeco.ttf); font-weight: bold; }]
> Allows use of specific fonts via CSS. *[C4, F3.5, S3.2, IE5, O10.1]*

> Referenced in Tip 25, *Working with Fonts*, on page 164

Transitions [transition: background 0.3s ease]
> Gradually transition a CSS property from one value to another over time. *[C4, F3.5, S4, IE10]*

> Referenced in Tip 26, *Making Things Move with Transitions and Animations*, on page 169

Animations [animation: shake 0.5s 1;]
> Gradually transition a CSS property from one value to another over time using defined keyframe animations. *[C4, F3.5, S4, IE10]*

> Referenced in Tip 26, *Making Things Move with Transitions and Animations*, on page 169

CSS Filter Effects [filter: blur(10px)]
> Allows effects like blur, grayscale, sepia tones, drop shadows, and more to be added to elements. *[C18, S6, O15, iOS6]*

> Referenced in Section 11.5, *Filter Effects*, on page 250

Flexible Box model
> Achieves better layout with CSS. *[C26, F22, S4, O10.6]*

> Referenced in Section 11.1, *Defining Layouts with the Flexible Box Model*, on page 240

A1.8 Client-Side Storage

localStorage
> Stores data in key/value pairs, tied to a domain, and persists across browser sessions. *[C5, F3.5, S4, IE8, O10.5, iOS, A]*

> Referenced in Tip 27, *Saving Preferences with Web Storage*, on page 185

sessionStorage
> Stores data in key/value pairs, tied to a domain, and is erased when a browser session ends. *[C5, F3.5, S4, IE8, O10.5, iOS, A]*

> Referenced in Tip 27, *Saving Preferences with Web Storage*, on page 185

IndexedDB
> An in-browser object store that persists across sessions. *[C25, F10, IE10]*

Web SQL Databases

Fully relational databases with support for creating tables, inserts, updates, deletes, and selects, with transactions. Tied to a domain and persistent across sessions. No longer an active specification. *[C5, S3.2, O10.5, iOS3.2, A2]*

Referenced in *Web SQL Databases---Awesome but Stalled*, on page 202

A1.9 Additional APIs

Offline Web Applications

Defines files to be cached for offline use, allowing applications to run without an Internet connection. *[C4, F3.5, S4, O10.6, iOS3.2, A2]*

Referenced in Tip 29, *Working Offline*, on page 203

History

Manages the browser history. *[C5, F3, S4, IE8, O10.1 iOS3.2, A2]*

Referenced in Tip 30, *Preserving History*, on page 209

Cross-Document Messaging

Sends messages between windows and <iframe>s with content loaded on different domains. *[C5, F4, S5, iOS4.1, A2]*

Referenced in Tip 31, *Talking across Domains*, on page 213

Web Sockets

Creates a stateful connection between a browser and a server. *[C5, F4, S5, iOS4.2]*

Referenced in Tip 32, *Chatting with Web Sockets*, on page 219

Geolocation

Gets latitude and longitude from the client's browser. *[C5, F3.5, S5, O10.6, iOS3.2, A2]*

Referenced in Tip 33, *Finding Yourself: Geolocation*, on page 227

Drag and Drop

API for drag-and-drop interaction. *[C3, F3.5, S4, IE6, A2]*

Referenced in Tip 34, *Getting It All Sorted Out with Drag and Drop*, on page 231

Cross-Origin Resource Sharing

Makes Ajax requests across domains. *[C4, S4, F3.5, IE10, O12.0, iOS3.2, A2.1]*

Web Workers

Process intensive or long running tasks in a background thread. *[C4, S4, F3.5, IE10, O12.1, iOS5, A2.1]*

Referenced in Section 11.3, *Web Workers*, on page 243

Server-Sent Events

Allows one-way messaging from the server to connected clients. *[C6, F6, S5, O11, iOS4]*

Referenced in Section 11.4, *Server-Sent Events*, on page 247

3D Canvas with WebGL[1]

Creates 3D objects on the canvas. *[C8, F4, S5.1, O12]*

Referenced in Section 11.6, *WebGL*, on page 252

---

1. This may be disabled by default or require the most recent video drivers to work properly.

jQuery Primer

Writing clean and concise JavaScript that works well across all web browsers is a difficult chore. Many libraries make it less painful, but jQuery is arguably the most popular. It's easy to use, has a wide array of existing plug-ins, and is a good fit for easily creating fallback solutions and complex web applications.

This appendix introduces you to the parts of the jQuery library that we use elsewhere in the book. It's not meant to be a replacement for jQuery's excellent documentation,[1] nor is it an exhaustive list of the features and methods available. It will, however, give you a good place to start.

jQuery makes Document Object Model (DOM) manipulation and event handling a breeze. jQuery uses CSS selectors to locate elements, wraps those elements in a special object, and then lets us alter the elements or add event listeners to them. Everything jQuery does can be done with plain old JavaScript, but jQuery's advantage is that it handles cross-browser issues for us and makes the syntax more uniform.

A2.1 Loading jQuery

We can grab the jQuery library from the jQuery website and link to the jQuery script directly,[2] but we'll load jQuery from Google's servers, like this:

jqueryprimer/simple_selection.html

```
<script
  src="http://ajax.googleapis.com/ajax/libs/jquery/1.9.1/jquery.min.js">
</script>
```

Browsers can make only a few connections to a server at a time. If we distribute our images and scripts to multiple servers, our users can download

---

1. http://docs.jquery.com
2. http://www.jquery.com

our pages faster. Using Google's content-delivery network has an additional benefit—since other sites link to the jQuery library at Google, our visitors may already have the library cached by their browsers. As you probably already know, browsers use a file's full URL to decide whether it has a cached copy. If you plan to work with jQuery on a laptop or on a computer without constant Internet access, you'll want to link to a local copy instead.

A2.2 jQuery Basics

Once you've loaded the jQuery library on your page, you can start working with elements. jQuery has a function called jQuery(), which lets us fetch elements using CSS selectors and wrap them in jQuery objects so we can manipulate those elements.

There's a short version of the jQuery() function, $();, and that's what we use in this book. Throughout this book, I refer to this as "the jQuery function." Here's how it works:

If you wanted to find the h1 tag on a page, you'd use the following:

jqueryprimer/simple_selection.html
```
$("h1");
```

If you wanted to find all of the <h1> tags on the page, you'd use the exact same thing. If you were looking for all elements with the class of important, you'd do this:

jqueryprimer/simple_selection.html
```
$(".important");
```

Look at that again. The only difference between it and the previous examples is the CSS selector we used. If we were looking for the element with the id of header, we'd simply do

```
var header = $("#header");
```

And if we wanted to find all links within the sidebar, we'd use the appropriate selector for that, which would be $("#sidebar a").

The jQuery function returns a jQuery object, which is a special JavaScript object containing an array of the DOM elements that match the selector. This object has many predefined methods we can use to manipulate the elements we selected. Let's take a look at a few of those in detail.

A2.3 Methods to Modify Content

We use several jQuery methods to modify our HTML content as we work through the projects in this book.

hide(), show(), and toggle()

The hide() and show() methods make it easy to hide and show user-interface elements. We can hide one or many elements on a page, like this:

jqueryprimer/simple_selection.html
```
$("h1").hide();
```

We use the hide() method throughout this book to hide page sections that need to appear only when JavaScript is disabled, such as transcripts or other fallback content. To show elements, we simply call the show() method instead.

We can use toggle() to easily toggle the visibility of an element.

If the jQuery function found several items that matched the selector, all of those items would be shown, hidden, or toggled. So the previous example doesn't just hide the first <h1> element; it hides all of them!

jqueryprimer/simple_selection.html
```
$("#sidebar a").hide();
```

html(), val(), and attr()

We use the html() method to get and set the inner content of the specified element.

jqueryprimer/methods.html
```
$("#message").html("Hello World!");
```

Here, we're setting the content between the opening and closing h1 tags to "Hello World!"

The val() method sets and retrieves the value from a form field. It works exactly like the html() method.

The attr() method lets us retrieve and set attributes on elements.

append(), prepend(), and wrap()

The append() method adds a new child element after the existing elements. Given we have a simple form and an empty unordered list, like this:

jqueryprimer/methods.html
```
<form id="task_form">
  <label for="task">Task</label>
  <input type="text" id="task" >
  <input type="submit" value="Add">
</form>
<ul id="tasks">
</ul>
```

we can create new elements in the list by appending these new elements when we submit the form.

jqueryprimer/methods.html
```
$(function(){
  $("#task_form").submit(function(event){
    event.preventDefault();
    var new_element = $("<li>" + $("#task").val() + "</li>");
    $("#tasks").append(new_element);
  });
});
```

The prepend() method works the same way as the append() method but inserts the new element before any of the existing ones. The wrap() method wraps the selected element with the element represented by the jQuery object you specify.

jqueryprimer/methods.html
```
var wrapper = $("#message").wrap("<div class='wrapper'></div>").parent();
```

In this book, we create a few complex structures programmatically using these techniques.

CSS and Classes

We can use the css() method to define styles on elements, like this:

jqueryprimer/methods.html
```
$("label").css("color", "#f00");
```

We can define these one at a time, but we can also use a JavaScript hash to assign many CSS rules to the element:

jqueryprimer/methods.html
```
$("h1").css( {"color" : "red",
              "text-decoration" : "underline"}
          );
```

However, it's not a good idea to mix style with scripts. We can use jQuery's addClass() and removeClass() methods to add and remove classes when certain events occur. We can then associate styles with these classes. We can combine jQuery events and classes to change the background on our form fields when they receive and lose focus.

jqueryprimer/methods.html
```
$("input").focus(function(event){
  $(this).addClass("focused");
});
$("input").blur(function(event){
  $(this).removeClass("focused");
});
```

This is a trivial example that can be replaced by the :focus pseudoclass in CSS3, but that's unsupported in some browsers.

Chaining

Methods on jQuery objects return jQuery objects, which means we can chain methods indefinitely, like this:

jqueryprimer/simple_selection.html
```
$("h2").addClass("hidden").removeClass("visible");
```

Take care not to abuse this—it can make code harder to follow.

A2.4 Creating and Removing Elements

From time to time, we need to create new HTML elements so we can insert them into our document. We can use the jQuery function to create elements. This is especially useful when these new elements need events or other behaviors added.

jqueryprimer/create_elements.html
```
var input = $("input");
```

Although we could use document.createElement("input"); to accomplish this, we can call additional methods easily if we use the jQuery function.

jqueryprimer/create_elements.html
```
var element = $("<p>Hello World</p>");
element.css("color", "#f00").insertAfter("#header");
```

This is another example where jQuery's chaining helps us build and manipulate structures quickly.

We also need to remove things from the DOM from time to time. By selecting an element using the jQuery function, we can easily remove all its children:

jqueryprimer/remove_elements.html
```
$("#animals").empty();
```

or remove the element itself:

jqueryprimer/remove_elements.html
```
$("#animals").remove();
```

This is quite handy at times when you're working with a more dynamic web application.

A2.5 Events

We often need to fire events when users interact with our page, and jQuery makes this very easy. In jQuery, many common events are simply methods on the jQuery object that take a function. For example, we can make all the links on a page with the class of popup open in a new window, like this:

jqueryprimer/popup.html

```
Line 1  var links = $("a.popup");
2  links.click(function(event){
3    var address = $(this).attr('href');
4    event.preventDefault();
5    window.open(address);
6  });
```

Inside our jQuery event handler, we can access the element we're working with by using the this keyword. On line 3, we pass this to the jQuery function so we can call the attr() method on it to quickly retrieve the link's destination address.

We use the preventDefault() function to keep the original event from firing so it doesn't interfere with what we're doing.

Binding Events

Some events don't have jQuery shortcuts, so we can use the on() method to handle those events. For example, when implementing the Drag and Drop part of the HTML5 specification, we need to cancel out the ondragover event. We use the on() like this:

jqueryprimer/events.html

```
target = $("#droparea")
target.on('dragover', function(event) {
  event.preventDefault();
  return false;
});
```

Notice that we drop the on prefix for the event we're watching.

Binding Events at a Higher Level

Adding click events to individual elements can make the page render more slowly and take up more resources than necessary. Instead of adding events on individual items, we listen for events on the element containing the items:

jqueryprimer/events.html

```
Line 1  var links = $("#links");
2  links.click(function(event){
3    link = event.target;
4    var address = $(link).attr('href');
5    event.preventDefault();
6    window.open(address);
7  });
```

On line 3, we use event.target to get a reference to the actual element the user clicked on. We can then wrap that with a jQuery object to work with it. This works even if we dynamically add new elements to this region.

Sometimes we need to be more specific about the events we watch, so we could define the event handler on the parent, but specify exactly what elements the event should apply to, like this:

```
links.on("click","a" , function(event){
  element = $(this);
  // more code
});
```

In this case we pass the selector as the second argument to on(). We get the same effect, but this gives us more flexibility; if we had a container with lots of elements and different events to watch, this method would let us easily make those connections, whereas simply looking for clicks on the parent element would catch all click events and bubble them up.

The Original Event

When we use any of the jQuery event functions like on() or click(), jQuery wraps the JavaScript event in its own object and makes only *some* of the properties available on the wrapper object. Sometimes we need to get to the actual event so we can access the properties that didn't get mapped. jQuery events give us access to the original event with the appropriately named originalEvent property. We can access the data property of the onmessage event like this:

```
$(window).on("message",function(event){
  var message_data = event.originalEvent.data;
});
```

You can use this technique to call any of the original event's properties or methods.

A2.6 Document Ready

The phrase "unobtrusive JavaScript" refers to JavaScript that's kept completely separate from the content. Instead of adding onclick attributes to our HTML elements, we use event handlers like we just explored in Section A2.5, *Events*, on page 267. We unobtrusively add behavior to our document without modifying the document itself.

One drawback to this method is that JavaScript can't "see" any of the elements in our document until they've been declared. If we loaded our JavaScript code inside the <head> section of the document, the JavaScript code would be immediately executed and none of the elements we want to interact with would be available to us because they haven't been rendered by the browser yet.

We could wrap our code in the window.onLoad() event handler, but that event gets fired after all the content has loaded. This could cause a delay, meaning your users could be interacting with things before your events have been attached. We need a way to add our events when the DOM is loaded but before it's been displayed.

jQuery's document.ready() event handler does exactly this, in a way that works across browsers. We use it like this:

```
jqueryprimer/ready.html
$(document).ready(function() {
  alert("Hi! I am a popup that displays when the page loads");
});
```

There's a shorthand version that you'll see a lot, which looks like this:

```
jqueryprimer/ready.html
$(function() {
  alert("Hi! I am a popup that displays when the page loads");
});
```

Loading scripts with document.ready() is an extremely popular design pattern in JavaScript apps. However, often we can avoid this altogether by placing the calls to external scripts at the *bottom* of the page, right before the closing <body> tag. As long as no scripts are asynchronously changing the DOM, we don't need to worry. But in cases where we don't control the load order of scripts, or elements are getting created on the fly, using document.ready() is the right choice.

A2.7 Use jQuery Wisely

jQuery is a big library and isn't always necessary. If you have a page where you only need to locate an element by its ID, stick with

```
navbar = document.getElementById("#navbar");
```

Loading jQuery for one or two things might be overkill. Modern browsers can already do a lot of what jQuery does with methods like document.querySelector() and document.querySelectorAll(), which are used in modern browsers to select elements using CSS selector syntax much like jQuery does:

```
links = document.querySelectorAll("a.popup");
```

Use jQuery when it makes your life easier, but don't be afraid to leave it out when that makes more sense.

This is only a small sample of what we can do with jQuery. Aside from the document-manipulation features, jQuery provides methods for serializing forms and making Ajax requests and includes some utility functions that make looping and DOM traversal much easier. Once you become more comfortable with its use, you'll no doubt find many more ways to use it in your projects.

Encoding Audio and Video for the Web

Encoding audio and video for use with HTML5's <audio> and <video> tags is a complex subject that's out of scope for this book, but this short appendix will get you going in the right direction if you ever need to prepare your own content.

A3.1 Encoding Audio

You'll need to encode your audio files in both MP3 and Vorbis formats to reach the widest possible audience, and to do that, you'll use a couple of tools.

For encoding MP3 files, LAME will give you the best quality.[1] You'll want to use a variable bit rate when you encode. You can get a high-quality encoding using something like this:

```
$ lame in.wav out.mp3 -V2 --vbr-new -q0 --lowpass 19.7
```

For Vorbis audio, you can use Oggenc.[2] To encode a good-sounding Vorbis file using a variable bit rate, you'd use something like this:

```
$ oggenc -q 3 inputfile.wav
```

You can learn more about MP3 and Vorbis encoding at Hydrogen Audio.[3] The information there is excellent, but you'll need to experiment with settings that will work for you and your listeners.

---

1. http://lame.sourceforge.net/
2. http://wiki.xiph.org/Vorbis-tools
3. MP3 encoding with LAME is covered at http://wiki.hydrogenaudio.org/index.php?title=Lame#Quick_start_.28short_answer.29 , and Vorbis encoding is at http://wiki.hydrogenaudio.org/index.php?title=Recommended_Ogg_Vorbis.

A3.2 Encoding Video

You need to encode your video files to multiple formats if you want to reach every platform when using HTML5 video. Encoding to H.264, Theora, and VP8 can be time-consuming, both in terms of setting up an open source encoder like FFmpeg and actually running the encoding jobs.[4] We don't have enough pages to properly explain this command, which converts a file to VP8 and Vorbis audio using the WebM container:

```
ffmpeg -i blur.mov
       -f webm -vcodec libvpx_vp8 -acodec libvorbis
       -ab 160000 -sameq
       blur.webm
```

If you don't want to mess with the settings yourself, you can use the web service Zencoder to encode your videos to all the formats necessary for use with HTML5 video.[5] You place your video on Amazon S3 or another location, and you can then set up jobs to encode that video file to multiple formats using the web interface or application programming interface calls. Zencoder will fetch the video files, do the encoding, and then transfer the new videos back to your servers. The service is not free, but it produces excellent results and can save you a great deal of time if you have a lot of content to encode.[6]

Miro Video Converter is an excellent, free option.[7] It has presets for converting your video files to multiple outputs and can do batch encoding.

Encoding video to multiple formats is a time-consuming process, so be sure your video is complete and correct before you press that Encode button. If possible, encode small chunks of your videos and test them to find the right settings.

---

4. http://www.ffmpeg.org/
5. http://www.zencoder.com/
6. Full disclosure: I know a couple of developers at Brightcove, the company that owns Zencoder. I would still recommend the service if that weren't the case.
7. www.mirovideoconverter.com/

Resources

Apple—HTML5 . . . . http://www.apple.com/html5/
Apple's page on HTML5 and web standards as supported by its Safari web browser.

Can I Use... . . . . http://caniuse.com/
Browser compatibility tables for HTML5, CSS3, and related technologies.

CSS3.Info http://www.css3.info/
Lots of background information and examples related to the various modules that make up CSS3.

Font Squirrel . . . . http://www.fontsquirrel.com
Provides royalty-free fonts in various formats suitable for distribution on the Web.

HTML5 . . . . http://www.w3.org/TR/html5/
The official HTML5 specification at the World Wide Web Consortium.

HTML5—Mozilla Developer Network . . . .
. . . . https://developer.mozilla.org/en/html/html5
Mozilla Developer Network's page on HTML5.

HTML5 Cross Browser Polyfills . . . .
. . . . https://github.com/Modernizr/Modernizr/wiki/HTML5-Cross-browser-Polyfills
A comprehensive list of polyfills for making HTML5 and CSS3 features work in unsupported browsers.

HTML5 Please http://html5please.com/
Quick advice on what features of HTML5 to use now, and what features to avoid.

Internet Explorer 10 Guide for Developers . . . .
. . . . http://msdn.microsoft.com/library/ie/hh673549.aspx
Provides details on HTML5, CSS3, and JavaScript features supported by Internet Explorer 10 and Windows Store applications.

Microsoft IE Test Drive . . . . http://ie.microsoft.com/testdrive/
Demonstrations of HTML5 (and related) features in Internet Explorer 10.

Kira's Web Toolbox: "Setting Up a Flash Socket Policy File" . . . .
. . . . http://www.lightsphere.com/dev/articles/flash_socket_policy.html
Contains a detailed description of Flash Socket Policy files needed for Web Socket fallback solutions.

Typekit . . . . http://www.typekit.com
Service that lets you use licensed fonts on your website using a simple Java-Script API.

Unit Interactive: "Better CSS Font Stacks" . . . .
. . . . http://unitinteractive.com/blog/2008/06/26/better-css-font-stacks/
Discussion of font stacks, with some excellent examples.

Video.js . . . . http://videojs.com
JavaScript library to aid in playing HTML5 videos.

WebPlatform.org . . . . http://webplatform.org/
Comprehensive documentation and tutorials for HTML5, CSS, JavaScript, and related technologies.

Bibliography

[Bur12]   Trevor Burnham. *Async JavaScript*. The Pragmatic Bookshelf, Raleigh, NC and Dallas, TX, 2012.

[Duc11]   Jon Duckett. *HTML and CSS: Design and Build Websites*. John Wiley & Sons, New York, NY, 2-11.

[HT00]   Andrew Hunt and David Thomas. *The Pragmatic Programmer: From Journeyman to Master*. Addison-Wesley, Reading, MA, 2000.

[Por10]   Christophe Porteneuve. *Pragmatic Guide to JavaScript*. The Pragmatic Bookshelf, Raleigh, NC and Dallas, TX, 2010.

[Zel09]   Jeffrey Zeldman. *Designing with Web Standards*. New Riders Press, Upper Saddle River, NJ, 2009.

Index

SYMBOLS

:: (double colon) syntax, 79–80

DIGITS

3D Canvas with WebGL, 240, 252

A

AAC (Advanced Audio Coding) codec, 135

accessibility, *see also* screen readers
  about interface, 91
  improved, 4
  improving table, 104–108
  interacting with websites, 6
  quick reference for, 255–256
  of video and audio files, 146–149

activateTab() method, 103

addTabToHistory() method, 209–210

addresses, getting, 228–230

Adobe Flash Player
  browsers participating in real-time chats using, 223
  delivering audio and video content, 132
  delivering video using, 148
  support of H.264 codec, 134
  supporting Flash-based fallback, 143

Video.js using, 145
working with containers and codecs, 135

Adobe Typekit, 166

Advanced Audio Coding (AAC) codec, 135

:after selector, 68, 78–80

Amazon S3, serving videos from, 142

Android browser
  about shorthand code for browser, xiii
  audio and video features supported in, 131
  Cross-Origin Resource Sharing supported by, 239
  features for storing data on client supported by, 184
  HTML5 APIs supported by, 207–208
  IndexedDB supported by, 201
  interface accessibility techniques supported by, 92
  selectors supported by, 67–68
  support for working offline in, 203
  Web SQL Databases API in, 202
  Web Workers supported by, 239

animate() function, 177

animationEnd() event, 176

animations
  about, 169

creating shake or rumble effect with, 173–176
handling with jQuery, 177
understanding timing functions, 170–172
using jQuery Color plug-in, 176

animations, user interface feature, 152

Apache, disable caching using, 205

APIs
  Cross-Document Messaging, 207, 213–218, 238
  Drag and Drop, 207–208, 231–238
  Geolocation, 208, 227
  History API, 207, 209–212
  quick reference of features, 260–261
  Web Socket, 207, 219–225
  Web SQL Databases, 202

appearance, user interface
  about, 151
  adding drop shadows to, 157, 160
  adding to backgrounds gradients for, 157, 159–160
  making things move, 169–178
  rotating elements in, 151, 157, 161–163
  rounding rough edges, 153–156
  working with fonts, 164–168

Apple, *see also* Safari on iOS;
Safari
adoption of CSS3 and
HTML5 by, 8
Flash Player not support-
ed by, 132
resources in HTML5 for,
275
applications, 4
ARIA roles
document structure, 96–
97
landmark, 93–95
providing navigation
hints with, 93–97
aria-atomic, 92
aria-describedby role, 92, 107–
108
aria-live
about, 92
polite and assertive updating using, 102
<article>
about, 14
in semantic markup for
blog, 19–20
vs. <section>, 19
<aside>
about, 14
in semantic markup for
blog, 20–22
assertive method of updating,
102
Async JavaScript (Burnham),
175
atomic updating, 102
attr() method, 196
attributes, *see also* contenteditable attribute
about future of new, 35
custom data, 14, 30–33
longdesc, 8
presentational, 7–8
profile, 8
quick reference for web
form field, 255
quick reference of fea-
tures, 254
audio
about, 4, 131
defining, 137
embedding, 137–140
encoding for Web, 273
fallback support for, 139

future of support, 149
making transcripts from,
146
audio codecs, 135
audio streams, containers
and, 135
autocomplete attribute, 51
autofocus support input type
about, 38
jumping to first field with,
49
autoplay attribute, 141

B
backgrounds
adding color to, 159–160
adding gradients to, 157,
159–160
creating fades, 169
making transparent,
162–163
backward compatibility, 1
bar graph
turning HTML into, 122–
123
using RGraph library for
drawing, 120–121
:before selector, 78–80
benefits of HTML5 and CSS3,
1–4
Bézier curve, cubic, 170–172
blog, building
about redefining using
semantic markup, 15–
25
<article> using in, 14, 19–
20
<aside> using in, 14, 20–
22
browser support of se-
mantic markup in, 24–
25
content describing web
page in, 19–20
creating doctype, 17
custom data attributes,
14
description lists, 14
<div> using in, 13
<footer> using in, 18
<header> using in, 14, 17
<meta> using in, 17
<meter> using in, 14
<nav> using in, 14, 18–19
<progress> using in, 14
<section> using in, 14, 19
sidebars, 22

structure for, 16
styling, 22–24
blur() filter effect, 250
border-radius, user interface
feature, 151, 155
box-shadow, user interface
feature, 151, 160
brightness() filter effect, 250
browsers
3D Canvas with WebGL
supported by, 240
about quick reference of
new elements support-
ed by, 253–254
adoption of CSS3 and
HTML5 in, 8
audio and video features
supported in, 131
audio codecs supported
by, 135
combinations of contain-
ers and codecs support-
ed by, 135
creating graphs using
canvas in, 120–125
creating vector graphics
with SVG in, 111, 126–
129
Cross-Origin Resource
Sharing supported by,
239
CSS Filter Effects supported by, 239
custom data attributes
support in, 33
dl tags support, 34
drawing on canvas in,
112–119
features for storing data
on client supported by,
184
Flexible Box model sup-
ported by, 239
fonts supported by, 165
handling contenteditable in,
65
IndexedDB supported by,
201
interface accessibility
techniques supported
by, 92
live regions supported by,
98
media queries support in,
83
meter tags support in,
27–29

participating in real-time chats using Flash Player, 223

playing MP4 files in, 145

polyfills resource for making features work in unsupported, 275

providing hints with placeholder text in, 52

resources, 275

selectors supported by, 67–68

semantic markup support in, 24–25

Server-Sent Events supported by, 239

shorthand code for, xiii

support for working offline in, 203

user interface features supported by, 151

using ExplorerCanvas library, 118

vendor-specific prefixes used in, 87–88

video codecs supported in, 133

VP8 codec supported by, 134

web form features supported by, 38

Web SQL Databases API in, 202

Web Workers supported by, 239

WebKit-based, 250–251

Burnham, Trevor, *Async JavaScript*, 175

C

cache, defining with manifest, 203–205

canPlayType() method, 140, 145

<canvas>

about, 111

about future of using, 129

creating graphs using, 120–125

drawing lines on, 115–116

drawing logo on, 112–119

drawing shapes and paths on, 116–117

<caption>, 92, 106

captions

adding to video, 146–148

explaining tables with, 106

card-sorting application, 231–237

challenges of HTML5 and CSS3, 5–9

chat servers, 225

chatting, using web sockets, 219–225

Chrome

3D Canvas with WebGL supported by, 240

about quick reference of new elements supported by, 253–254

about shorthand code for browser, xiii

adoption of HTML5 and CSS3 by, 8

alternative to drawing in, 111

audio and video features supported in, 131

audio codecs supported by, 135

combinations of containers and codecs supported by, 135

Cross-Origin Resource Sharing supported by, 239

CSS Filter Effects supported by, 239

features for storing data on client supported by, 184

Flexible Box model supported by, 239

fonts supported by, 165

HTML5 APIs supported by, 207–208

IndexedDB supported by, 201

interface accessibility techniques supported by, 92

media queries support in, 83

new elements supported by, 14

participating in real-time chats using, 223

providing hints with placeholder text in, 52

selectors supported by, 67–68

Server-Sent Events supported by, 239

support for working offline in, 203, 205–206

user interface features supported by, 151–152

vendor-specific prefixes used in, 88

video codecs supported in, 133

VP8 codec supported by, 134

web form features supported by, 38

Web SQL Databases API in, 202

Web VTT supported by, 147

Web Workers supported by, 239

Clark, Keith, 76

class attribute, 143

clearNotes() method, 200

click() method, 32–33

client-side storage, 5, 183, 259, *see also* data, storing on client

client-side web applications, talking across domains, 213–218

ClientLocation() method, 230

codecs

AAC, 135

H.264, 132–134

MP3, 135

OGG (Vorbis), 135

Theora, 133–134

Theora codec, 136

video, 133

Vorbis (OGG), 135

VP8, 133–134

working with containers, 135

color

adding to backgrounds, 158–159

filter effects changing, 250–251

input field, 43

input type, 38

using jQuery Color plug-in, 176

color picker, replacing, 44–47

column-rule: selector, 68

columns

aligning text, 72

headings associating with, 106
specifying widths, 88
splitting, 84–87
compatibility (backward), 1
configureTabSelection() method, 211
connectToDB() method, 194
contact list, creating, 214–215
containers
about, 133
working with codecs, 135
content
accessibility of, 91
describing web page, 19–20
displaying, 123
separating from behavior, 30–32
contenteditable attribute
Drag and Drop and, 235
in-place editing with, 38, 59–65
contrast() filter effect, 250
cookies, 183
Crafty library, 129
createDragAndDropEvents function(), 235
createMessageListeners() function, 247
createObjectStore() method, 194
cross-browser chatting, 225
cross-document messaging, 5
Cross-Document Messaging (Web Messaging) API
about, 207
about future of, 238
talking across domains, 213–218
Cross-Origin Resource Sharing, 239, 242–243
cross-site scripting, 5
CSS filter effects, 239, 250–252
CSS3
about, xi
benefits of, 1–4
challenges of, 5–9
quick reference for, 257–259
resources, 275

cubic-bezier() functions, 170–172
custom data attributes
about, 14
caution using, 33
creating pop-up windows with, 30–33

D

data, describing with HTML, 121–122
data() method, 196
data, storing on client, see also IndexedDB
about, 183–184
saving and loading settings with localStorage, 187–189
saving preferences with Web SQL Storage, 185–189
Web SQL Databases API, 202
working offline, 203–206
data-setup attribute, 143
date field input type
about, 38
recording, 41
dates with times input type, 38
delete() method, 200–201
deprecated tags, 6–8
description lists
about, 14
defining FAQs with, 34–35
descriptions, explaining tables with, 106–108
descriptive list (<dl>), 34–35
Designing with Web Standards (Zeldman), xiv
DirectX filters, emulating CSS3 transformations, gradients, and shadows with, 162–163
<div>
as container in HTML5 template, 241
in card-sorting application, 232–234
overuse of, 13
support for draggable elements using, 236–237
<dl> (descriptive list), 34–35

doctype
about, 17
declaration, 1–2
Document Object Model (DOM)
ExplorerCanvas library and, 119
Web Worker script accessing, 244, 247
document-structure roles, 96–97
DOM (Document Object Model)
ExplorerCanvas library and, 119
Web Worker script accessing, 244
domains, talking across, 213–218
done() callback, 174–175
double colon (::) syntax, 79–80
Drag and Drop API
about, 207–208
about future of, 238
events supported by, 234
using, 231–237
drawLogo() function, 119
drawing
graphs using RGraph library, 120–125
on canvas, 112–119
using SVG, 126–129
drop shadows
adding to elements, 157, 160
adding to text, 161
drop-shadow() filter effect, 250
DRY, definition of, 63
Duckett, Jon, *HTML and CSS: Design and Build Websites*, xiv

E

ease-in curve, 170
ease-in-out curve, 171
ease-out curve, 170–171
easing functions, 170
effects, visual, 4, 169, see also animations
elements, see also tags, new
adding drop shadows to, 157, 160
quick reference of features, 253

showing progress toward goal with meter, 26–29
turning into editable field, 60
using transformations to rotate, 157, 161
email field input type, 38, 42
<embed>, 131–132
Embedded OpenType (EOT), 165–166
encoding audio and video for Web, 273–274
EOT (Embedded OpenType), 165
EventSource, 249
EventSource object, 247
ExplorerCanvas library, 118–119, 124

F
fades, creating with transitions, 169
fail() callback, 175, 177
FAQs (frequently asked questions), defining with description list, 34–35
fetchNotes() method, 195, 197
filter effects, CSS, 239, 250–252
Firefox
    3D Canvas with WebGL supported by, 240
    about quick reference of new elements supported by, 253–254
    about shorthand code for browser, xiii
    adoption of CSS3 and HTML5 by, 8
    alternative to drawing in, 111
    audio and video features supported in, 131
    audio codecs supported by, 135
    combinations of containers and codecs supported by, 135
    Cross-Origin Resource Sharing supported by, 239
    features for storing data on client supported by, 184
    Flexible Box model supported by, 239

fonts supported by, 165
HTML5 APIs supported by, 207–208
IndexedDB supported by, 201
interface accessibility techniques supported by, 92
live regions supported by, 98
media queries support in, 83
new elements supported by, 14
participating in real-time chats using, 223
playing MP4 files, 145
providing hints with placeholder text in, 52
selectors supported by, 67–68
Server-Sent Events supported by, 239
support for working offline in, 203, 205–206
user interface features supported by, 151–152
vendor-specific prefixes used in, 88
VP8 codec supported by, 134
Web SQL Databases API and, 202
Web Workers supported by, 239
:first-child selector, 67
:first-of-type selector, 68
Flash Player
    browsers participating in real-time chats using, 223
    delivering audio and video content, 132
    delivering video using, 148
    support of H.264 codec, 134
    supporting Flash-based fallback, 143
    Video.js using, 145
    working with containers and codecs, 135
Flash Socket Policy file, 225, 276
flex items, in HTML5 template, 241
Flexible Box model
    about, 239

defining layouts with, 240–242
Flexie forcing, 242
focus effect, 61
    creating, 173
font stacks, 168, 276
@font-face directive
    about, 165
    redistribution rights and, 166
fonts
    about, 164
    about resources for, 276
    browsers supporting, 171–172
    changing, 165–167
    choosing in adding text to canvas, 116
    converting, 167
    @font-face directive, 165
    format of, 165
    rights and, 166
FontSquirrel font, 165, 275
<footer>
    about, 14
    in semantic markup for blog, 18
frames, support for, 7
frequently asked questions (FAQs), defining with description list, 34–35
future of HTML5 and CSS3, 9

G
Geolocation API
    about, 208
    discovering where people are with, 227–230
getContext() method, 112
getData() method, 235
getLatitudeAndLongitude() method, 229–230
getNote() method, 197
Google, see also Chrome
    adoption of HTML5 and CSS3 by, 8
    ClientLocation() method, 230
    fetching video from YouTube, 243–247
    Static Map API, 227–228
    VP8 and WebM supported by, 136
    YouTube support of H.264 codec, 134
Google Font API, 166

gradient fill, in styling meter element, 28–29

gradient objects, creating with canvas, 118

gradients, user interface feature
  about, 151
  adding to backgrounds, 157, 159–160

graphics
  creating with SVG, 126–129
  operations on elements, 250–252

graphs
  creating using canvas, 120–125
  turning HTML into bar graph, 122–124

grayscale() filter effect, 250

H

H.264 codec
  about, 133–134
  browsers supporting, 133
  encoding to, 274
  Flash Player and, 132

H5F library, building validation with, 57–58

handheld media type, 81

<header>
  about, 14
  assigning unique id to, 107
  in semantic markup for blog, 17

headings, associating with columns, 106

hide() method, 103

History API
  about, 207
  managing browser history using, 209–212

:hover, 69

:hover effect, 61, 251

href attribute, 31, 103, 209

HTML
  describing data with, 121–122
  turning into bar graph, 122–124

HTML and CSS: Design and Build Websites (Duckett), xiv

HTML5
  about, xi
  benefits of, 1–4
  challenges of, 5–9
  platform vs. specification, xi–xii
  specification for, 275
  template, 241

html5shiv, 25

html5shiv blog, 25

hue-rotate() filter effect, 251

Hydrogen Audio (website), 273

I

id attribute
  adding to <section>, 107
  assigning to header unique, 107

Impact library, 129

in-place editing, using contenteditable attribute, 38, 59–65

IndexedDB
  about, 184
  building interface, 190–192
  creating and connecting to database, 193–194
  creating records, 198–199
  creating table, 194
  deleting records, 200–201
  fetching specific record, 196–197
  loading application, 195–196
  storing data in client-side database using, 190
  updating records, 199

IndexedDBShim, 202

init() function, 211

input fields
  autofocus support, 38, 49
  building validation with required fields, 38, 57
  color, 38, 43
  creating using range with sliders, 40
  describing data with new, 39–48
  detecting features with Modernizr library, 47–48
  email, 38, 42
  handling numbers with spinboxes, 38, 40

providing hints with placeholder text, 38, 50–53
  recording dates, 38, 41
  replacing color picker, 44–47
  search field, 38
  URL, 43

insertNote() method, 198–199

interfaces, overview, 2

interfaces, user, see also screen readers
  about, 151
  adding drop shadows to, 157, 160
  adding to backgrounds gradients for, 157, 159–160
  making things move, 169–178
  rotating elements in, 151, 157, 161
  rounding rough edges, 153–156
  using media queries for building mobile, 81–83
  working with fonts, 164–168

Internet Explorer
  about quick reference of new elements supported by, 253–254
  about resources for, 276
  about shorthand code for browser, xiii
  adoption of CSS3 and HTML5 by, 8
  alternative to drawing in, 111
  audio and video features supported in, 131
  combinations of containers and codecs supported by, 135
  Cross-Document Messaging supported by, 218
  Cross-Origin Resource Sharing supported by, 239
  Drag and Drop supported by, 236
  features for storing data on client supported by, 184
  fonts supported by, 165
  handling old versions of, 5

HTML5 APIs supported by, 207–208

IndexedDB supported by, 201

interface accessibility techniques supported by, 92

live regions supported by, 98

media queries support in, 83

new elements supported by, 14

providing hints with placeholder text in, 52

rounding rough edges using, 155–156

selectors supported by, 67–68

support for working offline in, 203

user interface features supported by, 151–152

using ExplorerCanvas library, 118

using Video.js, 143–144

video codecs supported in, 133

VP8 codec supported by, 134

web form features supported by, 38

Web SQL Databases API and, 202

Web VTT supported by, 147

Web Workers supported by, 239

Internet Information Server, serving videos from, 142

invert() filter effect, 251

J

jQuery
basics of, 264
creating and removing elements, 267
document ready, 269
events, 267–269
handling animations with, 177
handling transitions with, 177
loading, 263–264
methods to modify, 265–267
primer for, 263–270

jQuery Color plug-in, 176

jQuery UI, 37, 237

jQuery library, persisting data using, 61–62

jQuery scripts, recommended practice in loading, xvi

jQuery-simple-color plug-in, 44, 48

JavaScript
issues of website accessibility using, 6
put shapes on canvas using, 112
validating user input without, 54–58

JavaScript APIs, exploring media content, 149

JavaScript scripts, recommended practice in loading, xvi

JAWS screen reader, 92, 97

L

landmark roles, 93–95

:last-child selector, 67, 73

:last-of-type selector, 68

latitude and longitude settings, 228

layouts, defining with Flexible Box model, 240–242

layouts, multicolumn, 84–89
creating, 84–89

Learning WebGL, 252

licenses and rights, of fonts, 166

linear curves, 170

linear-gradient, 160

lines
drawing on canvas, 115–116
using <polyline> in SVG to draw, 126–127

live regions, 98

load() function, 48, 57–58, 224

localStorage
about, 184
applying settings with, 188
saving and loading settings with, 187–189
sessionStorage vs., 189
storing data on client, 184

longdesc attribute, 8

longitude and latitude settings, 228

M

Macromedia, Flash Player, 132

manifest
caching and, 205
defining cache with, 203–205

markup
overuse of, 13
semantic, 15–25

matrix() method, 162

media queries
about, 68
building mobile interfaces with, 81–83

messages
posting, 215–216
receiving, 218

<meta>, in semantic markup for blog, 17

<meter>
about, 14
browser support of, 27–29
showing progress toward goal with, 26–27

Microsoft, adoption of CSS3 and HTML5 by, 8

Microsoft DirectX filters, emulating CSS3 transformations, gradients, and shadows with, 162–163

Microsoft Internet Information Server, serving videos from, 142

Miro Video Converter, converting video files using, 274

mobile interfaces, building with media queries, 81–83

Modernizr
testing for Geolocation, 230
using to detect animation support, 178

Modernizr library
checking audio availability, 140
detecting features with, 47–48
detecting placeholder support using, 53

loading H5F using, 57–58
using with load() function, 48, 224
Mozilla, *see also* Firefox
adoption of CSS3 and HTML5 by, 8
VP8 and WebM supported by, 136
Mozilla Developer Network, 275
MP3 codec, 135
MP3 files, encoding, 273
MP4 container, working with codecs, 135
MP4 files, playing if browser doesn't support Flash, 145
MPEG group, creating H.264 codec, 133
multimedia, *see also* audio; canvas; SVG (Scalable Vector Graphics); video
about, 4
quick reference for, 256–257

N

<nav>
about, 14
in semantic markup for blog, 18–19
navigation hints, providing with ARIA roles, 93–97
network, synchronizing local data and detecting connectivity of, 205
network connectivity, synchronizing local data and detecting, 205
noMeterSupport() function, 27
Node Packaged Modules (NPM), installing dependencies, xvi
Node.js, installing, xvi
NPM (Node Packaged Modules), installing dependencies, xvi
:nth-child selector, 67, 72
:nth-last-child selector, 67, 74
:nth-of-type selector, 67, 71
number input type
about, 38
spinboxes as, 40
NVDA screen reader, 97

O

<object>, <embed> tag and, 132
Offline Web Applications
about, 184
working offline using, 203–206
OGG (Vorbis) codec, 135
OGG container, working with codecs, 135
on() method, 218
onclick() method, separating from content behavior, 30–32
onclose() method, 222
ondrag() method, 234
ondragend() method, 234
ondragenter() method, 234
ondragleave() method, 234
ondragover() method, 234
ondragstart() method, 234
ondrop() method, 234
onmessage() method, 221–222, 244, 247
onopen() method, 221
onreadystatechange, 46
opacity() filter effect, 251
OpenType (OTF)
about, 165
browsers supporting, 165
Opera
about quick reference of new elements supported by, 253–254
about shorthand code for browser, xiii
alternative to drawing in, 111
audio and video features supported in, 131
audio codecs supported by, 135
combinations of containers and codecs supported by, 135
Cross-Origin Resource Sharing supported by, 239
CSS Filter Effects supported by, 239
features for storing data on client supported by, 184
Flexible Box model supported by, 239
fonts supported by, 165

HTML5 APIs supported by, 207–208
interface accessibility techniques supported by, 92
media queries support in, 83
new elements supported by, 14
providing hints with placeholder text in, 52
selectors supported by, 67–68
user interface features supported by, 151–152
vendor-specific prefixes used in, 88
VP8 codec supported by, 134
web form features supported by, 38
Web VTT supported by, 147
Web Workers supported by, 239
OTF (OpenType)
about, 165
browsers supporting, 165

P

pattern, validation with regular expressions using, 55–56
pattern attribute, building validation with, 57
placeholder support input type
about, 38
providing hints with, 50–53
platform vs. specification, HTML5, xi–xii
polite method of updating, 102
polyfills, resource for making features work in unsupported browsers, 275
<polyline>, 126
pop-up windows, creating with custom data attributes, 30–33
Porteneuve, Christophe, *Pragmatic Guide to Java-Script*, xiv
postMessage() method, 218, 244, 246–247
Pragmatic Guide to JavaScript, turning HTML into, 124

Pragmatic Guide to JavaScript (Porteneuve), xiv

preload attribute, 141

presentation role, improving table accessibility using, 104

printer-only style sheet, creating, 79

processLogin() function, 174–175, 177

processResults() method, 246

profile, attribute, 8

<progress>, about, 14

progress tags, showing progress toward goal with, 29

promises, using jQuery's support for, 175

pseudoclasses, styling tables with, 69–77
    about, 69–71
    aligning column text with :nth-child, 72–73
    bolding last row with :last-child, 73–74
    counting backward with :nth-last-child, 74–75
    striping rows with :nth-of-type selector, 71–72

pseudoelements, 78–80

pushState() method, 209

R

range (slider) type, 40

Raphaël library, 130

real-time interaction, 219

redistribution rights, of fonts, 166

regions, updatable
    hiding, 102–103
    polite and assertive updating, 102

regular expressions, validation with, 55–56

required fields input type, building validation with, 38, 57

Respond.js library, media queries support in, 83

rgb() function, 162

rgba support, user interface feature
    about, 151
    making transparent backgrounds, 162–163

RGraph library
    ExplorerCanvas library working with, 124
    graphing statistics with, 120–125

rights and licenses, of fonts, 166

rights, fonts and, 166

the role attribute, 92

rotate() method, 162

rotation, user interface feature, 151, 161

rough edges, rounding, in user interface, 153–156

rounding rough edges, in user interface, 153–156

rumble effect, creating, 173–176

S

sIFR, 164

Safari
    about quick reference of new elements supported by, 253–254
    about shorthand code for browser, xiii
    adoption of CSS3 and HTML5 by, 8
    alternative to drawing in, 111
    audio and video features supported in, 131
    audio codecs supported by, 135
    combinations of containers and codecs supported by, 135
    Cross-Origin Resource Sharing supported by, 239
    CSS Filter Effects supported by, 239
    features for storing data on client supported by, 184
    Flash Player not supported by, 132
    Flexible Box model supported by, 239
    fonts supported by, 165

HTML5 APIs supported by, 207–208

IndexedDB supported by, 201

interface accessibility techniques supported by, 92

live regions supported by, 98

media queries support in, 83

new elements supported by, 14

participating in real-time chats using, 223

providing hints with placeholder text in, 52

resources in HTML5 for, 275

selectors supported by, 67–68

Server-Sent Events supported by, 239

support for working offline in, 203, 205–206

vendor-specific prefixes used in, 88

video codecs supported in, 133

VP8 codec supported by, 134

web form features supported by, 38

Web SQL Databases API in, 202

Web VTT supported by, 147

Web Workers supported by, 239

Safari on iOS
    about shorthand code for browser, xiii
    alternative to drawing in, 111
    audio and video features supported in, 131
    audio codecs supported by, 135
    Cross-Origin Resource Sharing supported by, 239
    CSS Filter Effects supported by, 239
    features for storing data on client supported by, 184
    Flexible Box Model supported by, 239
    fonts supported by, 165

HTML5 APIs supported by, 207–208
IndexedDB supported by, 201
interface accessibility techniques supported by, 92
selectors supported by, 67–68
Server-Sent Events supported by, 239
support for working offline in, 203
video codecs supported in, 133
web form features supported by, 38
Web SQL Databases API in, 202
Web Workers supported by, 239
saturate() filter effect, 251
Scalable Vector Graphics (SVG)
    about element, 111
    about future of using, 129–130
    adding shapes using, 128
    browsers supporting, 165
    creating vector graphics with, 126–129
    drawing lines using <polyline> in, 126–127
<scope>, 92
scope attribute, 106
screen readers
    about, 91
    creating accessible updatable region, 98–103
    providing navigation hints with ARIA roles, 93–97
    survey on users of, 98
search field input type, 38
<section>
    about, 14
    adding id attribute to, 107
    in semantic markup for blog, 19
    vs. <article>, 19
Selectivizr library, using, 76
selectors
    about, 4
    :after, 68, 78–80
    :before, 78–80
    column-rule:, 68
    :first-child, 67

:first-of-type, 68
:last-child, 67, 73
:last-of-type, 68
:nth-child, 67, 72
:nth-last-child, 67, 74
:nth-of-type, 67, 71
semantic markup
    about redefining blog using, 15–25
    <article> using with, 14, 19–20
    <aside> using with, 14, 20–22
    browser support of, 24–25
    content describing web page in, 19–20
    creating doctype, 17
    custom data attributes, 14
    description lists, 14
    <div> using with, 13
    <footer> using with, 18
    <header> using with, 14, 17
    <meta> using with, 17
    <meter> using with, 14
    <nav> using with, 14, 18–19
    <progress> using with, 14
    <section> using with, 14, 19
    sidebars, 22
    styling, 22–24
sepia() filter effect, 250
Server-Sent Events, 239, 247–250
sessionStorage
    about, 184
    vs. localStorage, 189
setData() method, 234
setupChat() function, 222–223, 225
shadows
    adding to elements, 157, 160
    text, 161
shake effect, creating, 173–176
shapes
    adding using SVG, 128
    drawing on canvas paths and, 116–117
Sharp, Remy, 25
    html5shiv blog, 25
show() method, 103

showLocation() method, 228
showNote() method, 197
sidebars, in semantic markup for blog, 22
SimpleColor plug-in, 45
slider (range) input type, 40
sortable() method, 237
<source>, 131, 137, 139
<span>, 61
specification vs. platform, HTML5, xi–xii
spinboxes
    as number type, 38
    handling numbers with, 40
SQLite, 202
src: url, user interface feature
    about, 152
    changing font using, 165
    loading script using, 188
Static Map API, 227–228
storage, client-side, 5, 259
styling, in semantic markup for blog, 22–24
SVG (Scalable Vector Graphics)
    about element, 111
    about future of using, 129–130
    adding shapes using, 128
    creating vector graphics with, 126–129
    drawing lines using <polyline> in, 126–127

T

<table>, 106, 108
table accessibility, improving, 104–108
tables
    creating records using IndexedDB in, 198–199
    creating using IndexedDB, 194
    deleting records using IndexedDB in, 200–201
    updating records using IndexedDB in, 199
tables, styling with pseudo-classes, 69–77
    about, 69–71
    aligning column text with :nth-child, 72–73
    bolding last row with :last-child, 73–74

counting backward with :nth-last-child, 74–75
striping rows with :nth-of-type selector, 71–72
tags, new, *see also* elements
about future of, 35
<article>, 14, 19–20
<aside>, 14, 20–22
deprecated, 6–8
<div>, 13
<dl>, 34–35
<footer>, 18
<header>, 14, 17
<meta>, 17
<meter>, 14, 26–29
<nav>, 14, 18–19
overuse of, 13
<progress>, 14
<section>, 14, 19
text
adding in SVG, 127
adding in canvas, 116
aligning in columns, 72
shadows on, 161
splitting into columns, 84–87
<th>, 106–107
Theora codec
about, 134
browsers supporting, 133
containers working with, 136
encoding to, 274
timing functions, understanding, 170–172
title attribute, added to error message, 56
<track>, 131, 146–148
transcripts, making from video and audio, 146
transformations
making transparent backgrounds, 162–163
using to rotate elements, 157, 161
transition-timing-function property, 170
transitions
about, 169
about user interface feature, 152
creating, 172–173
handling with jQuery, 177
properties, 169

TrueType (TTF)
about, 165
browsers supporting, 165
<tspan>, 127
TTF (TrueType)
about, 165
browsers supporting, 165
Typekit, Adobe, 166

U
Unfortunately for us,Modernizr library, using to load jQuery UI, 236–237
updateNote() method, 199
URL field input type, 38, 43
user input, validating, 54–58
user interfaces, *see also* screen readers
about, 151
adding drop shadows to, 157, 160
adding to backgrounds gradients for, 157, 159–160
making things move, 169–178
rotating elements in, 151, 157, 161–163
rounding rough edges, 153–156
working with fonts, 164–168

V
validation via regex input pattern, 38
vector graphics
about, 4
creating with SVG, 126–129
vendor-specific prefixes, 87–88
video
about, 4, 131
adding captions to, 146–148
code testing browser support of MP4 files, 145
codecs, 133–134
defining, 141
embedding, 141–145
encoding for Web, 274
exploring media content, 149
fetching with Web Workers, 243–247

limitations of HTML5, 148
making accessible, 146–149
making transcripts from, 146
placing Flash object code within, 143
Video for Everybody (website), 143
Video.js library
resource for, 276
supporting video on all platforms, 143–145
<track> tag supported by, 147
using Flash as fallback for browsers, 145
visual effects, 4, 169, *see also* animations
Vorbis (OGG) codec, 135
Vorbis format, encoding in, 273
VP8 codec
about, 134
browsers supporting, 133
encoding to, 274

W
W3C Validator service, 8
WAI-ARIA specification
about, 91–92
future and, 108
live regions provided by, 98
web applications, creating interactive
about, 207
about future of, 238
chatting with web sockets, 219–225
discovering where people are, 227–230
managing browser history, 209–212
talking across domains, 213–218
using drag and drop, 231–237
web browsers, *see* browsers
web development, 1–4
web forms
about creating, 37–38
describing, 40–43
describing data with new input fields, 39–48
fields, 38

future of, 65–66
in-place editing with contenteditable attribute, 38, 59–65
jumping to first field with autofocus, 38, 49
overview, 3
providing hints with placeholder text, 38, 50–53
quick reference for field attributes, 255
quick reference of features, 254–255
validating user input, 54–58
Web Messaging (Cross-Document Messaging) API
about, 207
about future of, 238
talking across domains, 213–218
Web Open Font (WOFF), browsers supporting, 165

Web Socket API
about, 207
chatting using, 219–225
Web Sockets, about, 5
Web SQL Databases
about, 184
API, 202
Web SQL Storage, saving preferences with, 185–189
Web Video Text Tracks (Web VTT), 147, 149
Web Workers
about, 239
debugging, 247
fetching video from YouTube, 243–247
WebAIM, survey on users of screen readers, 98
WebGL, 3D Canvas with, 240, 252
WebKit-based browsers, graphic filter supported by, 250–251
WebM container, working with codecs, 135

WebPlatform.org, 276
websites, users interacting with, 6
WOFF (Web Open Font), browsers supporting, 165

X
XHTML self-closing tags, 3

Y
Yepnope library, load() function and, 48
YouTube
fetching video from, 243–247
support of H.264 codec, 134

Z
zebra striping, 71
Zeldman, Jeffrey, *Designing with Web Standards*, xiv
Zencoder, encoding video using, 274

More Web Development

From recipes for better web development to safe-and-sound JavaScript, we've got you covered.

Modern web development takes more than just HTML and CSS with a little JavaScript mixed in. Clients want more responsive sites with faster interfaces that work on multiple devices, and you need the latest tools and techniques to make that happen. This book gives you more than 40 concise, tried-and-true solutions to today's web development problems, and introduces new workflows that will expand your skillset.

Brian P. Hogan, Chris Warren, Mike Weber, Chris Johnson, Aaron Godin
(344 pages) ISBN: 9781934356838. $35
http://pragprog.com/book/wbdev

With the advent of HTML5, front-end MVC, and Node.js, JavaScript is ubiquitous—and still messy. This book will give you a solid foundation for managing async tasks without losing your sanity in a tangle of callbacks. It's a fast-paced guide to the most essential techniques for dealing with async behavior, including PubSub, evented models, and Promises. With these tricks up your sleeve, you'll be better prepared to manage the complexity of large web apps and deliver responsive code.

Trevor Burnham
(104 pages) ISBN: 9781937785277. $17
http://pragprog.com/book/tbajs

The Joy of Math and Healthy Programming

Rediscover the joy and fascinating weirdness of pure mathematics, and learn how to take a healthier approach to programming.

Mathematics is beautiful—and it can be fun and exciting as well as practical. *Good Math* is your guide to some of the most intriguing topics from two thousand years of mathematics: from Egyptian fractions to Turing machines; from the real meaning of numbers to proof trees, group symmetry, and mechanical computation. If you've ever wondered what lay beyond the proofs you struggled to complete in high school geometry, or what limits the capabilities of the computer on your desk, this is the book for you.

Mark C. Chu-Carroll
(282 pages) ISBN: 9781937785338. $34
http://pragprog.com/book/mcmath

To keep doing what you love, you need to maintain your own systems, not just the ones you write code for. Regular exercise and proper nutrition help you learn, remember, concentrate, and be creative—skills critical to doing your job well. Learn how to change your work habits, master exercises that make working at a computer more comfortable, and develop a plan to keep fit, healthy, and sharp for years to come.

This book is intended only as an informative guide for those wishing to know more about health issues. In no way is this book intended to replace, countermand, or conflict with the advice given to you by your own healthcare provider including Physician, Nurse Practitioner, Physician Assistant, Registered Dietician, and other licensed professionals.

Joe Kutner
(254 pages) ISBN: 9781937785314. $36
http://pragprog.com/book/jkthp

Long Live the Command Line!

Use tmux and Vim for incredible mouse-free productivity.

Your mouse is slowing you down. The time you spend context switching between your editor and your consoles eats away at your productivity. Take control of your environment with tmux, a terminal multiplexer that you can tailor to your workflow. Learn how to customize, script, and leverage tmux's unique abilities and keep your fingers on your keyboard's home row.

Brian P. Hogan
(88 pages) ISBN: 9781934356968. $16.25
http://pragprog.com/book/bhtmux

Vim is a fast and efficient text editor that will make you a faster and more efficient developer. It's available on almost every OS—if you master the techniques in this book, you'll never need another text editor. In more than 100 Vim tips, you'll quickly learn the editor's core functionality and tackle your trickiest editing and writing tasks.

Drew Neil
(346 pages) ISBN: 9781934356982. $29
http://pragprog.com/book/dnvim

Seven Databases, Seven Languages

There's so much new to learn with the latest crop of NoSQL databases. And instead of learning a language a year, how about seven?

Data is getting bigger and more complex by the day, and so are your choices in handling it. From traditional RDBMS to newer NoSQL approaches, *Seven Databases in Seven Weeks* takes you on a tour of some of the hottest open source databases today. In the tradition of Bruce A. Tate's *Seven Languages in Seven Weeks*, this book goes beyond your basic tutorial to explore the essential concepts at the core of each technology.

Eric Redmond and Jim R. Wilson
(354 pages) ISBN: 9781934356920. $35
http://pragprog.com/book/rwdata

You should learn a programming language every year, as recommended by *The Pragmatic Programmer*. But if one per year is good, how about *Seven Languages in Seven Weeks*? In this book you'll get a hands-on tour of Clojure, Haskell, Io, Prolog, Scala, Erlang, and Ruby. Whether or not your favorite language is on that list, you'll broaden your perspective of programming by examining these languages side-by-side. You'll learn something new from each, and best of all, you'll learn how to learn a language quickly.

Bruce A. Tate
(330 pages) ISBN: 9781934356593. $34.95
http://pragprog.com/book/btlang

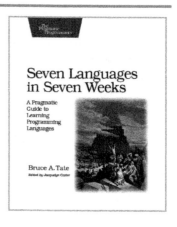

Tinker, Tailor, Solder, and DIY!

Get into the DIY spirit with Raspberry Pi or Arduino. Who knows what you'll build next...

The Raspberry Pi is a $35, full-blown micro computer that runs Linux. Use its video, audio, network, and digital I/O to create media centers, web servers, interfaces to external hardware—you name it. And this book gives you everything you need to get started.

Maik Schmidt
(149 pages) ISBN: 9781937785048. $17
http://pragprog.com/book/msraspi

Arduino is an open-source platform that makes DIY electronics projects easier than ever. Even if you have no electronics experience, you'll be creating your first gadgets within a few minutes. Step-by-step instructions show you how to build a universal remote, a motion-sensing game controller, and many other fun, useful projects. This book has now been updated for Arduino 1.0, with revised code, examples, and screenshots throughout. We've changed all the book's examples and added new examples showing how to use the Arduino IDE's new features.

Maik Schmidt
(272 pages) ISBN: 9781934356661. $35
http://pragprog.com/book/msard

The Pragmatic Bookshelf

The Pragmatic Bookshelf features books written by developers for developers. The titles continue the well-known Pragmatic Programmer style and continue to garner awards and rave reviews. As development gets more and more difficult, the Pragmatic Programmers will be there with more titles and products to help you stay on top of your game.

Visit Us Online

This Book's Home Page
http://pragprog.com/book/bhh52e
Source code from this book, errata, and other resources. Come give us feedback, too!

Register for Updates
http://pragprog.com/updates
Be notified when updates and new books become available.

Join the Community
http://pragprog.com/community
Read our weblogs, join our online discussions, participate in our mailing list, interact with our wiki, and benefit from the experience of other Pragmatic Programmers.

New and Noteworthy
http://pragprog.com/news
Check out the latest pragmatic developments, new titles and other offerings.

Save on the eBook

Save on the eBook versions of this title. Owning the paper version of this book entitles you to purchase the electronic versions at a terrific discount.

PDFs are great for carrying around on your laptop—they are hyperlinked, have color, and are fully searchable. Most titles are also available for the iPhone and iPod touch, Amazon Kindle, and other popular e-book readers.

Buy now at *http://pragprog.com/coupon*

Contact Us

Online Orders:	*http://pragprog.com/catalog*
Customer Service:	*support@pragprog.com*
International Rights:	*translations@pragprog.com*
Academic Use:	*academic@pragprog.com*
Write for Us:	*http://pragprog.com/write-for-us*
Or Call:	+1 800-699-7764

CPSIA information can be obtained at www.ICGtesting.com
Printed in the USA
BVOW09s1425250515

401659BV00007B/38/P